FIVE TIMES MISSING

Five Times Missing

TOMMY SAMPLE

SERENDIPITY

First published in 2004 by
Serendipity
Suite 530
37 Store Street
Bloomsbury
London

British Library Cataloguing-in-Publication data
A catalogue record for this book is available from the British Library

ISBN 1-84394-084-1

Printed and bound by Alden Group, Oxford

Dedication

To my son Brian, daughter Christine and both their families And in memory of my comrades of the Royal Northumberland Fusiliers who did not return home. Their dedication and inspiration I shall remember with pride all my life.

Also my brother Stephen who was killed on HMS *Bleam Oran*, 6 December 1942; 19½ years old.

They shall not grow old as we that are left grow old
Age shall not weary them, nor the years condemn
At the going down of the sun, and in the evening
We will remember them

I would like to thank my friends of the Royal Regiment of Fusiliers Association (Newcastle Branch) and the Royal British Legion (Forest Hall Branch) for their comradeship, hospitality and support, the wonderful hand of friendship that has given me comfort and security, in particular:

Major (ret.) Bill Campbell, President, The Royal British Legion

Mr Dave Reynolds, Chairman, The Royal Regiment of Fusiliers.

The following people also helped with my book:

Alison Robinson

Lenny Szrama

Wendy Todd

Douglas Todd

Jackie Wheaton

Tony Wheaton

Amanda Cardwell

Leslie Cardwell (Heard, seen and told)

I dedicate these page to my late darling wife,
Edith (Edie) Sample

An empty table,
An empty chair,
Where have you gone, my dear.
I had to go away
When I wanted to stay
And left you on you own;
I am all alone and forlorn,
You were in such pain
I had to let you go again.
Your love will always live in my heart
As my love will stay like it did from the very start.

Edith Robinson, 1941

Thomas Sample, 1945

Edith Sample, 1995

Thomas Sample, 1995

Photos copyright *Isle of Man Picture Box*

Author's Note

First Time Missing

This is when I sent a card to my parents to say I was alive, from Benghazi, Libya. I had to wait a long time before getting into a proper camp: Camp 65 Bari, Italy, when I was able to send a letter and a card to tell my parents and my fiancée that I was safe

Second Time Missing

I left Camp 65 and went by train to Rimini, still in Italy. Here I could again communicate with my parents and could receive Red Cross parcels.

Third Time Missing

I went by train to a place outside Bolzano, Italy, to a small village with a fruit farm. Here there were no letter forms to send home and no parcels but we did not need them as there was plenty of food. We stayed here till the capitulation of Italy, when the Germans put us on cattle wagons to travel seven nights and six days to Moosburg in East Germany. Here we received a number and were photographed with this number round our neck. We got Red Cross parcels but still were not able to send mail home. After a while there we were once more loaded onto cattle wagons, this time for six nights and seven days, to Sagan in Poland. Here we could at last send letters home and end my third time missing

Fourth Time Missing

We were sent on another working party, place unknown, in a sugar beet factory, working very long hours. This was until 4 January 1944 when we travelled to Malsh-on-Oder in Germany to work in a paper factory. Here we could send home letters to tell our families we were safe, and also received parcels.

Fifth Time Missing

With the advance of the Russians we were suddenly evacuated from Malsh on 8 January 1945, taking our food parcels on a sledge through the snow. We went on the Death March, a thousand miles across Germany to Hannover where we worked on the railway until we managed to get out to Fallingbostel on 16 April 1945. Here we had parcels but no mail; and were finally released by the 7th Armoured Division. We flew home from Minden and a telegram was sent from a hospital to my family to say that I was safe.

Chapter 1

I enlisted on 16 October 1940 and had to report to Fenham Barracks, Newcastle. I reported to the guard house for instructions and was sent to another room for clothing distribution and given my Army number. Then we were marched in some sort of style to the new barracks and each given a bed and a locker. In the evening we were given a pass till midnight.

On guard duty we had to use baseball bats, guarding motor vehicles in the parking area. We had to do rifle drill, marching and counter marching. This was weeks later. There was grenade-throwing, machine-gun practice and PT, then marching, maybe 5 and 10 mile marches, with full packs and machine-guns to carry. Everybody got their turn in the column.

We had instructions on how to drive a motor vehicle and had to take a three-month crash course, learning how to drive and remember weekly maintenance and about carrying spare parts and topping up batteries. I failed this course, probably because they had their allocation and wanted many more for replacements in the battalions abroad. This took place on two afternoons a week, with an instructor. The next time out, we drove round Newcastle then went back to the depot to hand the vehicle back to the sergeant in charge. Next came my final driving test. A Sergeant MD gave me a check before I left the depot, that the lights were not covered by anything. I checked the tailboard, lights, wheels and flaps on either side. Just as I pulled away there was a shrill whistle for me to stop. I stopped the 15 cwt truck and the sergeant shouted, 'Get out and look for yourself. You left the tailboard hanging. You should have done a further check on your 15-cwt.' That is why he failed me.

The Horseshoe Draft was taken on a ten-mile march, with all our equipment, including rifles. Everyone had to take his turn carrying the machine-gun parts, tripod, barrel, ammunition boxes and so on.

I had been laid up with swollen feet and blisters. I was put on the sick list so I could not get down to Forest Hall to see my parents or girlfriend. My mother and Edie came to see me but were not allowed inside the barracks. A soldier came to my section and told me they wanted to know what was the matter with me. The guard said, 'They cannot come inside the barracks. You will have to see them outside and then only for ten minutes.' When they saw me hobbling they knew something was wrong. I was very very pleased indeed to see them.

One Saturday afternoon I was detailed to go the Palace near the Haymarket to go on stage with Jack Warner at the Garrison Theatre. I was to meet Edie and Ned, my best friend, at the Empire theatre for the first show and then go on to the Palace for the second half. I could not get in touch with Edie, but would try to explain when I saw her on Sunday afternoon. I tried to find her in the blackout, but couldn't, and there I was stuck in case they were looking for me.

We did a training session at Otterburn, Harlow Hill. Our 'day and night' training included crawling along the ground. We were split into two teams, a home side and the enemy. I was captured, but I enjoyed the day.

On the following Sunday I went to church. After that, I decided to go to the slit machine-gun hole in the wall. I was quite slim and I could get through; I had done it a few times. On the other side however there was a Redcap waiting.

He asked, 'Have you a pen or a pencil?'

I said, 'No, I haven't any.'

'Well, come into the guardroom. And where is your respirator?'

'In the barracks.'

'Paybook?'

'The same.'

So in the guardroom he wrote all this down and then said, 'Come here every hour until 11 o'clock tonight. In the morning I want you here at 7 a.m., then 8 a.m., then see the officer at 9 as you will be on a charge from yesterday.'

The captain was not too pleased with me and put me on seven days jankers.

On my third day, around 5 o'clock, this sergeant said to me, 'Go and round up the Horseshoe Draft and tell them to come on parade.'

I said, 'Sergeant, I am not a cowboy!'

He just gave a good laugh. Away I went to get the lads from the block and they came with me to the parade ground. We stood in files of threes. The sergeant made us come to attention and told us, 'Tomorrow we will be going to Scotland, but you must not tell anyone.' He dismissed us and everyone could go home.

We ran all the way to Sandhurst block. I got my overcoat; I had cleaned all my buttons that morning. Before I got to the guardroom I put my coat on and went up to the guard.

'You go back!'

So I did. I just went round the corner and stayed a while then went back to the guardhouse. This time it was all right. I could not believe it – he had lost me my tram to Forest Hall. I just ran all the way to Oxford Galleries and got the tram there. It kept stopping all the way but eventually arrived at the station and I ran all the way to Rocket Way.

When I knocked at Edie's she came to the door. I just gave her a hug and a kiss and said, 'I have something important to tell you later.'

She said, 'I am going for my coat.'

Her mother said, 'Before you go, there are dishes to do!'

So we both got stuck in and did them.

At my mother's house, Edie said, 'You better call in as this may be the last time she sees you for a time.'

I agreed. So we went in and told her I was going to another camp. 'We do not know which camp as they have not told us yet, but I will call again later before I go back to the barracks.'

Edie and I went to our usual place beside the railway line and I said to her quietly, 'I am going to Scotland tomorrow.' She told me she had written a letter to her Aunt Mary in Scotland who told her we could get married at sixteen there.

I said to her, 'This is good news.'

She said, 'Why don't you make me pregnant?'

I said, 'No! This would be a stigma and with people calling you names. Also, I cannot support you on ten shillings and you would not get any help from the Army as you have to be married for that.'

She said, 'I want to!,' but I said 'No!' We just left it at that. I just gave her kisses and hugs, as many as I could. My mate Ned passed on his way to his mother's. He said, 'Be careful!' We said that we were and away he went.

It was starting to get dark and cold so we went back to our mothers' houses before I went back to the barracks.

Next day was 24 March 1941. We were all up early for breakfast and then got our kitbags to get on the trucks on the parade ground. We made our way to the parade ground and the Scottish sergeant was waiting for us to form in threes. This we did, then at ease, then the band went towards the gate and we followed behind and marched down to the Central Station for the troop train. It moved off with people waving as we went. It stopped at Forest Hall station. I got off with this lad Ben and saw my cousin Greta going through the small gate.

I said, 'My girlfriend nearly always goes to work about this time.'

Just then someone tapped my shoulder and said, 'Where do you live?'

I said, 'Here, Sir.'

'Well, you'd better get on this train now.'

I had been going to do a runner but the officer beat me to it.

We passed many stations on the way north and then we were in Scotland. Then it started to slow down and pulled into a siding, right onto a platform. This was Portobello. Most of us decided to have our sandwiches and we were waiting for trucks to take us the rest of the way. We waited a long time until they came and we got aboard them and they put our kitbags on too. Away we went through Edinburgh – we could see through the flaps.

We were out in the countryside. It was a good while before we got to Glasgow and then we carried on for a while again until we came to docks at Gourock.

Everyone got out of their trucks and waited. Lighters started taking troops on board these big ships in the Clyde. Ours was called *Louis Pasteur*, a French ship about 34,000 tons. They took us to our quarters on B deck. So that had been Scotland. Now we were going abroad somewhere.

We had sailed down the Clyde on 26 March 1941 towards the Irish Sea, where we met the convoy. That evening we sailed up the Scottish coast and in all my life I had never seen such a beautiful sight as the purple heather colour. It started to get dark and they put shutters up, in case anyone lit up. We had been told by the Captain not to as enemy ships or submarines might spot the light and endanger lives on board.

Next morning we were told that we had gone past a good few islands and were on our way to Greenland. While on board I was strolling along the deck and saw these lads playing solo – it seemed a very interesting game. Then I saw another group playing dominoes where I lost my pay, which was 10s. a week. My mother also received 4s. It I had been killed she would have got a pension from the Army

We passed Iceland and Greenland and were on our way towards Canada. It was rather stormy weather and at least they put the shutters up to keep B deck dry. The ship's crew said we might be going towards Newfoundland.

I was just sitting on B deck when I saw this lad coming towards me and I could not believe it – it was John Leighton from West Allotment. I had lived there from 1927 to 1936 before the family moved to Forest Hall. We had a good chat and then he left – I saw him once or twice more during the voyage.

There were twenty-six ships in the convoy including battleships *Nelson*, *Rodney*, *Warspite*, *Repulse* and *Renown*. There were 6 destroyers, of which 4 were English and the others Polish and Danish. The cruisers were *Newcastle* and *Sheffield*. A few days later the *Renown*, with the RAF on board, left the convoy, making their way to Canada. We just steamed ahead, blowing our sirens at them and waving.

A day or so later we were about a hundred miles from New York and headed into a storm. The waves were nearly sixty feet high and the ships were going up and down; it was unbelievable what a ship could do. This lasted two days, then it calmed down a bit though still with a good swell.

One of the destroyers was dropping depth charges and others joined in. There must have been an enemy submarine in the area. The next thing we heard was the sirens from the Polish destroyer and the others joined in so they must have got it.

I had been trying to write a page and a half every day to Edie, just to tell her I was really disappointed not to be in Scotland. If I was we could have married, but it was not to be. I told her how much I loved her, with all my heart and soul.

I learned a lesson, after I had lost my week's wages, not to gamble any more as I could not get a cup of tea or coffee or even a cigarette. I had to borrow till I got paid again.

A few days later we came across a number of islands, probably the Azores, and after that a lot more sea. We saw flying fish and porpoises following behind some of the ships. The sea was a lot calmer and I was now enjoying this cruise. I decided to get a bit of suntan but fell asleep and was burned all over my shoulders, back and legs. I had to go the ambulance room to get treatment.

When I saw the sergeant he said to me, 'I am going to take three weeks' wages from you. You have inflicted damage on yourself, which is a serious crime in the Army.'

I was really suffering and I swore never to do it again. I could only lie on my side and if I rolled on my back I gave a yelp as it was very sore indeed.

A few of us decided to play Solo but not for money. I tried hard until I mastered it and got better and better each time so we played for most of the journey.

Eventually someone said that he could see land and we saw the ships lining up to go into port. This was West Africa, one of the crew told us, and the port was Freetown in Sierra Leone. There were black children asking for a silver sixpence; they dived off their small boat for the coins, but some people used silver paper off their cigarettes and put a threepenny coin inside. The children went mad, then, waving their hands at us.

We were not allowed on shore. We stayed there for two days to replenish food. There were supply ships inside the harbour and the lighters went to and from them. The coloured people had all types of fruit to sell but we were not allowed to buy any. If anyone had been caught he would have been severely punished. It was very hot here and next day we sailed away. Our meals were much better now than during that storm, when the food was not nice at all but better than going hungry.

Much later when we woke up we were in harbour; we must have

arrived during the night. We could see Table Mountain through the portholes and one of the crew, who was giving us our breakfast, said that this was Cape Town.

Some of us were detailed to go ashore for the afternoon. When we got to the dockside our legs were a bit wobbly as it was a long time since we'd been on land. There were cars standing by with people willing to take us into town. They dropped us off near the pub but gave us instructions about people to avoid, such as prostitutes and 'hangers-on' asking for money. The beer was dreadful. I had a half pint and was very sick. We decided to go to a cinema – Errol Flynn in *Dodge City* – and it was very comfortable in there. Then we went to a café for a meal and a cup of coffee and some cake. As we went to pay for it someone on the next table said, 'We will pay for these lads' meal.' One came over and said. 'Would you like to go to a pool to see swimming competitions?' They paid for us there too, and then said, 'Would you like to go up Table Mountain?'

We all went in two cars. When we were halfway up, however, the cloud covered the mountain top so we came down and they took us back to the ship. We thanked those people very much for their hospitality. Everyone shook hands and away they went. When we got on board it was 10.30 p.m. We could not believe it, but they said they would pick us up again.

As good as their word, next day they were waiting for us. We had to wait for permission, but within ten minutes we were on our way down the gangplank. They said, 'Today we are taking you to our home.' They drove us along some dirt tracks then we came to some tarmac roads. After quite a while we could see this large farmhouse. We got out of the cars and thanked them very much for bringing us to their home. They had servants doing all the work and within ten minutes had put on a lovely meal. The soup was out of this world and the rest was like a Sunday dinner but with no Yorkshire puddings and as much meat as you could eat.

They wanted us to stay the night but we told them we must get back to the ship to report in. As we were going back, it started to rain.

At the dock area we got out and thanked them for our lovely day. At the bottom of the gangplank were Navy MPs asking us the password.

The four of us agreed we had been very lucky meeting these people; if we had not gone into that café we would not have had such a good time.

Well, everything was just going great; the next day we were down town just looking at shops and things of interest. We had a meal and then another stroll. As we were getting tired of walking and our funds were running low by now, we went back to the ship and decided to spend more time on board.

As we were approaching we were met by a Naval officer who said we had to report back to the ship. They carried on to give this message to other soldiers. When everyone was on board, the Captain explained why we had to cut short our stay. 'Rommel has broken through and is making his way to Benghazi. We must get to the Suez Canal area as soon as possible.'

Chapter 2

A day or so passed and we were coming towards Mozambique. It is quite a big island and we could just see the outline of the African coast. We were still full steam ahead in the Indian Ocean. Everyone was wondering what was going on as we were getting very little information. One of the crew served us dinner: very few vegetables and small bits of meat and potatoes. Maybe everyone was doing extra duties as one could never tell if there was a flap on. The ships were going at full steam but the main ships were well in front. The ones that couldn't keep up were escorted by a destroyer or a cruiser.

Eventually we arrived at Port Tufic. We were called early to get breakfast and ready to get off the boat. We had to wait for lighters to take us to the dock area. There were already three big ships there and one was the *Queen Mary*; this was unbelievable, a great sight to see. They had been bringing troops from different places in England and Canada. We were taken by truck to the Suez canal area, I think it was called Genifa, Ismaila, near the Blue Kettle.

It was very hot. Our legs just buckled in the heat. A sergeant detailed us to each tent. He said, 'Each day, everyone must move to a different place, then there will be no fights. Tomorrow you will all be up at 4.30 a.m.'

That was to go up those hills in the distance. Everyone was advised to have an early night as we would do this every day at the same time; and we were told not to put matchsticks or butt ends into the sand because if the officer in charge found any the culprits would be dealt with.

Next morning, as good as the sergeant's word, we were up and running round in our PT kit. These hills were quite a distance. The sergeant kept shouting at us to get a move on. We were all over the place, with being at sea for six weeks. Our poor legs were aching but the sergeant kept shouting, 'When you have done this you can have a nice dip in the Suez Canal. Then you can have a cup of iced tea and that will quench your thirst.'

We all reached the top of the hills and it was good to come down again slowly, much easier than climbing, but it was a good way to the Canal. I did not go in as I could not swim, but I went to a café for iced tea. It was in a half pint glass and was like manna from heaven.

After this the sergeant said. 'Right, lads, back to the tents and get your breakfast.'

Again our legs were wobbling. We had a job finding our tent as they were not marked. The sergeant kept saying, 'If you don't find your tent soon I am going to put you on a double run tomorrow.' That made us more determined and we succeeded eventually.

We had our breakfast in our mess tins, food in one, tea or coffee in the other.

The sergeant said, 'Outside in ten minutes – machine-gun practice. I want everyone to strip the gun, then put it back together again. I do not care if it takes all day as this is most important. I want everyone to be as quick as possible because if the enemy sees you are slow he will be the winner each time. So we must practise every day. We will then do it blindfold as you could be in the desert in the dark when you can't see your hand in front of you. You must train hard at all times as your life is at stake.'

A couple of days later we were once again up early on this run up the three hills, then down to the Canal. Each day we felt better with less pain in our legs.

Each day, two of us had to keep our area clean from matchsticks and butt ends. We also had to sweep it with a brush made of thin sticks, to make the sand smooth for inspection. Once a duty officer came and with his stick kept turning the sand over. He came across a cigarette butt and matchsticks.

'Right, who is on duty today?'

I said, 'Me, Sir.'

'Right. For this you will lose a day's pay.'

We did some machine-gun training until teatime. Later three of us went down to the NAAFI tent for a game of Lotto. Much later I saw a lad from West Allotment. I just could not believe it.

'Billy Blewitt!' I said.

'Tommy Sample!' he said, 'I never thought I would meet you here.'

I told him we had only been here a few days. I said, 'Come over here with your mates and have a drink. My mate has just won the Lotto and there are bottles of Australian beer.'

We stayed till closing time – 9 o'clock at night.

Next minute, there were searchlights everywhere in the sky, looking for this lone plane. Billy said, 'It will be an Italian one. They're always causing a nuisance.'

Just then one of my mates fell into this six-foot trench then I did the same as I was trying to pull him out. All of the lads had a great laugh at our downfall because we had had too much to drink.

Next day we did our usual trip to the hills and then down to the Canal. After our tea, then breakfast, the sergeant took me and another lad and told us to go with him. Next thing we knew we were told, 'Go towards the road. A truck will pick you up and take you to an Italian prisoner of war camp. You will be on guard for 24 hours.'

Amongst the lads was one that I had worked with in a pit called Algernon, near Old Allotment. I knew he was in the Horseshoe Draft but he was in a different block. I managed to sit beside him and by Jove, it was a hot day, 100 degrees in the shade. We had to do two hours on and two off and he was picked with me and two others to patrol round the compound. Everything was fine till Joe decided to take his topee off. Next thing he had collapsed and was taken to the hospital, so we were one man short. The one in charge said we had to do extra duty. The food was very good but we were glad when the job was done. At night time it was not too bad as lights were on all the time. They sent another chap to take Joe's place.

Joe was put on a charge for disobeying orders. He had to see the officer in charge next morning and he got a good telling off and lost a fortnight's pay.

A week or so later when Crete was invaded we were taken by truck to an airfield to guard it with six machine guns. There were hundreds of crates of aeroplane parts – wings, tails, propellers – but no engines, which had been sunk on their way from America. This was only for one day and next we went down to the Suez Canal for a dip. A lad, Ben, from London tried to teach me to swim. I felt great as it was lovely and cool.

The Italian planes came over very high because our AckAck guns were so good. We still had to do everyday training with the machine guns as there were over 350 parts to assemble, sometimes blindfold. We also had to do rifle practice in the hills, imagining that objects were enemy soldiers.

After our lesson was over for the day we went for dinner with our mess tins, trying to avoid the 'shite hawks'; as you were carrying a tin in each hand all you could do was shout at them. Once a sandstorm blew up over the food and there was nothing you could do but throw it away and use your pay to buy a meal at the canteen.

We stayed there from 8 May to 23 June 1941.

On 24 June we left by train just outside the Blue Kettle, Ismaila. On the train, an officer said to everyone, 'Please do not buy anything off these Egyptians.' Later, I just bought a small bottle for 2s. 6d. I thought it was whisky and just kept taking a sip now and again. Two days later my throat started to swell so I was taken by truck to Alexandria hospital. The bottle had been tampered with. They told me my throat had been burnt. They asked me how it had happened and of course I had to tell them. I could not eat or drink anything, not even soup. I was in hospital for my 21st birthday, 5 July 1941. I was really cursing myself for not taking heed of the officer. On 7 July I was taken back by truck to Amiraya and lost a fortnight's money.

A couple of days later I was detailed with some other Fusiliers to go to a place outside Amiraya to guard people who had been absent without leave. Some who had run away from prison camps in other countries had been sent here for punishment.

W went to a small billet and had just settled down when the sergeant major came in and said if they tried to escape, just to shoot them in the arm or leg as we were marksmen sent there. This other chap and I went with him around the compound. There was a hill of sand which we passed; we saw people going up the hill with sandbags and emptying them at the top. They did this for eight hours a day, with only five minutes break every hour, and you should have heard them shout, 'Get me back to the front line!'

The sergeant-major shouted to them, 'If you do come back here, it will be double time, up and down this hill. You may have broke your mother's heart but you will not break mine.'

As the day wore on, the sun was very hot indeed. No water for them, just that short break. We were glad when this was over and we had got back to Amiraya.

The next day we were given leave to go to Alexandria. They gave us £2 to go there. We went straight to a bar and had a few drinks and most of the lads went to get tattoos. I said, 'I have had enough needles to last me a lifetime.'

They said, 'You must be scared.'

I said, 'No, I do not want my body covered with tattoos.'

So I and this lad Ben went to look at the shops. I said, 'I wouldn't mind a cheap watch and a gold ring – not too expensive as I have only thirty shillings left.'

We went from shop to shop and we found a small one. He had some dear ones, so the lad said, 'I will try and barter with him and have some fun at the same time.'

The shopkeeper tried to sell us one for £2 but the lad said, 'No, too expensive.'

I said I would offer £1 10s. but my mate said, 'No, we'll try £1.'

The shopkeeper said, 'No.'

We made our way out but the shopkeeper ran after us and said, 'Yes!' so I gave him £1. Then my mate Ben saw this ring and said, 'How much?' and the man said '£1 5s.' Again the shopkeeper said all right. I got the two for just under £1 10s. and was over the moon.

At the pick-up point we saw the lads who came down with us. Some were drunk as lords and some holding their arms and bodies where they had their tattoos.

Chapter 3

The next day the Horseshoe Draft were told they would be leaving for a new place. Everyone was on tenterhooks, but someone said. 'When we get there we will know!' Everyone had a laugh, but little did we know we were going back to Alexandria to a boat.

We pulled alongside in the trucks to board HMS *Hotspur*, a destroyer which had been in battle earlier at Narvik. We marched to the shop area and as we got on the gangplank we were given a tin of corned beef and some hard biscuits for our tea. It pulled away and before long it was dark. No one was allowed to smoke on board in case it gave a plane or submarine a chance to spot us. It was a good job we had our Army topcoats handy as it was getting very cold, especially as the boat steamed ahead.

It was early morning when we arrived at Tobruk harbour where there were a lot of ships sunk. One that was badly damaged, the *Ladybird*, could still fire its guns. I was told that she could also fire a wire which would be tangled in the propellers of aircraft and pull them down, most effective against Stukas as they dived towards the harbour.

The ship was guided in by someone with a small hand lamp and we were taken to bunkers inside the hillside. We were just settling down when there was a terrible explosion from a German gun. Someone said it was either Bardia Bill or Derna Sal. People were killed or wounded.

As it got lighter we were detailed to different companies – W, X, Y and Z; I was in X Company. There was a truck to take us into the Tobruk area, then to our sections. Mine was near a white escarpment, Fort Pilastrino, and German troops were there. On our left were the remains of a Gloster Gladiator that had been shot down; the pilot had been killed. The trip there was quite nice but I got really tired of bully beef and biscuits so dumped some of it in the sea. Little did I know that they were in case you were short during the next 24 hours, so I had to go without until next day.

Much later, a lad said, 'Did you see a small ship? That was a sloop with a gun on board. It sank, firing the gun at the Stukas. They are dive bombers with just one or two bombs. It's the sirens they have on when diving and they frighten the hell out of you.'

I could not get accustomed to the shells. One chap said, 'So long as you can hear them coming you're OK, it's the ones you don't hear you have to worry about.'

Things had been quiet for a few days then hell let loose one evening. They were sending shells over thick and fast but none fell beside us. They were shelling the fig tree where the Polish troops were and they were getting a real bashing. We got into dugouts round the perimeter, With our guns overlapping theirs, any enemy coming into our areas would have been slaughtered. In fact all guns could be called at a minute's notice. Those not on machine guns had rifles, hand grenades, Brens and guns that could fire a 5 inch shell, mostly for armoured cars. Sometimes they came walking beside tanks, other times they came on their bellies. No one could tell until they were seen from our signals at the front or by phone. It was pretty cold during the night and you had to wear your overcoat to keep warm.

One afternoon the sergeant said, 'We may be going up towards the front, taking wood planks and corrugated sheeting, just to help the lads there with some protection against mortars and shell splinters.'

We had another raid by Stukas for about an hour, mostly where the Aussies were dug in. Sometimes one of them would drive a 15 cwt., making it appear like there was something astir when there wasn't; then the Jerries would shell around them. They were a great bunch of lads. If you were short of anything they were glad to help and it was the same with us.

We saw some Aussies playing around with an old Italian gun, and eventually they got it to go. Somehow it just went haywire and one or two were hit by exploding shells. It was terrible.

The following day a lad and I were coming back from there with shovels and rifles when we came across a snake. The lad said, 'Come on, let's see if we can kill it!' But somehow just as I lifted the shovel to strike, he said, 'Don't! Your heel is just above a mine.' We just crept back in our footprints and scrambled back onto the road. By, we did get a fright.

The officer and the sergeant came along to have a chat about what was going to happen that night. We were going to take the two machine guns to within reach of the front line, as the Aussies were going to attack the front. Another two machine guns were going to give cover further away from us. They were going to attack with bangalows, to take the wire fences away. But it never happened because something went wrong; maybe an officer gave the wrong order to fire or maybe the elevation was low and caught the Aussies as some came out wounded and some were killed. We stayed till sunrise and then made our way back to our dugouts.

After breakfast the sergeant said, 'I want you two to clean your gun sometime today after all the sand blowing into it.' The other lad was inside the gun emplacement and I decided to go out of the dugout and clean the front, the barrel and the sights which he couldn't reach. This took me a while with just a piece of cloth. At the end I asked him if the gun was clear; he said 'I will try it and see.' With me standing with my legs apart, he pressed the trigger and a bullet went between my legs. It was a good job I was tall; if I'd been shorter I might have had my private parts blown off. He came round to see if I was all right and I gave him a good blasting for being careless. He asked me not to tell the sergeant about it.

A few days later, a lad and I had been detailed to go to a new cookhouse. We got new canisters, one for tea, one for soup. It was about two miles away. We stayed for a chat, talking about leave in Cairo or Alexandria. I started on my way and the other lad came later and caught me up. All of a sudden Jerry started shelling. We just dropped the canisters and ran back to the cookhouse. It was an awful sight. One lad was killed outright – he was the cook, about 21 years old. The sergeant had received injuries in his backside as he was lying on top of the dugout and one lad from Ashington was all right but his brother, who was in the Signals, attached to us, was badly wounded and died in his brother's arms.

Another day a lad was killed and that night the sergeant made us go and pick up his pieces and put them into black bags. Someone found a boot and inside was his foot. It was about midnight when we finished. The sergeant shone a small torch with a cross on it, so it would not give our position away.

A few days later I saw some lads playing football with some grey and red objects. I thought, 'Those are Italian grenades,' but they still kept kicking them until one exploded. One got wounds in his face, another to his chest and another, all his legs. They had to be taken to Tobruk Hospital for treatment. They would have got a good talking to and a heavy fine or more.

I had been asking about Edie. The sergeant said, 'Is your girlfriend pregnant?'

I said, 'No.'

'It's a pity. If she was you both could have been married as a date would have been arranged.'

I asked, 'Sergeant, can I get engaged to my girlfriend?' I told him she was 17 years old in May that year.

The sergeant said, 'This can be arranged straight away. How much do you wish to spend?'

'Would five pounds be enough?'

'Five pounds would be more than enough. I can take it out of your pay that is lying.'

The sergeant said he would have to go through the CO about this and I gave him Edie's address and he told me she would receive it very soon. I was over the moon.

We were into September 1941 and things were not too bad, pretty quiet. The corporal told us to get some corrugated sheets and trail them to this area where that night we were going to dig a new dugout and machine gun emplacement. In the darkness we made our way to the front line, creeping on our bellies past fixed German machine guns. 'If you do not get low enough you will get shot,' he said. The sheeting kept bending as we were trying not to cause any noise. Eventually we got through and the one I was carrying slipped as the corporal shouted in a low voice unexpectedly. We had to get it all done before sunrise, digging down to 5 or 6 feet to get the sheets down the side and then to get it covered as soon as possible. We had this arrangement in England as Anderson shelters. They were not bomb proof but would keep out shell or mortar fragments.

That evening my arm was aching. I must have banged it with one of the corrugated sheets. The next day it was really painful so told the corporal. I lifted my shirt sleeve and he said, 'You have large lump under your arm. You will have to see the sergeant,' and the sergeant sent me to a hospital in Tobruk.

On the way I looked at my letter from Edie; inside it was a photograph. She was a lovely lass and I would carry it with me no matter what happened. I hoped she received my engagement ring.

Eventually we arrived at the hospital. I saw one of the male nurses and told him I had a wound on my elbow. He said, 'Wait in this room and a doctor will see you.'

I waited a good while and then an officer came over and I pulled my sleeve up.

'That is a nasty wound,' he said. 'How did you do it?'

'I was carrying corrugated sheets into the front line the other night.'

'You have a lot of sand in your wound and I have no anaesthetic to give you.'

I said, 'Just do what is necessary.'

He asked, 'Do you want a piece of wood to bite on?'

'No, because I don't think I shall feel it as my arm is so numb.'

When he finished, he bandaged it right down to the wrist. It was really good with very little pain. He said, 'I am going to keep you here for a day or so. Here are some tablets to ease the pain. It may take a month or six weeks to heal.' He then put my arm in a sling and said, 'Do be careful you do not knock it as that might open the wound.'

After a really good meal I was taken to a tent with three people inside. One had a hand wound, one a leg wound and one had broken his ankle. Below the escarpment was a lovely beach. We went to look, but another lad said, 'We are not allowed to go outside the tent area.'

One morning he said, 'Let's go for a stroll along the top of the escarpment and get some prickly pears.' We were collecting some in our jumpers when suddenly we heard aeroplane engines and firing at the people below. The planes had come out of the blue and started machine gunning people on the beach and in the sea. There was blood all over, a massacre. They would have been lads on 24-hour leave, just enjoying themselves. We lay down with the pears in our jumpers and we were covered in prickles but we were the lucky ones.

We were into November 1941 and an officer came to the hospital and asked for volunteers for the front line. About eight of us accepted but this major came on the scene and asked me, 'What are you doing?'

I said, 'I have volunteered for the front line.'

'Your arm is not ready, you could damage it. Never mind, take great care of it.' The major who did my arm gave me a white bible.

On the way back to W Company we hit a shell hole and unlucky for me, I fell off the 15 cwt. onto a rocky surface. Everyone had a good laugh at my expense. I fell onto my helmet, and it jammed on my head. Someone shouted I had fallen off so the driver had to reverse back towards me.

Chapter 4

Later I was introduced to other Fusiliers and one of them said, 'Welcome to W Company. The Commander is Captain Jackman,'

I arrived at the platoon quarters and got shaking hands with everyone. I then had something to eat as I had had nothing since dinnertime. Later Robert Young and I had a good chinwag about Tobruk. I told him I had been with X Company, then in hospital. 'What do they call this area?'

'This is Fort Solaro.'

Robert Young was in the same platoon. I told him how I had met John Leighton and Billy Blewitt in different places, John on the boat and Billy in the Genifera area. Then there was Joe Pyle from Shiremoor who came over with the Horseshoe Draft. Robert said he had been out here since the beginning of the year. Joe had been in my class at Shiremoor Modern School.

There was to be an attack during the early morning so we had to be up early. The sergeant said that we might attack Butch and Captain Jackman gave them orders. We never knew what we would attack until the sergeant or the corporal said. Maybe they did not want us to know in case we were captured. Our area was for mopping up, making it safe until the next part of the battalion took over for the next approach to the next place.

It was quiet for a while then our guns started shelling the Germans and Italians and we went in with the tanks. We just lay back as the rest of the company went in in case the enemy came out. We either took them prisoner or shot to kill or wound them because no one knew what would happen if they had been cornered.

The next attack was Jill and was next morning. We began as before and it was a nasty battle which went on for some time and we were glad when it was over. We lost a truck or two. Later we found one old soldier, one that must have joined long before the war. He had been badly wounded and had his tin helmet between his teeth; he must have been in a lot of pain. No one knew how long he had been lying there.

Next morning we attacked our next objective – Jack. It was not so bad this time. Maybe Jerry had pulled out in the night and made it easier for us. One or two were left behind to hinder us but we just kept plugging away. We were all glad to rest down but had no word of casualties.

We had just finished having something to eat when the sergeant said, 'We will have to dig trenches as deep as we can.' We hit solid rock so we just put sand around and tried as best we could. It was a peaceful night, then just before we stood-to, the Jerries started shelling. We saw trucks and tanks hit and on fire. The shelling stopped about 200 yards from us.

Our tanks started to move forward, then the corporals said, 'We will be having another attack this morning.' The tanks had all-over camouflage nets on them and we were going to Tiger to attack. We crept forward, and after an hour of so of shelling they seemed to fade away, so that was another place we had taken. Later we just consolidated and rested up for the night after a cup of tea and some soup and sandwiches.

The day before we had to attack Lion, a corporal told us to go and get some ammunition with him. We took the dirt track because if you wandered you might meet trouble; it was lined with tin drums to guide us. On our way we came across a vehicle with soldiers on board, from the Yorks and Lancs Regiment. They had stayed off the track into a minefield and everyone had been killed. They lay in many positions as if they were trying to save themselves.

The ammunition was too much for us to carry in our small truck so they supplied us with another. The corporal left word about the dead soldiers.

All the ammunition was to attack Lion. Captain Jackman with his whip and cheese-cutter hat was waving us on, giving cover for those going towards the enemy. There were quite a few prisoners and this was again a bloody battle and went on for some time. You could see other companies attacking at the same time and they were getting shelled. We were pleased when this one was over.

Later, in the afternoon I met two lads, one with a rifle, as we were going to do our business. When people went to the place where the toilet was, a chap always stood by with a rifle, in case. There was a sand storm blowing. Just then we heard planes, very low; they started dropping cocktail bombs which explode as they hit the deck. The two of us put them out with handfuls of sand. The lad with the rifle started shooting at them and one plane crashed with an explosion. The lad kept saying, 'I brought that plane down!' We said, 'Don't be daft. Its engine kept missing a beat.'

Once again we were awakened by gunfire and it turned into a real battle with the Jerries. We lost a few tanks and some 15 cwts. on the way in but Captain Jackman, with no tin helmet, just a cheese-cutter hat on and his stick in his hand, just kept shouting at us to get a move on. The tanks were gaining on the Germans and everyone was trying their very best and we kept going till we reached our object, El Duda. At the bottom of the embankment we took off our machine gun and tripod and a box of ammunition and started putting it together. Captain Jackman shouted to the second lieutenant to get it all back into the truck and then all of a sudden a whistling sound came; we all dived under the truck for cover. But the shell just slithered along the rock base and did not go off. We were very lucky again.

When it was over, we approached the Axis Road. The lieutenant said, 'We must all go towards the escarpment and get ready for anything.' We got into a wadi and set up the two guns. The ones in front of us must have knocked out a mortar launcher as we saw these dead German soldiers. They must have just been putting a shell in. Their machine guns were just below the escarpment; you could just see the barrels. We got ammunition for our rifles and shells for the Pait gun which could fire a 5-inch shell to hit a tank track. If you got a direct hit within 50 yards or so, you could disable them.

I was No 3 and this lad from Blyth was No 4; we brought ammo boxes upwards where No 2 could fed it into the machine gun chamber. As night began to fall the corporal put three men on standby as sentries, one east and one west of the Axis Road and another facing the flat plain overlooking another escarpment in the distance.

In the morning the dead Germans were gone. We could not believe it.

Later in the afternoon we heard what sounded like a tank coming from the east side of the Axis Road but it was a motor bike with two Italians; it had a sidecar with a machine gun on the front but we had our Pait gun. We went over to see, but they were dead so we left them at the side of the road. The corporal phoned the second lieutenant who said they would get someone to dispose of the bodies later. In the evening, just after this had happened, we heard another vehicle and this time it was a rather large van. We had a Bren gun and rifles with 33 rounds; some fired high and some at the tyres and it stopped and toppled over onto its side into a small wadi. The two Italian drivers were dead.

Next day Jerry decided to do some shelling round the area and one lad got wounded; he had been inside the van we had knocked out, for shelter. He was from Blyth and a bit of shrapnel had hit him in the arm. The corporal got the First Aid box and tried to get the shrapnel out but it just kept bleeding. He put a heavy bandage on and put the arm in a sling. This was all we needed, to be a man down, but the lad said, 'I will do my best to carry on.' We thought it very brave of him.

Later that afternoon we heard plane engines heading for us. We dropped to the ground and they released their bombs but they landed a good way from us. Later we were told that 17 soldiers and 2 officers had been killed.

The lad with the wounded arm said it was very painful and he hoped a truck would come to pick him up soon. The corporal tried again to remove the shrapnel but it was too deep and there were no tweezers in the box. He told him just to rest and if he needed anything to give him a shout.

After a quiet night, as usual we did the cleaning of the ammo ready for action; some were in the sanger and some outside. I decided to put on my tin helmet, but one of the corporals said to me, 'Before you put that on, just give it a bang on the ground in case a snake has got inside.' I banged it on the ground, and sure enough, out came a snake. I couldn't believe it. It had happened to him once, apparently. The corporal said, 'You never know what's inside.' I replied, 'You're dead right!' We had a laugh.

Suddenly the lookout, looking west, gave a shout. Everyone crawled to the machine guns and saw the trucks getting hit by bullets and tracer. Some saw trucks on fire and opened fire as the enemy was coming along the Trigh Capuzzo track in the distance, going north. The No 4 lad was trying to pull ammo boxes towards us with his feet so as not to raise his head. One gun stopped, then the other. A lot of people were jumping out of their vehicles, so we had done some damage.

As things quietened down we took out a machine gun to clean and strip and then we did the next one. We all mucked in as it made it a lot easier for everybody, and that's how comradeship should be. Later we were told that Captain Jackman had been given the Victoria Cross. We were pleased for him as he was a good officer and always looked after his men. Later however we heard that Captain Jackman and Sergeant Hedley had been killed during the afternoon when the Jerries had been shelling, which was really sad news.

During the morning I got a letter. I decided to read it later and just put it in my pocket. We had our breakfast and about an hour of peace then all hell let loose. The corporal tried to get the second lieutenant on the phone in the other section as two armoured cars were heading in his direction, but could not get through.

He said, 'I'm afraid that I'll have to detail someone to go down the wadi to tell them, someone who is not married. Who is married and who is not?'

I said I was not and the corporal said, 'I'm sorry, but you will have to go.'

So away I went like a snake, crawling into shell holes on the way to the other wadi, with rifle shots whizzing over me. I did not know whether they were friend or foe, I just kept crawling. I got to a bend and there were a lot of mangled bodies, some without legs, headless, just ripped apart. They must have been victims of that earlier shelling. I kept on till I met this officer and I could hardly speak to him for shock. When I got my breath back I told him as quickly as I could about the armoured cars, but he said, 'I know all about them. We have knocked them out,' and offered me a cup of tea before I made my way back.

A sergeant said, 'Where are you going?'

I answered, 'My platoon of machine-gunners over by the Axis Road.'

He said, 'We got a hell of a hammering this morning by the German mortars. We lost twenty or thirty men.' I just said, 'Cheerio, Sergeant,' and off I went and I had to pass those bodies again.

Later one of the corporals said, 'Do you fancy a cognac?' They had found a bottle in the van we knocked out. They asked if I felt all right but I never answered; I was just shaking like a leaf.

One of the lads said, 'Someone out there is shouting, '*Aqua*.' Someone said it meant 'water'. He kept shouting so someone said, 'Why don't you have a go at him?' I went into the sanger and got my rifle; the corporal gave me five rounds so I just put the clip in and fired at him as he shouted '*Aqua*.' We believed it was a ruse to lure us into a trap. He never shouted again.

I never told anyone about my letter. I got a chance to open it and got a terrible shock. It said, 'Your girlfriend is going around with a married man.' I was dumbstruck. I could have lost my life that morning, and someone had done that to me.

As I was reading it someone came into the sanger and said they could see red lights on vehicles going past our wadi. I asked if I could have a go, but the corporal said we must not give our position away but just stand by the guns in case. I was glad I had had the cognac as it did help me a great deal. I put the letter beside Edie's picture in my bible.

This was the fourth day we had held this place; we had done really well. I asked Robert Taylor where his 15 cwt. was.

'It is back there in the wadi.'

'Can we not take it if an emergency arises?'

He said, 'I am in charge of this vehicle, besides, I have no maps and would not know where to drive to. You know it is dangerous out there through the minefields.'

The injured lad still had no vehicle to take him to the hospital and the corporal had another go at his wound. They put some cognac on to help prevent infection, but still he could not get the shrapnel out. As darkness fell, the corporal said, 'We must get ourselves ready to stand-to just in case Jerry decides to attack us.' But it did stay quiet. The next morning he said that after stand-to and breakfast there would be an attack by the Australians going towards the south of us. We were to give covering fire. We moved the machine guns into place and awaited orders, but the attack was cancelled so we had an early dinner. We had just got the guns back to the sanger when the corporal came over and said, 'I am afraid we have to destroy all guns, machine-guns, Paits and rifles and bury or destroy all ammunition. All the troops that were going to attack have been withdrawn, leaving one and a half platoons beside us in the wadi. This afternoon we will be taken prisoner by the Germans.'

Later that afternoon the army coming towards us from the west along a track known as Trigh Cappuzzo was the South African 1st Army. We all thought we were going to get released by them but were downhearted when they dispersed and the German tanks and motorised units came towards us. That afternoon about 3.30 we were taken prisoners of war. Some Tiger tanks approached along the Axis Road and along the bottom of the wadi were another three. A German officer approached us and said in English, 'I am afraid for you Tommies the war is over,' (and by, was he wrong!). He had a chestful of medals, maybe from the First War.

We got into different armoured half-tracks and just got settled when an anti-personnel shell burst above us. A German got hit in the shoulder and so did the lad from Blyth and Jimmy Hirst; but it missed me. Of course the Germans got treated straight away but our lads didn't and they were in a lot of pain when we got to El Adem.

Chapter 5

We were handed over to the Italians who searched us. We all had different things on us – I had sixty Capstan cigarettes, two tins of fruit and some photos. They gave me back Edie's photo and one of my mother but the others they destroyed. They gave me my letter and my bible. They took my ring and watch.

We left El Adem by truck to Acroma, getting there just before dusk. The Italians gave us a tin meal, bully beef and two hard tack biscuits, and later led us to a place inside a barbed wire stockade, with camouflage ground sheets for bedding. They were soaking wet with the rain we had had that afternoon. We could not sleep at all because we were so cold and we had very little protection from this sodden material. We were glad when the sun came up.

Within half an hour we were put on trucks and trailers and taken to our next stop, Derna. One road was a long pass which was very steep and winding. One truck ahead of us just went over the top and dropped down the side, a long way. It turned over and over till it reached the bottom and the screams were terrible from those soldiers.

We ourselves made it to Derna in one piece and they put us straight into a compound. After one night there we were again put into trucks and went all the way up that frightening pass again. At the top we could see on our left a big aerodrome. It must have had a bashing because there were bits of planes all over the place. We could not say anything because the Italians were a bit jumpy but there were great big smiles on our faces.

We met some paratroopers and a sergeant major who had been on a mission to try and catch Rommel, by land and sea. The day they were dropped a strong wind blew them off course, and after wandering for days, one lad found a truck and drank water from it. He went crazy and later took his revolver and shot himself. This was the story from this sergeant major. They were seen by some Italian trucks as they were in a bad way, and taken to Derna that day.

Now we were on our way to Benghazi to a prisoner of war camp. It was a rather nice area with lots of greenery, palm trees and dates, but a hellhole of a camp. There were hundreds of prisoners. They had a great big trough for a toilet with a narrow wood bar across. One day we were doing our business when the bar snapped and we fell into the cesspit. I was lucky, I fell feet first, but some went in head first and when we all got out they had to hose us down. This was quite refreshing on a hot day. Within the hour our clothes were dry.

We were here for a few days and it was really hot but by gum, it was really cold at night. There were only old blankets and camouflage sheets and the food was not very good. An Italian gave everyone a card and told us to write and tell our parents that we had been taken prisoner and that we were getting good treatment which we were not.

Then on 8 December we were taken to the docks at Benghazi, straight onto a ship. Somehow we knew our destination would be Italy. We were just sailing along nicely when some of the crew came and asked so many at a time to go up on deck for some fresh air. One of the crew came over and said in a low voice, 'The Japanese have bombed Pearl Harbour. A lot of ships have been sunk.' He added, 'I am an American Italian and was over here in Italy for a holiday. They said I had to join up and put me on this ship.'

During the night of 9 December 1941, these coloured South Africans were chanting, which was a bad omen as the next day was the afternoon we were torpedoed. That morning I moved to another place and this deck was made of steel; but people in the place we had been earlier were killed. That was a very stormy time.

A little while later there was suddenly a most almighty bang. The whole ship shuddered, there was a lot of screaming and shouting and when I looked up there was no stairway. We tried to account for who was missing. We had been torpedoed. We got up to the top deck by a rope they had dropped to us which had a lot of knots in it. I took off my boots and left them as it was easier to climb with just my socks. You just kept going, your foot on one knot, your hand on another, till you managed to reach the top. Just as I got there the ship jolted and something caught me in the back of the neck and head and knocked me out for twenty minutes. As I was coming round, I found everyone saying there was a Kiwi with ginger hair who had his legs trapped in a capstan which had broken away.

Later a chap from our section said that a German officer, probably Gestapo or SS, had shot the Italian captain of the ship because he was getting into a lifeboat with his crew. The small boat tried to get further out to sea but the ship's propeller and the waves kept pulling them in and the boat ran into the propeller. Their bodies were thrown all over the sea.

We just roamed about the ship until it was beached on the shores of Greece; this was way after midnight and there was a long queue to get down the rope. It must have been 1.35 when it was my turn. I let go and dropped into the sea and as I could not swim I went down once then twice, and the last time I managed to catch the rope and pulled myself out onto Greek soil. I heard a lot of people shouting, 'Save me!' but it was too dark to see them.

We had to go into a large cabin. My cigarettes were soaking wet but we could dry them off and have the first smoke for ages. The cabin was nearly bursting at the seams and there were a good few Italian soldiers guarding us, and in each corner was a light machine-gun. In the middle was a brazier and we were all just milling around hoping to get warm. I only had a jacket, shirt, and shorts, with socks and no boots.

At daylight we were lined up and marched through the small village. A Greek lady came towards us and saw this lad with no trousers on. She tried to give him a sack to wrap round himself but the guard tried to chase her. She threw it across and one of the lads caught it and passed it down the line to the young lad. The villagers just gave a big grin. At the top of the steep track they opened a large iron gate and we were led into some naval barracks, then mustered into groups of about forty and put into large cells.

We had had nothing to eat or drink since we were torpedoed and it was quite a while before we got a drink that afternoon. When it came to our turn, I looked and said, 'Don't drink that, there are little beetles floating in it.' Another lad had a taste and said it was awful. Later they brought small buns and one ladle of soup, just like dishwater.

Next day quite a lot of the lads were quite poorly. There were no toilets so we kept a place in the corner to do our business. Some had dysentery and the smell was getting terrible but we just had to grin and bear it. Some were sick as well; these were probably the ones who had drunk the contaminated water.

Much later they came round with the dishwater soup – at least it was hot. The next day was much the same routine. That afternoon a single plane arrived in low; guns started to fire at it but it just came on. All of a sudden it dropped a bomb and next thing we saw smoke.

We had a bit of a singsong at night time, just to keep our morale up and let the Italians know we were not a beaten nation. We stayed at this place about ten days. Each morning we had a roll call, checking if everyone was present. They must have thought we had keys!

Days went very slowly as we had nowhere to go: just to watch the sky and see the clouds roll by. Nearly every day was the same routine and the stench was terrible. They never came once to clean the place, not even a hose pipe to swill it. We were glad when they opened the iron grills of the pen; it was lovely just to be counted out. Then an Italian officer told us we were going by truck to another place and escorted us down a small track. On each side were about a battalion of soldiers, covering us all the way down. At the bottom there were a number of trucks; someone asked how many people had been on the ship and it was about two thousand. A party had been taken to the ship and brought back boots, shirts, pants and coats. I got a pair of Kiwi boots which were a size too big but better than nothing

There were lemon trees by the side of the road and I thought it would be all right to eat them as we had them in cakes and things at home. We peeled one or two and tried them, but later became very sick indeed.

Our destination was Patras. They called us into lines to be counted but it was many times before they let us into this huge warehouse which was meant for drying grapes. There were wooden slats to lie on which were very uncomfortable.

The next morning we were all paraded outside so they could count us again. We all stood for a very long time and then suddenly it just poured down with rain. We had very little to protect ourselves against the weather. We were standing around for four and a half hours before we could go in, very wet indeed. We were given a supply of two buns per person and this was our daily ration. After tea we all had to go out again and this time it was snowing. Once while I was outside I found half a spoon handle sticking out of the snow and picked it up. I wasn't sure at that time what I could use it for.

Beneath the snow were lovely green shoots of grass so I put some in my pocket. This chap asked, 'What is that for?'

I said, 'If cows can eat it, why can't we?'

When we received our buns, I opened mine and put the grass in it; it tasted lovely as we had not had any greens for a very long time.

The people of Greece were very helpful. For a single bun they would give eight pieces of flat currant slices, so we nearly all bartered a bun each.

Some of the lads had been up the mountainside to a First Aid station. The Italian soldier there had not a clue what he was doing as he was using the same scalpel on each man, not even cleaning, it, and they were afraid of getting an infection. One said, 'I do not know what I am going to do as I am not going back to that place again. Do you know anyone with a bit of First Aid?'

'Well.' I said, 'I passed a small First Aid course when I was at Backworth Colliery. Come with me,' and I took Jimmy Hirst to where they were cooking our meal that night. One of the lads beside me gave me a piece of his shirt and I scalded it in the hot water. Jimmy's wound was really in a bad way. The only thing I could do was to put the cloth, not too hot, on it and squeeze the fluid out. I was careful as I could as I didn't like hurting him. He said, 'As long as I can get some sleep tonight I will be more than happy.' I kept pressing the cloth and seemed to get out a lot of pus. I must have spent half an hour and he said, 'That time attending to my wound was the best yet. I never received much treatment from the Italians.'

I then did what I could for this other chap from Blyth. I must have spent an hour with him, cleaning his wounds. I don't know if the shrapnel was out by then.

I found a use for the spoon handle which I would sterilise and use to apply pressure to the boiling cloth on their wounds to ease out the pus. Jimmy Hirst was beginning to get along fine but it was a still a long way to go with the lad from Blyth though he too gradually began to improve with treatment. Another lad had carbuncles but his was a longer job. I managed to get out a piece six or seven inches long. One chap said to me, 'Try salt water on all wounds, that might help,' so the next day I went down to the cookhouse and asked one of the lads for some. He said he would ask the Italian guard. All our meals must have been made without salt. I kept working on my three patients all the time at that camp.

It was now approaching Christmas 1941 and the following week would be New Year 1942. Christmas would only be a day like any other. Some rumours said that we would get double rations but many said we would just have to wait and see. However, nothing did happen; it was just the same: two buns and a small bowl of skilly like dishwater. We remembered the lovely dinners we had had at home. Such lovely broth soups and Sunday dinners; we longed for a good feed with a lovely cup of tea. We only ever got cold water. We just reminisced about all the good times we had spent with our families and loved ones: the Christmases and New Years. They were good memories to fall back on which kept you going for another day.

Roll call was as usual two or three hours waiting around; sometimes it was blowing a gale with rain and sleet just lashing down. Standing in this weather was awful. We were wondering if anybody would come down with flu and were really glad to get indoors, just for some warmth. Lying around with wet clothes was just not on, but these Italians didn't care at all. They counted us again and again and still could not get it right. Inside we would strip off our clothes and wring them out, then put them over the rail near the top of the building, hoping they would get dry before the next roll call. Some of us were poorly with sneezing, coughing and shivering but you could not get any help at all; you just had to grin and bear it.

I had been a prisoner for just over a month and so much had happened. The lads came down to the cookhouse and I took a last look at Jimmy's wound. It was coming along great, no pus at all, just raw flesh, but I put a light warm cloth around the edge in case of infection. He said he could not thank me enough. I said, 'At least it gave me something to do; the other guys must be sick as chips, lying around day after day.'

The lad from Blyth took off his shirt, which was rather short with taking pieces to do his back and arm and he too was healing nicely. The lad with carbuncles said, 'It will be great when I can lie on my back with no pain.' I started with medium hot cloths to get some more of the core out. I said, 'There aren't many left to do.'

He said, 'If I stay a bit longer, you could put another hot cloth on the ones that are left and maybe you could work on those; you'd have less to do tomorrow,' and I agreed.

Well, a New Year dawned and we hoped we would get away from this place but no one knew where we were to go next. We all wanted to get into a permanent camp. No one knew how long we were to be prisoners; the way things were going it could be years. We were missing Old England and homes in other countries: all different nations were fighting the Nazis, the Italians, and now the Japanese. We got very little information. The Italians kept mum about what was going on; all you got from them was that they would win the war. In the desert they gave themselves up by the thousands to the Aussies and British; they were very poor fighters though good in artillery. You got a few who might make a stand but they were just slaughtered or maimed. Mostly they surrendered with a white flag but you had to be careful in case they had a grenade in the other hand.

Another reason for wanting to go to another place was maybe we could get a good wash in the morning. With so many people wanting the taps here, which were on for only a short time, there was a rush to get to the small basins. It was not drinking water, maybe from the sea. Sometimes it was dirty and I would sooner go without, like many other people, frightened of getting some disease. You just had to go dirty. The lads and I were lucky; we could get a wash nearly every day with a nice warm cloth when we finished doing the wounds.

The next day I took a stroll down to the cookhouse and surprise, someone had brought a small amount of salt, so when the lads arrived I used it together with the hot cloths and it was very soothing. By the end of the third week in January, after the same routine, the lads were improving with their wounds and carbuncles but left with nasty scars.

Chapter 6

We stayed in Patras for fifty-seven days and then heard we would be moving sometime that day. They said we would be going by lorry to the docks to board a ship. We were glad to be getting away from that hell-hole. They told us to take our belongings, and in my case that was not much, just a little bag I had made with my photos of Edie and my parents. The soldiers called a roll call, which would be the last here, and it was rather a pleasant day.

The lorries arrived and we all started getting on the tailboards; some were open and some had covers on. There were about fifteen on each, plus four guards, and about six or eight lorries. One of the guards said, 'We are taking you to Italy.' The Greek people tried to smile as we passed and one of the lads put his hand out of the slit in the back and gave them a wave.

It did not take long to get to the docks, then we were marshalled like a herd of cattle onto this coastal tramp steamer, just over a thousand tons and by, it was a scruffy old tub. We went up the ramp along a gangway into a hold then down some ladders right to the bottom of the ship. There were some wood batons to lie on with two small lights in our corner and two more beside the ladders and the damn thing was swaying very badly. Some of the lads were saying we were in for a rough ride; maybe some of them had been working in the shipyards. People were still coming down the ladders. I do not know how many holds there were but it seemed to take a long time.

Eventually we all settled down, hoping we would get something to eat and drink. What they did drop was a rope and on it was a big can of skilly. There was a mad rush and though they dropped half a dozen cans some got fed and some did not. There was one hell of a commotion and a sailor said, I think, that they were sorry but that was all they had for that night. Jimmy managed to get some for us four. Most of us got

34

two buns in the morning, so those who had had no skilly would have to wait till then. We could not complain because they were in control over us. We just had to grin and bear it. If we complained we might not get anything the next day. Everyone started to settle down for the night but it was very cold and damp. The boat was swaying about and we were glad when morning came.

But next day the same thing happened. They sent bags with buns and we all agreed we should put someone near the steps to dish out the food and no one could eat anything till everyone had at least one bun, and if there were more we would share, even if it meant one and a half buns for all. A staff sergeant was in charge. Meanwhile an Italian sailor asked if we wanted water and a few medium sized cans of water came down. We had little alloy dixies and the sergeant said he would distribute small portions of water to everyone.

Suddenly the engines started and we moved from the canal. All of us thought, 'Right, we are on our way to Italy.' We seemed to travel about an hour then the engines stopped again.

One lad on board said he had been in Greece since the start of the campaign, fighting first the Italians and then the Germans. Around June 1941 they met some Greek people who hid them for a time and later, dressed as Greeks and having started to learn the language, they could mix with the locals. They were in a very small village in the mountains near Athens. After many months they decided to move on; they travelled looking for work just to get some food and a place to sleep. Now they were getting braver and decided to go into Athens. They went into a tavern and there met a woman who took them to a brothel to stay. Some nights German officers and soldiers went there. Sometimes they asked the prostitutes to get information to be passed on. Eventually there was a raid and they got caught. One was an Aussie, one from the Sheffield area and one from Scotland. They had a rough time with the Germans who asked about why they were living in Greece and it was lucky they still had their dog tags or they might have been shot as spies.

Later in the day the rope came down with packages on and the food was shared out. We were supposed to get a ration of food a fraction below that of an ordinary soldier there: maybe half, but nobody really knew. If you asked an Italian they would say, 'Maybe the day after tomorrow,' but when the day came there was nothing.

The next day passed with the same routine, people talking about their different experiences and how they were captured. Some were taken at Sollum Barida and other places near the Egyptian and Libyan borders. A few chaps were caught at Hell Fire Pass.

It was beginning to smell as though there was a lavatory in the corner there was no water, just some newspaper for the necessary things you had to do. We all hoped we would be sailing soon but there was no movement. It was the third day on board and the same routine. The sergeant stood at the bottom of the line and took the bags off and some of the lads gave him a hand to stack them. We all hoped and prayed we would get plenty of buns. We had received just one so somebody was going to be short unless they put extra ones in. The sergeant said, 'I want the names of people who only got one; don't think of not telling the truth as tomorrow you would not get any.' Jimmy got two buns so he and I shared the second one. Better to have one and a half than just one because you have not got any mates.

The next day we were still short of food and that night we again did not sleep well because two or three lads were ill, crying and shouting with pain. We were all sick of the smell; maybe that was what was causing people to be ill. You'd think they would drop a hose pipe to clear it all away and the sergeant said he would see if he could find an officer or the Captain about it. Within the hour, we heard movement with the hold hatch opening. It was the sailor and the sergeant tried to talk with him but he said, 'I am rather busy at the moment; I will talk to you later if I can.' He dropped the rope with bags on so at least we might get something to eat.

The sergeant was getting really angry and shouted again. He said, 'Where are we?'

The sailor replied, 'Corinth Canal.'

The sergeant asked, 'When will you come and clean up down here as I have some chaps ill. If you don't, I will report you to the Red Cross in Switzerland.'

The sailor said, 'I will see about it tomorrow.'

The sergeant replied, 'And I would like to see the Captain.'

'It will be tomorrow. He went ashore this afternoon.'

The next day was just the same but eventually the Captain came and they conversed as best they could. Within half an hour, two chaps came down with hose pipes and started clearing up the mess. The sailor said, 'Tomorrow we may be sailing,' and we all agreed it would be great to get away from that dingy hole.

Up to now there were still no engines running and once again it was a waiting game. The rations were cut. When the sergeant asked, the reply was that they were expecting another ship with supplies and that they could not sail without them. We got one and a half buns again, which was better than nothing.

We lay down and tried to get some sleep. We had not got much the night before because of people being ill. You started thinking of home and the lovely meals you had with your family – roast beef, potatoes, peas, carrots, turnip, cauliflower, cabbage; maybe apple pie with custard; and teatime with scones, teacakes and buns of different kinds. When I woke up it was not far from skilly time and we still were not sailing. It was another night of short rations. Again it took time to dish it out and we stood in a queue to get served. The sergeant had us in sections; different sections went up at different time each night. It was a good system and quite orderly, no pushing or bad tempers. If there were the sergeant said, 'Any more of this and every night you will be last.'

Afterwards we had a little chatter as no singing was allowed, then we settled down for the night. I had to go to the loo in the corner as the skilly went right through me. It was uncomfortable passing people in their beds – if that's what you could call bare boards on deck.

The rations got even smaller, only one bun each. The sergeant made another complaint and eventually the Captain appeared and was told what we wanted. He said, 'I am sorry, the food rations, that is all we can do and we are also cutting back, as the boat did not arrive. If we sail away to another port we may get some there.' He did say he would send some men down to clear up the mess. At least the sergeant was getting something done; maybe the Captain remembered the threat about the Red Cross. The Captain said we might sail later today or early tomorrow. This would be just over a week since we had arrived on board.

At any rate, it looked as if we were in for a rough ride. Something was making them scared, perhaps they were frightened to leave. I wondered who gave them their orders, the Italians or the Germans; the first boat had a Nazi officer though it was Italian manned. If they were on that ship perhaps they were on others.

During the night someone shouted, 'I think the engines are starting to rev!' All of a sudden we started to move. So the old Captain was right. It was quite calm, as might be expected in a canal. At least we were on the move and at the next port we might get some extra food. It would be terrible if not. The sergeant would have a large book to write about our complaints.

The boat was acting all right unless it was hugging the coast to keep away from the submarines. It was soon time to have our bun or buns. When the door hatch was opened maybe we could find out where we were, unless they were keeping it secret. Then they started to open the hatch. We had not had any water since we came on board, just the watery skilly. On the rope were very few bags; it looked like one bun each only. The sergeant shouted up, 'Where are we going?' and the sailor replied, 'Corfu.'

Someone said, 'I hope we land there, it's such a small island and a very nice place; I've been on holiday there with my parents.'

It was quite calm sailing along; maybe it was a nice calm hot day. I wondered if we would cross the Adriatic or go round the coast all the way. We didn't know how far it was across but it would take longer all round the countries: Greece, Albania, Yugoslavia.

We arrived at Corfu very late and stayed there till early morning. We moved on then, very smoothly; at least it was better than lying in harbour. It would be nice to have some food as there had been no sign of any. It approached midday then on to one o'clock; it seemed odd because every day between 12 o'clock and 12.30 we got our food. Now it was 2 o'clock and no sign of food. It was very frightening not getting anything at all, but you could never trust the Italians – as I said before, tomorrow or the day after. We were still travelling on, then we might arrive at another port and stop.

We got over the first day without food. Some of the lads were down with dysentery, others with the runs and by, when you got it it was non-stop to the toilet.

Two more days went by and still there was no food. One or two lads were very ill indeed. They had the runs since leaving Corfu and might die because there was no way to get any attention from above. It was just a matter of time. In fact many more would die before we got to our destination. It was really terrible down there with the heat, no fresh air, the stench which was unbearable and people getting ill all the time. You just lay down hoping to get some rest and that we would arrive soon. During that night six people died.

By the fourth day since leaving Corfu, we could not stand much more. We were in God's hands for survival; it was a crying shame that so many young lads like myself had got to die because of stupid people in command. It would have been nice just to see the sky, even the sea or the places we passed. We all hoped we would reach land soon. The boat was moving on and the hunger pains were getting worse as each hour passed. Most were sleeping all the time just to while the hours away.

On the sixth day something happened. The boat slowed down. At last there was a glimmer of hope. Everyone was on their feet hoping that this was the end of the journey. Some were too weak to stand and were just kneeling and so pleased that we all would get ashore. Maybe some of the men that were ill could be taken to a hospital to get help. Mostly, there would be food, even if it was only a little. That was what our bodies were crying out for.

The boat got even slower. We didn't know if it was daylight or darkness. It would take us a while to acclimatise to the light. All of a sudden the engines stopped and we could hear voices from above. Within half an hour the hatch was opened and we were very glad to get some fresh air – it smelled like heaven. Unfortunately three or four more lads had died during the night.

The sailor shouted down, 'We have landed at Bari, Italy!'

We all shouted at him for not giving us any food but he blamed the Captain. We were concerned now to get out of this hellhole and on to land. Most of the lads said it would be a long time before they would get on another boat.

They dropped the ladders but it was a slow process as only a few at a time could go up at once; there were eight hundred men or less on board. It was late in the afternoon when I got up. It was really nice to see a lovely day but you had to shade your eyes because the sun was so strong.

Chapter 7

They took us along this street in Bari. Someone spotted Mussolini pictured on the wall and he started picking up stones from the street and throwing them at it. The Italians saw this and began firing shots above our heads. The sergeant shouted, 'Stop, or someone is going to get killed by a foolish trick like that!' So it quietened down a bit. As we were passing one house there was a small round of bread and one chap went over and took it. He snapped it in half and gave his mate some.

We were kept waiting for transport to take us somewhere for the night; some people had already gone. We stood for a while and still no one had any food. One or two lads started dropping to the ground, exhausted; even I just sat down for my legs were like jelly. Quite a while later we saw some trucks coming down the main street and we all shouted, 'About time too!' We kept going along the coast, then into the country and along a road. Half an hour later we were again on the coast. We passed a signpost to Brindisi then once again turned off into the country. Half an hour later we pulled into a field with three large huts and when we got out we were given some skilly straight away and it was the first food for days and really nice to have a hot meal.

There was quite a range of troops: Indians, Australians and New Zealanders and some sailors who had been captured from a submarine in Libya. The field was very small and with lots of barbed wire fencing around an area of 200 by 120 yards,

Later in the day we went around to see if there was anything we could eat. There were one or two trees, different types of weeds and some grass, some very young, some old and tough. Some of the weeds could be used in soup; it was really trial and error. If you are hungry you will eat anything. We picked some and put them in an Italian dixie – a small metal container which held one helping of skilly. We collected some timber from around the trees and got a fire going; then started boiling water in the dixie. The first sample was really terrible; it tasted sour and rotten. In fact it was all a disaster; none of our efforts came to anything.

The next morning some Italian soldiers knocked on the three huts. Just at the entrance to the field were three soldiers with big steaming cans. We thought it would be another helping of skilly, but no – we were to get a ladle each morning of hot cognac and water because the mornings were very cold indeed. We all had a mug and by, it did warm you up.

Later we all went into the field for roll call and the sun started to rise. It was getting warmer by the hour. Afterwards we wanted to go in out of the sun but were not allowed into the huts in daytime. So most of us wandered about the field and none of us had any cigarettes, so I said, 'Why not try some bark and see if we can make cigs out of it?' One of the lads had a piece of glass, so we managed to get off small pieces and rolled them in some paper and it wasn't too bad, not when you hadn't any others at all. We were rather short of paper though and there did not seem to be any nicotine, but it was just like having a real ciggy in your hand.

On the third day one of the guards told us all to get outside. Then he gave us the news that nine or ten people had died during the night with meningitis. They started putting stuff into our mouths; we found out they were sulphur tablets, the size of a half-crown and half an inch thick and you had to swallow them without water which was quite a struggle. We were in the field all day until 6 o'clock at night, with two roll calls; we were pleased it did not rain.

A wagon came into the compound and the soldiers started to unload it. There were camouflage sheets to make tents which had to be assembled using a mallet. Jimmy Hirst and I put the wooden poles into the ground then the Italians dished out lengths of rope to tie each pole. Time was getting on and we needed to get it finished before dark. Quite a few didn't make it so they just had to lie on the sheets till morning. We made it in the nick of time but had to sleep on the ground, which was not too bad: better than the wooden slats at Patras.

It took ages to settle down and Jimmy and I told stories about where we had lived. I worked at the Algernon Pit near West Allotment and

Jimmy and his sister ran a business shop in Winlaton. He was a few years older than me. I worked at the pit from when I was fourteen till I was twenty, when I was called up. Women were hardly ever mentioned. I kept my private life to myself and I tried to keep from making pals with anybody because I thought if you didn't get attached then if anything happened you wouldn't get hurt. We stayed as friends for quite a while, mind; just that it was best not to get too involved.

Next morning broke quite sunny and I went towards the gate to get our hot cognac. There was quite a queue but it was quite nice to wait for something hot. On my way back I got lost as there were so many tents all alike. I just kept calling Jimmy's name until at last he shouted, 'I'm over here.' I had been going the wrong way. We wondered what we could do about this and finally broke a piece of branch and tied it to the pole.

About midday our buns came as usual and this took the hunger pangs away while we wandered around the compound talking; this we did many times. Living in these conditions was terrible. When it rained the place was like a mire; you had to sit in you tent or lie on straw that they gave us but this didn't stop the water coming in. Mostly you had to kneel or your clothes got wet. We talked about what we had done at school. Jimmy was a bright lad; I was just a dunce compared to him. I was good at history, geography and sport and I enjoyed gardening. Woodwork was poor but we were not taught properly. Our teacher used to leave us to get on with things while he said, 'I'm away to see someone.' We knew who – Miss Pinder, the French and music teacher. She did sometimes take children outside to talk about flowers, trees and birds, which was interesting.

After skilly a lorry pulled up with bundles of straw in. We opened the bales and took some to our tents. Jimmy and I put some in our tent – it was still warm. Later we had a nice lie-down on it and within half an hour we were fast asleep.

Next morning, Jimmy said, 'By, lad, I'm bit to pieces. I wonder if there are any flies.'

He stripped and on his shirt were some lice right along the crease. He lit a ciggy and started burning along the edge and you could hear them crack. Everyone was doing it as the bales of straw were wick with lice.

After our dinner time buns an Italian officer came through the gate and shouted he wanted everyone to form lines. They told us we would not be allowed back in the huts but didn't explain why not. Still more straw arrived and we got some; we took all the old straw out of the hut tent and put it in a heap; half an hour later an Italian soldier set fire to it. Because everyone was doing the same thing, my, what a blaze there was. They must have wanted to light it before it got dark in case a plane came over.

The stinking farmer and his farm were about two or three hundred yards away. The farmhouse was built somehow on stilts and part was a lean-to where the cattle and others sheltered. He had all sorts of animals – cattle, goats, sheep, dogs, cats, you name it: we all thought he had Noah's Ark. When the wind blew from the Brindisi direction it smelt terrible.

The next morning was the start of a new month, April 1942. It was surprising to think what we had already been through and we wondered when our luck would turn. I don't know if this was the start of Ramadan because there was a lot of praying and chanting going on that morning from the Indians.

Chapter 8

We had our usual cognac and hot water and were waiting for our buns which usually came about twelve. We did some more delousing to pass the time. Just after our buns some lorries turned up and they started putting our lads on them; then they drove away. Another batch arrived and more of us were loaded, starting at the top sections. So we were going to a different abode.

We went along the same route that we had come from Bari but before the town we turned off into a smaller road, rather winding. It was a nice change from being penned up. We arrived at a field where the tents were already up, thank god, because it was already getting a bit dark. There was no straw, but we settled down; got some skilly but within half an hour the heavens opened and the tents started to flood. Once again we had to squat; and there was very little sleep that night. But at least we were under the tent, unlike some others whose tent collapsed during the night. All through the next day it rained and many people were getting to the end of their tether, Night time approached again and it was going to be another terrible night.

Everyone was looking forward to their cognac. Later there seemed to be a bit of blue sky and the rain came down more slowly. I thought if the sun broke through it would be wonderful and maybe we would get some dry straw as we had passed plenty of farms. It did brighten up and everyone came out to see what they could do, all helping each other.

A bunch of Italian soldiers came in with shovels and told us to make channels so that if it started to rain again it might avoid our tents. We dug down about a foot and a half while the rain kept off. Some of the soldiers helped those whose tents were down or lying at an angle. It didn't take long to put everything right and it put the morning in lovely.

A bread lorry came to just outside the gate. It was lovely to have something to eat again but it didn't take long as we were tired, weary and hungry.

Later we were given fresh bales of straw which were again covered in lice but kept us dry. We still had to have two roll calls a day with nothing to do but twiddle your thumbs; it lasted an hour and a half, just to count two hundred people, ridiculous. They should have put us into groups of fifty, but they insisted on doing us all together and making mistakes.

But as the day drew to a close, we knew it would be a better night's sleep. The moon was bright and there were stars in the sky. We had our skilly and sat to take it easy.

The rain stayed away for a while, then a couple of days later it started again and we were very pleased with our work; it just went down the channels we had dug out.

We had been here nearly a week and some bright spark said he had heard a rumour we would be moving again. We just hoped and prayed we would get to a proper camp, though everyone was at that time quite happy staying here as it was rather nice compared to the last place we were in.

The next day arrived and as usual we had our early morning cognac and hot water, then Jimmy Hurst and I had a stroll round the camp, as it was a lovely morning. He talked about his sister keeping their shop in Winlaton and how she was coping with the rations being so tight. He was not courting which seemed rather funny as he was about 28 years old; unless he had someone and did not want to talk about it. I was always talking about my girlfriend, what were her tastes, what good times we had had at the Palace and the Empire in Newcastle, some of the shows we had seen.

As we were approaching our tent we saw this major coming into the compound with two soldiers. He later addressed the compound of men and told us that we would be going back to that smelly farm site again within the next day or so. Everybody was disappointed but as we always said: just grin and bear it as there was nothing we could do. We all really wanted to go to a camp and get settled and get in touch with our families again. I specially wanted to find out if my girlfriend had received the engagement money I sent from Tobruk, as I did love her very much.

I still had her photograph and was always looking at it. When I came down the ship's rope it really did get a good soaking and it was a good while before I got it into shape as it was very crumpled.

We spent the early morning just talking about food: what lovely meals our parents made us on weekdays and for Sunday dinners; really, it was mouthwatering just talking about it. Then we discussed the Newcastle team, just before the war started. Some of the lads had been to the matches because they had good jobs and money; others came from big families whose mothers could not afford to give them much. I had been 17 years old, doing a man's work but getting a young lad's money; I earned 17s. 6d. a week and my mother only gave back 1s. 9d. from this as I was the only worker in the house.

It was approaching bun time as came towards the gate and there was the van with the buns on board. The Italian soldiers started to unload and Sergeant Bertram asked for volunteers to help them carry the baskets to the distribution area. When we four finished this chore, we received an extra bun; we could not believe it but it was very welcome. It did not happen again however as the sergeant announced later that we would leave tomorrow morning when trucks would be laid on to take us back to the farm. All our bits and pieces would have to be shown to the soldiers at the gate.

Next day the trucks were waiting just outside the compound. At least we had had our early cognac which always warmed us. Some started to get on board. There were a lot of Italian soldiers around, about a company, milling around with hats and feathers sticking out on their silly uniforms. They looked like a bunch of unruly peasants, not smart like the British soldiers.

Four trucks went and we waited to see if any more would appear and it was much later in the afternoon that we eventually boarded. There was quite a column of trucks with escort motor cycles in front and beside, even behind, the convoy. It was quite a nice trip, but what a place to end up in. We travelled along towards Brindisi, all hoping we would arrive before it got dark as we didn't know if our tents would still be there.

When we arrived it was not too bad because the earlier arrivals had helped putting tents up; at least we would not be lying in the open field again. We were very near the main entrance which was good as we would not have to travel far for our grub, which again would be late as it was approaching 7.30 p.m. With no lights allowed it was going to be really terrible. These people didn't care about anyone but themselves. We were really hungry – anything would do so long as it was hot, and with something to drink.

There was some movement at the main gate where some men had started to form a line with their small soup cups. The truck dropped its tailboard and we all went to get served. We had to keep blowing on the soup to get it cool before it got dark.

Actually, things did not go wrong that night and there was no roll call; and next day we got our morning cognac. This time it was really hot because we were beside the gate. After a while the main gates opened and the soldiers started coming in. Sergeant Bertram called us to form in lines to make it easy to count us, so we formed three lines. However, what did the Italians do but make us form into different groups as before and once again they started counting and got it all wrong and we had to stand till they counted us again. We were outside in the rain for over an hour and a half. We had not much clothing on – I had a pair of short trousers, holes in my socks and boots that were starting to let water in. Again they made a mistake and we had to get counted again. We were all soaked to the skin and it was getting to be past our bun time.

Suddenly an officer came in and gave a command. All the Italians went running towards him and he told them all off; then the parade was stood down.

We went into the tents soaking wet, cold and miserable. Jimmy and I took our shirts off and tried to dry them with the straw, wringing them out first outside the tent, but to no avail. We had very little sleep with the cold. Surely this could not go on for ever. There must be a silver lining on the horizon.

Just then we saw the sun rising in the east. This was our only hope of getting warm, and we might get a bit of sleep later, in turns so as not to miss our bun ration. By midday the sun was really hot and our clothes were beginning to get dry. Nearly everyone was going around in the nude but at least we were warm.

48

Next morning the cognac seemed really strong. Someone must have put extra rations in. Jimmy said, 'Do you know what, them bloody lice have come again in my shirt, I thought we had got rid of them as the last place had none at all; it must be this filthy farm we are getting the straw from.'

Once again we were smoking whatever we could get from the tree, burning them out of the creases in trousers and shirts. This delousing was not a pretty sight; nearly everyone again with all their clothes off. If it wasn't rain it was these rotten lice. Our next meal of skilly was just dishwater, just coloured nothing at all with not even a piece of macaroni. Still, it was hot.

Now it was the end of April with every day much the same, still hoping to get word of moving to a proper camp. It was really nice to sit in the sunshine and get brown though sometimes too hot, and also too hot inside the tent. We sometimes walked around the compound talking of things we had done when we were youngsters: football, cricket and other things like hopscotch, knocky door nine and rounders.

On the last day of April, after the usual hot cognac and roll call, an officer came into the compound accompanied by three soldiers and the interpreter. They called all the sergeants to them for a private talk. It was quite a while before the sergeants came away, and then one called our group over to tell us what had been said.

In a few days time we would be moving to a camp in Bari which had been being built. It would be quite a big camp, holding thousands of prisoners from different places around the country. There would be proper billets and a bed for everyone. We would be able to send letters to loved ones and families, and most of all there would be Red Cross parcels. Everyone cheered and all were asking different questions, some of which he was unable to answer; but he said there would be water taps to wash ourselves and our clothes and to shave; and once a month a shop would be open to sell things like fruit. He told us not to build our hopes up as sometimes their tomorrows never came.

Chapter 9

He was right as it was 6 May before a lot of trucks were lined up. An officer asked for Sergeant Bertram and told him to form a batch of men with their things. He said that this new camp was right in the middle of nowhere and by God he was right; but never mind, it was good to get away from this stinking place.

We got on our way, the same route as before at first, but then a different route. It was quite a nice journey into the country. Then in the distance we saw this massive camp, blocks of concrete housing. When we arrived we could see big drums of cooking and people milling around with little cups. It smelt really nice and we had only had two little buns at midday.

Then we were allocated our billets. Inside there were three-tier beds, with laths across the length of each bed. Then we had to go and get our food, but there was quite a queue and it was some time before we got served. We had hardly got it down when Sergeant Bertram told us to line up to get some palliasses. This did not take long because there was a pile of them and you all helped yourselves.

My bed was top one and you had to be fit to get up. Because of what we had been through, we needed a lift up. Maybe after few days of good food it would be all right and with all the talk of Red Cross parcels, that would be lovely, just to taste some English food.

Next day we received a card and a letter card to write home. The card was very small, about nine lines; the other had about fifteen. I thought I would send the small one to my fiancée and the other to my parents. I had my Dear John letter in my hand and while strolling around the compound I showed it to one of the lads. He said, 'It's not fair on you, her going around with a married man while you're stuck in here; if I was you I'd break off the relationship.' So I took his advice and wrote that I was finishing with her. As I was writing my eyes welled up and

I started to cry because I really loved her very much. I still carried her photo around with me so at least she was near me and I could talk to her when nobody was around. I never gave her a chance to tell her story and it was really hurting very much. I wished I could turn the clock back and not have sent that card to her. She was a wonderful person. These people did a terrible thing to two persons in love. Maybe I would see her again when I got back to England, but God knew when that would be. Just to hold her in my arms and give her a long lovely kiss. Why did I let her go, because of someone putting a knife into my heart.

Things were looking up in this camp; meals were a bit better and regular, and the Red Cross parcels did help a great deal; Jimmy and I got one to share. He was on the bottom bunk. The toilets were quite a way away but there you could get a wash and shave and a haircut now and again. There was a hole about 12 inches wide and you had to stand on two concrete foot marks. Every day two men were detailed to put in a hose pipe and swill it down so it was always nice and clean. The wash basins were one large trough and many blokes could get in to wash though it was terrible if too many tried to get in at once.

Someone came up with an idea to make tea involving a milk tin cut into strips to make a pipe and another for charcoal and paper. Another tin had the water. It was bad when the smoke started filling the room though.

I was vexed with myself for what I did to Edie and asked my mother to give my address to Edward Blake to see if he could shed any light on it. It was hard waiting to see how things went. On Edie's birthday I was so miserable, thinking about her all day and about how we were so happy in each other's company, talking about having children if we got married, how we would look after each other no matter what. I wished I had ripped up that Dear John letter right away; someone had put poison between us. I could only hope something came out of this when I got home and I could only say to myself. 'Have a lovely birthday and my love goes to you.'

I would walk round the compound two or three times just to fill the time.

I met Jimmy and said that I had met one of our lads from Whickham, and he had said, 'What have you in your hand?' I said a letter and told him that I could not understand what it meant as I could hardly read or write. 'If I was you just write and break it off,' which I did. Jimmy said, 'What a pity. If you had told me I would have said just carry on.'

The roll calls were twice a day and they must have thought we were going to run away because there must have been a battalion of troops around the camp. Some had machine guns in the high sentry box and there was a trip wire which if you crossed they had a right to shoot you. If a ball went over, you had to put your hands up then retrieve it. One day a soldier went out without putting his hands up and got shot, and later died of his wound.

At dinner time when they dished out the buns I used to make a meal for Jimmy and me with one bun; then at tea time we would have the other, with maybe a slice of corned beef or some cheese from the Red Cross parcel. Late in the day we got our skilly between six and seven o'clock. The food was a bit better than in the other places, but the days were long with nothing to do but sit around and sometimes sunbathe. Sometimes we were allotted a cold shower with a hose pipe attached to the wall.

Once a fortnight we got a card that we could fill in with very few words – just the place is all right, food good and so on. The only excitement was getting the Red Cross parcels and Sergeant Bertram said we might get a supply of cigs as we had not had any since we arrived. Each block was to be allotted a day to go to the shop with coupons to buy things like fruit and maybe vegetables like carrots. I got two oranges and two apples this first month.

As we lay in the sun I thought of the good days I had with my family, down at Whitley Bay on a bank holiday which was full of people from the North East and Scotland, hearing the sellers shouting 'Get your Walls ice cream here!' Kiddies would be paddling in the sea, playing with a bucket and spade making sand castles. My mother brought plenty of sandwiches and tea cakes and meat pies. Everyone had their own carrier bag to put their things in.

It was lovely lying in the sun, getting very brown indeed; we were all down to our trunks. Roll call was still twice a day and it took them quite a while to count us. Why didn't they come round and make everybody stand by their beds? We had to go outside and stand in the hot sun and some of the lads fell down with the heat, not being used to it; we had had a new intake of men who had been captured a few months ago in the desert. They were looking depressed as they had also had a hard time but things were looking up now.

You were scared stiff especially on rainy days in case you got flu as some chaps did, and they lay in bed hoping some Italian doctor would come to see them, which was not very often, so you just had to grin and bear it, hoping God was on your side. In another block one chap died and within an hour or so they took his body away in a horse and cart.

One rainy day someone said they were giving out Red Cross parcels so we went out to see if that was right. By, the lad was right and there was a great long queue. As I joined it the lads were passing all smiles; he said these ones were from Canada; this was a great change from English parcels and there was one between two persons. The first thing we opened was the Klim tin (milk backwards); it was really creamy and our tea tasted quite different; we had two biscuits each and the butter was quite good too. There was a portion of cheese so we split it between us and really enjoyed it, having not tasted any at all during our captivity.

Every day was like one all rolled into each other. It was no good complaining as things were looking up – it was a lot nice here than anywhere we had been before. Still, it got really boring with nothing to do but have a stroll round the camp and look forward to our Canadian parcels and letters from home. They must have been going through a lot there with us being missing, wondering where we were, not knowing if we were alive or dead.

One day a couple of Italian soldiers came into our block and Stephen, a lad from London, started speaking to them in Italian; he gave them something out of his Red Cross parcel and they gave him some lira. The next thing was that this lad Ron was digging a piece of the wall away and putting the pieces in his jumper and taking them outside. Eventually Ron broke through and he started putting things inside it while Stephen would keep a lookout. He seemed to be learning more Italian from a dictionary.

I was just talking to Sergeant Bertram and asking if he had heard anything and we spoke of how welcome the Canadian parcels were. He said he hoped there were plenty in the storeroom. Just then two Italian soldiers came through the gate and demanded that we formed in lines, then an officer followed them. It seemed earlier than usual; maybe he had assembled us to tell us something, maybe the war was over. But instead he said that they were cutting rations to one bun each instead of two as there was a shortage of flour in the area. We all thought something must be going on, and later the London lad, Stephen, said that Foggia had been bombed during the night. We hoped they wouldn't cut our skilly as well.

The Italian soldiers came into our block and went straight over to find Stephen. Jimmy said he'd not seen them since that morning, but we thought he must be bartering. Later he and his mate came in carrying something up their jumpers but they put up a blanket so no one could see what was going on. Much later the roll call came but Ron never went on parade. I think he must have had some hold over the Italians.

We were having a cold drink at bedtime from the creamy Klim. The guards had stopped us using the contraption we had been making tea in; they must have thought we would set fire to the place but they were quite wrong – why should we set fire to it as it was our only shelter from the rain and wind. Just after, while I was in the queue for skilly, it all of a sudden started to rain, just steady at first but by the time I got served the heavens had opened and I got a real soaking. My shoes started to take in water. I only had a blanket to keep me warm that night and I was perished so I sat up and wrapped it round me. There was no heating in the buildings, so I did not know what we were going to do in the winter. I was very glad when morning came and I could have my nice cup of cognac and hot water. All my clothes – shirt, trousers, army jacket – were still soaking wet and would take some drying. At roll call other people like myself were wrapped in blankets.

The Canadian parcels were nearly finished and we would have to make them stretch out as God knows when we would get the next one, even if they were in the store. There was just a little jam and one tin of meat left and I had had no cigs for a few days.

We decided to have a stroll round the compound and on our way met a lad who had been at Tobruk; he was caught just outside Derna in

1941. He had had a rough time in different camps; we told him about our bad times. He said he could not say what was happening in the desert so we didn't press him in any way.

It was ages before I had any clothes to wear after their soaking as the sun was not as hot as on other days, but after my skilly I had an early night and went straight to sleep. In the morning I kept feeling cold in the queue and wondered if I was in for a dose of flu or a cold, which I could do without. When I got into the block Jimmy said, 'You don't look too good.' I lay down and Jimmy put both our blankets on me. I had my cognac and Jimmy went to tell Sergeant Bertram that I was ill and in bed. That day Jimmy said he would go and get what was necessary as long as I was not well. He said I had to try and get better by staying in bed after the soaking I'd had.

I must have dropped off to sleep but I woke up to hear someone shouting that the soldiers were dishing out parcels. Jimmy said he would get both; he would stand in one line and get the buns and then the next queue and get the parcel. It could not have come at a better time. He made me a cup of milk with a drop of sugar and two or three biscuits with cheese spread, and then I fell asleep again. I said that if there were any tins of soup I wouldn't mind that, but it would not be fair if I had it to myself, but Jimmy said we could come to some arrangement about that. The soup made me quite warm and again I dropped off to sleep. Jimmy insisted that I stayed in bed for a few days. I had small portions of the meals he made and some milky coffee. While I was lying there during roll call I realised that Stephen was still there, looking after his hole in the wall. God only knows what he had inside.

Jimmy seemed to be away a long time and when he came in he said that the skilly was late with some hold-up. He was not in a very good mood, having been standing for nearly an hour.

The 1 June looked as if it was going to be a real scorcher and I felt better than I had for days. After my cognac I thought I could get up and just walk round the room, and Jimmy and another man took me to the toilet. I lay for a while on Jimmy's bottom bunk and he said that I could have his place until I got better. I was frightened in case I fell off the top bunk.

Another day arrived. I hoped I might go down to the toilets and have a wash and a shave. Jimmy went for the cognac and asked me to try and take some as I had not had any yesterday; I must have fallen asleep before he came back. Jimmy drank it instead, not to waste it. 'That's all right,' I said, remembering seeing the empty cup and thinking I had drunk it, 'it's no use wasting stuff.'

'But it's not right, me eating your rations under these conditions. I'll try and give you a bit extra when you feel well enough.'

'All right, Jimmy, because you will need feeding up as you have lost a lot of weight.'

When he had gone I dropped off to sleep again. But when Jimmy came back after waiting over two hours for buns, he said that he would make a cup of tea, or some milk. I had half a bun, the most I'd eaten for a week, though I'd had skilly, cognac and the odd cup of tea or milk.

Jimmy went out for roll call and again he seemed to be quite a while, especially when I was on my own, because Ron, on the other side, never said anything at all. Without a watch, time seemed to stand still. He said it was a long roll call, two and a half hours, but it was a lovely day, the sun was red hot and he was going to go out again and meet some of the lads from the regiment. I was on my own once again, so again I lay down and went to sleep. Well, it must be doing me good.

The next day I thought I would have a small walk round the beds to see what I could do, so I got hold of the bed post and managed to take a few steps on my own. After my cognac and while Jimmy was getting the buns, I managed to walk three bed lengths. Later I walked some more and it felt a little better than the first time. When Jimmy brought the buns, I said, 'Give them here and I will butter them,' and Jimmy said, 'All right, but I will make the tea.' It was nice to have something to do again. Jimmy took me down to the toilets; it was quite an effort but I managed with his help. It was wonderful just to be out in the sunshine, and though it took quite a while, as they said later, you have all the time in the world.

Someone in the block said they were receiving mail. He must have heard someone talking about this; there are many things said and sometimes they are true but nearly always wrong. I started to get out of bed and I felt better than I had for a while, so I decided to take a stroll round the beds and I was quite amazed as I was not holding on.

While Jimmy and the lads were at roll call I tried the full length of the block. When they came back Jimmy said he had heard that people had received letters from England and we hoped that we would be getting some mail from our loved ones though not me as I had made a mess of things by not waiting to see what Edie had to say. How I wished I had torn up that Dear John letter, or lost it when I was in the water off Piraeus.

Then I went for a small stroll around the compound and when I had had enough I sat down with my back to the block and then went in to the toilet.

Meanwhile some Italian soldiers came through the main gates; Jimmy said it could not be roll call yet; it was too early. But another couple of soldiers strolling round the block started to rant and rave at us. Jimmy said they must be out their minds but what we did not see was a young lad wounded; he must have stepped over the trip wire, trying to get a ball, and one of the soldiers must have shot him. Sometimes you did hear shots, because some of the Italians were trigger-happy. He was taken away in a small wagon, where to, no one knew. They had put a blanket over him so no one could see what kind of wound he had. You should give the sentry a signal if you were going over the trip wire.

I was looking forward to my skilly as I was feeling hungry, maybe I was getting better. I didn't feel as weak as I had a few days before. I made a cup of tea to go with it. Later they all started to sing; maybe something triggered this, perhaps that everyone was going to get letters from home. It was lovely as there had not been singing for a while.

Three days later I was going along fine. We still had not heard anything about the lad who was shot. The Italian soldiers had probably been told to keep their mouths shut. I took a stroll with Jimmy down to the toilets and it was really nice to be back in circulation and meeting some of the lads from our regiment who I had not seen for quite a while. Just to feel the razor going across my face was such a lovely feeling, and a wash all over my body.

We had just returned to the block when two Italians came in, asking for Stephen, but someone said he had gone out ten minutes before. It was time for roll call and it did look funny seeing so many people after this long time.

We got into groups and Sergeant Bertram said that the officer had told him that another batch of mail had arrived. After a relatively short roll call, under two hours, the interpreter shouted out that all sergeants were required by the officer. Sergeant Bertram then came and said that we would be getting Red Cross parcels as well, one between two people while stocks lasted. He also said there could be twenty cigarettes for each of us. Somebody shouted, 'What about a pint of beer?' and we laughed our heads off.

Later the sergeant came into our block with mail; Jimmy got one, Stephen got one but I got none, but the sergeant said there was quite a bundle still so there was still hope.

Jimmy went off to get the buns and I got the water boiling to make the tea. I was starting to eat a lot better and to go for much longer walks around the compound. Next day I was better still and I told Jimmy that the next day I would be the one to get the cognac.

Then they started to open the warehouse where the parcels were stored and the sergeants went forward and a lot of people were lining up. It was a lovely day, just standing with Jimmy enjoying the sun, though I did not take my shirt off as I was afraid of getting burnt. It was nice to know that we had extra rations for five or six days. It all depended on what articles there were in the parcel and where they came from: perhaps Scotland or London or different places in England.

At the moment there was no mail for me; only one chap received a card the previous day. I suppose it took a while to get them shipped out, probably by Red Cross people in Switzerland. That next day I went to get the cognac and it was going to be a very nice day. Later Sergeant Bertram came over to our block and said that they were going to see the officer of the day, what about he did not know but he might be able to give us some information later. I knew that the shop would be open sometime that afternoon and we could go and get something, even if it was only fruit.

This was six weeks since we had arrived, nearly every day the same. It got really monotonous, but what could we do? As day after day went by, it might get us nearer home but no one could tell when the war was going to end; it could be years. But then I received my first letter; Jimmy had two, one from his sister and one from his parents. I was quite pleased with mine. At least everyone was quite all right, with something about 'Uncle Joe', meaning the Russians. We were wondering how things were going in the war zones; we got very little information.

Once again roll call started late and then took over two and a half hours and we were going to be late for our buns which were dished out about 12.30. All of a sudden the officer appeared and gave them a good telling off, but we waited for another half an hour before the interpreter said, 'Fall out, everybody.'

I went for the buns and it was great just going for them and I said I would go the next day too, just to give him a break. Jimmy made coffee for a change. I felt a bit itchy so I said to Jimmy, 'I am going to have a look and see if there are any lice; it is a while since we had any. Maybe those new lads who came yesterday brought them in.'

I took off my shirt which was quite worn but nevertheless kept me warm and there by the seam were quite a few. Out came the cigs and I kept burning them; then I took my pants off and there were some there as well. You had to control them as soon as possible or you got riddled with them.

Quite a lot of the lads had received letters but I was still waiting. Jimmy said one of his letters was mostly blanked out. As we were strolling around, we asked Sergeant Bertram if he had any news of the lad who was shot, but he had had no word at all. Later he came to our block and said that he had died with his wound during the night; he had been shot in the stomach. The sergeant said that his parents would have received one letter saying he was all right and now another one saying he was dead. It was a real shock and so sad for his parents. The sergeant went from block to block to tell everyone in the camp. After a few days we heard that he was going to be buried in Bari.

Three new lads came in who had been taken at Benghazi and could give us some news. They said it was terrible when you didn't know where the Germans were as the people who were in front of them just disappeared, leaving them on their own; nearly two platoons got captured.

I also heard that one of the Horseshoe draft, Lyle Dodds, had died of dysentery in a camp near Naples and that was a shock. He had lived in Forest Hall near me. This would be a shock for his parents – buried in a foreign country. He was very young and they would never have dreamt that he would die. There was also Billy Blewitt who was in a camp in Bologna.

It was still only one bun per person. While I was leaving the queue I met Sergeant Bertram who said they would be getting a very big consignment of parcels in the next few days and also some letters or cards to send home. I still wished I had not said anything to anybody as I still felt guilty. I wished we had got married in Scotland then I knew things would have been all right. My mind was in such a turmoil. Most of my mother's card had been blanked out.

Jimmy's letter said that his sister was keeping the shop on; that things were not so good with the rationing. He said that he would like to expand his business when he returned to England. I said that I had no idea how to run a shop but that my fiancée had worked in a shop in Forest Hall.

During a stroll I met Johnnie Ward who said he had had a letter from his brother Bill who was my Auntie Eva's husband, who said everything was fine and that they were asking about me, so we went round a few times together. Just as it was getting dark, all of a sudden the heavens opened and we got a bit wet; unfortunately it was nearly skilly time so once again I was going to get a good soaking. After skilly we had a singsong, just to keep our spirits up.

Another day dawned and my things were still damp. I was pleased it was Jimmy's turn to get the cognac and it would be nice to have something warm. I went to the toilets in my damp shirt and trousers and met some mates. Then later I laid my shirt out on the ground and it was lovely and dry in three quarters of an hour so I took my trousers off to do the same hoping that when I went back for them they would still be in the same place.

As we were going to roll call two Italian soldiers came through the main gate and straight to our block, maybe to see Stephen, the lad from London; maybe he was doing some bartering. He was getting well into the Italian language. We got into groups for roll call and an officer came into the compound and started shouting at the guards. As time went on it was just pathetic watching them perform, losing the count again and again. The interpreter called the sergeants over and hands were flying in that Italian way. Our tea was the last biscuit and portion of cheese; later Sergeant Bertram told us that there would be a delay in the consignment; that is why they were complaining as it was going to be hard for us with the cut in rations and maybe they should bring back the bun we lost some time ago.

In the meantime there was another post delivery. He was shouting out names and Jimmy's came; there were not many left but then he shouted my name and there was a letter from my mother and father. Again some was blacked out so when I wrote back I told her that she was writing things she should not. There was no mention of Edie at all, which was rather fishy since the letter I wrote from Tobruk said Edie was looking after her during the air raids. My mother was a bit deaf and was always frightened in case the Germans dropped into the country by plane. My father was still working, which was good and she said 'Fred …' then a blank. Out in the compound Johnny Ward said that his brother Bill was not very well at the moment and I told Johnny to give him my best.

Two soldiers came into the compound shouting and in a filthy mood; everyone just tried to get out of their way in case one of them started hitting with his rifle which was rare but you never knew.

The sunrise was beautiful coming through our window as it faced east. In a week's time it would be my birthday and I would be 22 years old. Last time I was in Alexandria. Then back to the block to make my bed as I did every morning – it didn't take long, just to give the mattress a shake and fold your blanket and put the small pillow at the top of the bed. Jimmy had his own bed back by now and I was back on the top tier. I did some washing but my clothes were full of holes and might not last very long.

Someone was sorting the mail and within ten minutes Jimmy's name came from the bloke, but I'm afraid none for me. I was still fed up with sending that card. She might explain everything if I ever got home, because no one knows what day brings illness; when you are in a weak state you might get any sort of germs, We only had a bit of butter left and never any from the Italians, so it would be dry buns from now on until we got a batch of Red Cross parcels.

As we went round the compound, one of the lads said there was going to be a boxing match in another compound. This could be the highlight of the evening. Jimmy said he used to go to Saint James Boxing Club. I had been with my father to a boxing booth at the hoppenings at Shiremoor – it was called the Children's Treat. It was rather one-sided. I think the bloke that went in had had a good drink and his mates were teasing him on to enter. it was rather one-sided as he was out in the second round. But he would have got £10 if he had won which was a lot of money. The man he had to beat was a better boxer than all his opponents unless they had been to the Saint James.

The sergeant asked us who would like to go to the match and three or four of us agreed. Shortly we had to go to the main gate and some guards would take us over to the other compound. There a boxing ring had been erected by the Italians. It was rather high so Jimmy and I stayed back a bit to get a better view. There were about six or seven matches from featherweight to middle-heavyweight and they were three-minute rounds. Then we went back to our block just in time for skilly and a singsong. It had been a really good day and some very good boxing; someone said they would like it every week if possible.

My next letter from my mother still had three or four lines crossed out, so there was very little news and though I was pleased everyone was well – this was our biggest concern – there was still no news of Edie. But the sergeant said there was some good news; there was a consignment of parcels on their way in one or two days' time.

On 5 July was my birthday, my second since I left home. There would be no greetings from my family; but never mind, we just had to get on with things. I went to get my cognac on a lovely day and then had a stroll.

While we were having a sit-down we saw an Italian civilian digging a hole not far from us, about three feet down. On top of the hole was a red spotted bandanna with his lunch in. At about eleven o'clock he opened the handkerchief, sat on the edge of the hole and ate some of his bread and cheese; there seemed not to be any butter or margarine. There was an apple there as well. Later we saw him again; while he was digging a young lad, just ambling along, pounced onto the hanky and ran away with it. That poor soul would not have any lunch or tea.

Later we saw this big truck arrive and parcels were put in the store room so we might get our parcels the next day. People started shouting and chanting, they were so pleased. Everyone was smiling, just like kids at Christmas time. We only had enough tea left for perhaps one watery cup each. Sergeant Bertram was really pleased that there would be no more long faces. The interpreter was telling the soldiers to hurry up with their counting but we did not now mind what time they spent with us. Next thing we knew, the soldiers had their coats off and really got stuck into these Red Cross parcels; it was quite a good load, maybe three or four weeks' supply. We seemed to have a new spring in our steps as we circled the compound.

Some of the lads joined us and we talked of different things – food mostly – broth stotties and pease pudding and ham sandwiches.

Next day was my birthday. When Jimmy came back with the cognac I said what a pity it was not a proper drink like a nice glass of beer, really cool like we had it in Alexandria. it was two years since I had met Edie. It would have been nice just to hold her in my arms and give her a lovely kiss. I wanted to keep writing about her as this was my only outlet. Jimmy wished me a happy birthday.

After roll call we stood in a line to get our Red Cross parcels. It was one between two people which thrilled us because you heard so many rumours going about. We made a meal and my, did we make a nice cup of coffee instead of tea, so it was a sunny birthday after all. Much later we had our skilly and a singsong and my, we almost brought the roof in with everyone singing or whistling and everyone was in a very happy mood for a change. The food parcels came from places in England I had never heard of, and some from Canada. The Canadian ones were very good: not many items but good quality and with lots of vitamins. They usually had cigarettes, maybe five or ten. The non-smokers bartered theirs for food; smokers would eat very little just to have a cigarette.

Next day we saw Italian guards going round the outer wire and stopped to see what was happening. Late we were told that someone from another compound had tried to escape but got caught and was talking to the officer. He would be for the high jump – he was stupid, especially in broad daylight; perhaps there was something wrong with him. We thought later that he had had shell shock. He was lucky not to have been shot. A few days later Sergeant Bertram said that the story of him trying to escape was just hogwash; someone was said to have seen him try and that was how the rumour started.

That day there were different soldiers with the interpreter, with different markings on their clothes, and these were younger, perhaps only 16 or 17 years. Perhaps the others were being taken to the front. You still had to be careful as they might be trigger happy.

One of the sergeants came into our block laden with parcels from home; Jimmy and I did not get any, but I got a letter from my parents though most of it was blacked out. I was pleased that everyone was all right. There was a bit about Johnny Ward; they thought it was funny that we were in the same camp and said that his brother Billie was not in very good health. Still no mention of Edie, which really puzzled me; indeed they never asked why I had broken off the engagement. I really wished they would tell me one way or another; well, they say no news is good news. Later I passed on their good wishes to Johnny and was in a dilemma as to whether to tell him about his brother but in the end decided not to.

We went off to have a shower – not really a shower, just a hose pipe and the water was cold; but we tried to spray each other with a hand over it. We were lucky because there was no queue. The soap was terrible, with no lather at all, about an inch and a half in length and half an inch wide and very thin indeed. It also had pieces of grit in. We had to dry ourselves with our shirts as there were no towels; then we laid our shirts on the ground to dry. Jimmy said that his shop was coming along in leaps and bounds; even with the rationing they had sweets and cigarettes. I said, 'That is very good, Jimmy; at least you have something to go back to.'

That night the Welsh lad Terry from the bottom of the room started singing; he had a canny voice.

We had not had much news for quite a while as no new intake. Most of the time their news was of ships that had been sunk in the Far East: India, Burma, Singapore, and that the Japanese had taken some of these places. You didn't know if really big ships were still afloat, like the *Hood, Repulse, Rodney, Nelson* and *King George V*: destroyers and cruisers, and many merchant ships as well. Some of the other Fusiliers talked of the times in Alexandria and one day in Cairo when they were camped nearby just before the Italian attack in 1940. They said they had quite a fight but they were no match for us as we had better equipment and theirs was very poor indeed. They went right past Benghazi and further to El Agheila but were pushed back by the Germans and ended up at Tobruk in April 1941, and were in the siege, till we broke out in November 1941.

We heard some good news, that we were going to go back to two buns a day. We all had smiles as long as we could stretch, so with some Red Cross parcels due the next day and that extra bun we would be very happy. It did your morale lots of good and made the day go along nicely and let you look forward to the next day.

The next day everybody was in a good mood as I went to get the cognac, and someone must have slipped up as it was quite strong. After a visit to the toilet area, a stroll and roll call we got into our groups for the parcels. The soldiers were waiting by the store room for the office to hand them the keys. When we got the parcels there was a nice cup of coffee for a change and a nice meal as well. It was exciting to open the parcel because every one was different. We were grateful for people for sending them; it was our lifeline and without them people could not have survived as we could not live on what the Italians gave us. Many would have been dead by now.

The singsong after skilly time showed that the Italians could not get us down; we had at all times to try to keep our spirits up even in those dark days; still, there is always light at the end of a tunnel.

After our usual morning routine (we got our two buns) that Monday we saw Sergeant Bertram go through the main gate with a soldier and hoped it was good news. In fact after roll call and a lovely cup of coffee he came into the block with a bundle of letters; I got a letter and even a parcel. I was over the moon getting two things, and when I opened the parcel it was two hundred cigarettes from the Salvation Army. It was wonderful and I gave Jimmy fifty of them. We each smoked one and then went round the compound and when I met some of the lads I gave them five each and they were pleased as they were getting a bit short. Usually when you had a cig you just smoked half, and within a couple of days I was back at that routine because you never knew when the next ration could be.

My letter was from a relative, Eva, who lived in Birmingham, which was a good surprise. She said she was really choked when she heard I was a prisoner of war and was really pleased to hear I was all right. The next bit was blacked out, then she said my Uncle Tom and the rest of the family were all right. I could send her a card when next I had one. I had only ever seen her twice as she lived so far away but she used to live in Wallsend before they went south to get work, which she and her brother found within weeks. In the North-East the situation was terrible: only the pits, shipyards, the railways or the shops.

A few days later we were walking round the compound when we saw Sergeant Bertram and an Italian soldier going towards the officer's office, so we wondered what was up. Within half an hour they were coming through with bundles of letters and boxes of cigarettes. We got ten cigarettes each, and were told that the shop would open twice a week, though with very little change, so at least we could get another supply of food and even some fruit which was most welcome.

Just before the end of the mail hand-out I received a card and I recall feeling very pleased, just hoping it was from my loved one, then I remembered that I had told them not to give my address to her. I had written to my mate and said I would not mind her having my address after all so long as my family did not know about it. This card was from him and it gave very little news and two lines blacked out. It seemed I could not rely on anyone giving me information about Edie. Later I did send him another card saying again would he give her my address; I told him I had received a Dear John letter when I was at El Duda in November 1941.

One day towards the end of the month, just as I got back to the block from getting the cognac it started to rain; I was really pleased I was not still standing in the queue. But the time came when we had to go to roll call and it was still raining so within half an hour of standing in our groups we were soaking wet and God knew when we would get dry again. We hoped the sun would come out, but as it did not we would have to put our wet clothes on again. We sat inside and made our dinner: not much, just a bit of corned beef and a tin of soup plus a bun each; afterwards a lovely cup of tea and a cig each. I still had a few left from the two hundred I had received. We tried to dry our shirts by hanging them up on the posts of the three-tiered bed. Even the floor was soaking wet. Then it was time for roll call again. We had been standing for over an hour and the Italians were still counting. But the officer, who was standing with the interpreter, suddenly called the sergeants to come to attention and then the sergeants said, 'Fall out, everybody.' We were really glad this was the last of the day as everyone would be lying with little on that night; it would be very cold and we would get very little sleep. I just hoped I would not get another cold like before, because the food was not full of vitamins to help us through an illness.

Next day it was Jimmy's turn to get the cognac. Just as he got to the doorway he shouted back, 'It has stopped raining!' We could go out in our shorts, even though they were still wet, if only we could get our shirts dry. Many holes were appearing in our shorts but we had nothing to mend them with; we thought if only we could get some needles and thread from England we could try to darn them.

The sergeant said that maybe there would be another boxing match, and there would be more information later. We all hoped it would be staged as it really would be a great event one afternoon, just to have some action. It was hot again and we got a bit sunburnt as the weather seemed to be coming from the African coast. We strolled around and saw some Italian soldiers hammering posts into the ground, so we stopped and watched. They had the four posts up and then started to put the ropes around the bottom.

Then it was skilly time. The soldiers carried a large drum of food with two big handles and a bit of wood put through to carry it. Everyone got in line and they dished out a small ladle of skilly to each man.

After this back to our block for a singsong. The Welsh lad, Terry, who had a lovely voice always started us off, with no music – it was magic. One lad, Norman, had a comb and found a piece of paper and started playing that; then Ken had the loan of a mouth organ and by Jove he could really play it. It was a shame really, when someone could play like that, that he could not have one of his own; he should have sent away to his home or the Salvation Army to ask for one. It was a really enjoyable night, though the next day I felt I had a nasty cold coming on, as you might expect with one day raining, the next day red hot.

We were told that only so many out of each block could go to the boxing match, and those that went before would not be able to go this time. We said that would be understandable, as everyone should get a chance to go. Later they said that no one from our block could go as there were two or three blocks that did not go at all last time.

Once again we had lice. Where they came from nobody knew, unless it was when the clothes were drying. It looked like delousing time again. You could not smoke on parade or we would have started straight away. By, they do give you a nice bite, just suck your blood. To burn them and their eggs with a cigarette is the only way, because if you didn't they would multiply.

With the next mail I had a card from my brother Stephen, again with much of it blacked out so not much in news but at least I knew he was all right. He was at the NAAFI at Hexham. He had gone in at the beginning of the war and as that position was exempted, he would not be called up into the Forces. He had just turned 19 years old.

Sergeant Bertram said we would be getting more parcels within a fortnight, so at least we knew that was the longest we would wait, just to keep our spirits up. They started counting in the roll call and we just stood there very hot indeed, sweat pouring down our faces, but at least it was better than rain. My cold had retreated to a sniffle and I was pleased because I had thought I was going to be laid up again.

Chapter 10

One day at the beginning of August the sergeant came in and said that on Monday there would be a party going out of the compound. We all thought this was a great idea. Then he said he would be along later with some cards and letter forms and that we could send them to whoever we liked. I was still debating whether to send a card to Edie; but on the other hand she might have found someone else. I was still in a demented state, not knowing what the situation was and nobody would tell me, so once again I put of sending one.

The Italian was in again talking to Stephen; we only hoped he was getting some news. He was speaking quite good Italian now and had a book with some phrases in, to help them along. You would think the officer would play war with them but no. I thought the lad might give us some news but he said he had asked but they had said 'No'. They would not bend in any way; maybe he was frightened in case they lost their connections as they were bartering together two or three times a week. it depended on the parcels; it might be coffee, salmon, tea or sometimes milk.

The sergeant came back and had a list of names of people who were going out of the compound on Monday and mine was among them. There were only ten for each block. We had to be ready to get to the gate and be counted.

On Monday the fifty of us had to be at the gate by eight o'clock. Outside the gate there must have been a whole company of Italian soldiers. At eight thirty they started letting us through, five men at a time; they must have thought we would try and escape. After a mile or so the mist started coming down quite thick so they made us turn round and headed us back to the compound; it was a real farce. Outside the compound it was very stony but it was great just to be outside and we were really enjoying the walk until that blinking fog had to come in thick. Twenty minutes later we were back in the compound and they started counting us in one at a time. Then there was a small corridor, then another gate into the compound. So back to the old routine.

At least we must be keeping a company or so looking after us. Some were very young, about 17 to 19 years old, ill trained and more like cannon fodder but they would not get any training with us.

The fog kept on rolling in so we hoped that the roll call would be called off. The sergeant came in and said he was going to ask if he could take four or five men to collect the buns instead of us all lining up but it all depended on the soldiers. They liked to make all the decisions themselves and hated to be told about anything. Never mind; we would have our dinner and if the fog kept up I thought they would be doubling the guards around the perimeter, and maybe during the night as well in case someone should try to escape. But every door was locked. We had buckets inside and had to empty them every morning, about half a dozen of them, in a little offshoot with just room for one man at a time. There was a rota to take them to the toilets; sometimes they were very full. There was a small notice board just beside the door as you came in telling you who was detailed to do this, or to use the hose pipe. If you didn't check someone else would tell you.

The fog was still thick in the afternoon so there was no roll call and we were all pleased just to stay indoors, making tea and sometimes having a snooze; but people still had to go out to the toilets or to get water. The cup was made out of a Canadian milk tin as it seemed to keep clean the longest, and when it got dirty you discarded it and got an English soup tin, which was smaller.

Jimmy and some of the lads and I wanted to question the sergeant about having to use the pail inside during the night; it could be because we just have these young soldiers guarding us now; maybe the older ones have been sent to the front. Jimmy said he would ask; it was no use everyone shouting at once. He said to the sergeant that the pail in the block was not hygienic and the smell was terrible. The sergeant said he would see what he could do. it was my turn to go down with the pail and while I was there I had a good wash down with cold water, very refreshing, because my body smelt of the bucket.

It was very cold standing around at roll call that day. The guards seemed a bit quicker than usual; maybe they were getting cold like us; their clothes were very thin. Our clothes were also getting very thin and we hoped it would not rain. We didn't know if we would receive any clothes from the Italians.

After roll call the sergeant said he had had a word about the pail of slops and told them how we felt about it, but nothing could be done yet; it had to go to a higher officer. He said that we would be getting cards and letters to sent home but that there was no word yet about the Red Cross parcels. Our rations were nearly at an end. We were using tea four or five times until it was really drinking hot water. We never drank cold water because one never knew if the pipes were clean.

The soldiers that day seemed much older; the other ones must have gone for training, unless it was that these were not fit for the front line. We all thought that at least we would get done quicker, but that was not to be; it was nearly half an hour to a group and twenty-five blocks to count, so it was going to be a long time. Eventually when they had just started the sixth group, we just started to mill around as it was getting a bit chilly. Some wanted to go to the toilet, so we just called everyone to turn their backs till he was finished and a few in each squad were doing what comes naturally. These two were still counting after two hours and there were still twelve groups left. The officer was really vexed with them. There is nothing worse than standing wanting the toilet. After three and a half hours they still had five groups to do and we were getting really hungry. The officer was shouting at them to hurry up but they still strolled along at their normal pace. It was more than five hours at the finish. I had to run down to the toilet and only just made it; another minute and would have wet my pants.

A fortnight went by and it was a very good morning with the sun just coming through the clouds. Roll call was just over two hours, the quickest they had been for some time. The sergeant came with some letters and cards to send home. These were always bad times for me, wondering if I did the right thing, but my heart was almost broken by the person that did this, to people very much in love with each other. How I wished I had never received that letter; it had been a thorn in my side; in Tobruk they were saying that she had been very good in helping my mother. And then to do this. I had been in the dark all the time. It just filled me with anger. Well, I would just write to my parents and send a card to my brother in Hexham. It was hard to know what to say, so just that I was all right and wishing I we home, but that could be a long way off. it was not receiving any news that was so depressing.

Later the sergeant came back with letters and parcels but we did not receive any: just the luck of the draw. He said there was no news about the slop bucket, nor any Red Cross parcels so we would have to live on our Italian rations. He said he would have a word with the interpreter straight away as these were poor indeed, with us only just getting along, always hungry.

We had only a spoonful of tea left; that might do that day teatime and dinner and teatime the next day, with perhaps two weak cups the day after; so it would be hot water then until the parcels came. When the soldiers brought the big cauldron of skilly we got served nearly straight away and that done we were back at our block. Terry broke into song and when he had finished that one, he shouted, 'Don't let the Italians get us down, we must keep our spirits up,' and once again he started to sing. We joined in when we had had our skilly. It didn't matter if you were good at it, you just joined in.

I never said that this was Camp 65: this was the address our parcels and letters from England were addressed to.

I was down to my last three cigs and when they were gone there were going to be long faces unless the Italians supplied us with any. We had some of theirs before: half tobacco, the rest cardboard – you just lit it, three puffs and it was gone; still it took the nicotine craving away for and hour or so.

During roll call someone shouted, 'There is a big wagon coming in the other gate!' so we couldn't help thinking it was the Red Cross parcels. It came to a standstill just outside the storeroom and everybody shouted and clapped and all the smiles came out just like Cheshire cats. We all crowded round the main gates to see. By luck they showed us a parcel and they were Canadian and we were pleased as they were good quality: twelve things inside including milk, biscuits, coffee, sometimes tea, good meat tins, cheese. Well, they would be received with open arms and we could only hope there were cigarettes as well, though food was our main concern.

Jimmy and I decided to do some washing because it was our block's turn. Within an hour we had it back on quite dry and it felt a lot fresher, even just being washed in cold water.

The next day I went to get the buns while Jimmy queued for the Red Cross parcel. We had a ham sandwich and a nice cup of coffee with the lovely creamy milk. then we had our last cigarettes. But food was more important as cigarettes do not feed you at all.

At the beginning of roll call, when we were waiting, all of a sudden the interpreter was shouting something, calling all sergeants towards him. This seemed funny as it had not happened before. He took them to the store room and each one came out with a box; everyone was concerned as to what they could be. At the end of the roll call, the officer called 'Dismiss!' in English; everyone was amazed as no one had ever heard him utter one word of English before. Maybe he had overheard the sergeants saying it to us. Later the sergeant came into the block with his box and gave everyone a cigar. He said, 'I'm sorry, but they have only sent cigars.' They were medium sized which was not bad. Some people started pulling them to pieces to make a cigarette with a piece of paper. Later I had a few puffs at my cigar. They were very strong indeed, a few puffs was more than enough.

I had a letter from my brother Stephen and one from my mother and father, but still no news about Edie. It really seemed funny, not mentioning her name at all. I just started thinking that perhaps she knew something about that Dear John letter; if she knew the person who did this and was frightened to say anything about it. I still wished I had not sent that letter; it was eating me up all the time. I still loved her very much and would never love anyone else. I wished we had had sex and I had made her pregnant; at least I would have been married when I was in Tobruk.

While we were walking round the compound, Jimmy said, 'What is the matter, you seem in a very bad mood?'

I said. 'Jimmy, I cannot tell you at this moment, as I am waiting for a letter from someone who is very precious to me.'

He said, 'This has been bothering you for quite a while,' so I told him about the Dear John letter and the chap who told me to finish with her. He said this lad's friend who received a Dear John letter, and it said your wife is expecting a baby by another man, and on this ship he climbed over the rails and jumped into the sea and drowned himself, and he was the Battalion's best swimmer. He said that he felt very sorry for me. I told Jimmy I loved no one but her and that we were going to get married if I had stayed in Scotland, but instead I went aboard the ship and sailed for the Middle East. I never said any more about that, but said that I had had a letter from my parents and one from my brother but much of it was blacked out. My mother never mentioned Edie at all.

It would soon be September, so the months were getting along all right but it would be better if we were released. There was a rumour that some people who were ill were being sent back to England if they had wounds and were not fit for war. They could be repatriated in exchange for enemy prisoners in the same predicament. Good luck to them; it was not nice to go home that way.

We would use our tea leaves four or five times as we didn't want to run out like last time; it may have been weak but it was better than hot water. A can substituted for a tea pot; we made a handle by cutting another can into strips then joining it from the top to the bottom; we used a piece of wood like a hammer and anvil to nip the tins together. It took time, but was something to do as it was boring sitting around doing nothing.

We tried rolling cigar tobacco in paper. We just cut it into strips and tried to roll it. It took a while because you had to wet it to make it stick but if it was too wet it took a while to light. Never mind, it was better than nothing at all. Really it was nicer than ordinary cigs because there was less nicotine this way. It was just a smoke to us, wonderful.

Our Red Cross parcels were between two which was good because if you opened anything it went off in the heat. A tin of Spam would do two meals so we had to keep it in the tin wrapped in some sort of cloth or paper or cardboard. Sometimes we would make sandwiches and take them to the roll call.

Later came some letters and Jimmy even had a parcel. This had 200 cigarettes from his sister who was looking after his shop, and within a few minutes he gave fifty of them to me. They got plenty from the Wills' factory, because they knew someone there.

I had a card from my mate Edward Blake but there was still no mention of Edie. I know he had a soft spot for her but she did not like him at all, why I do not know, because she mentioned in one of her letters I received in Tobruk that he made some kind of remark to her. I expected him to say he had given the address of my camp to her, but he did not mention anything at all, just saying that all his family was all right and that he was still working at the same job, at the Algernon Pit near West Allotment, where I had worked before I was called up.

I wondered as we waited for roll call whether Edie was still single, as she was quite a lovely lass with a heart of gold, always helping people just like my mother who is deaf in one ear and it was beginning to affect the other. When I was at Fenham Barracks Edie took my mother to the pictures and looked after her during an air raid. The Council had put an Anderson shelter into everyone's back garden at the beginning of 1939. They were a godsend because when the AckAck went off beside old Whitley Road you got covered with shrapnel and once or twice we had to huddle together there. If I had my tin helmet I would put it on her head, just in case she got hit by something.

While waiting for my cognac next morning I was talking to a chap from another block who told me about another bloke who had had a letter from the Government telling him that his parents had been killed by a German bomb which fell on their remote farm. This lad could not control himself from crying. He was the only son and would claim the property. Jimmy said later that he must be devastated getting news like that.

We were hoping that the shop would open again soon but sometimes there was just fruit and vegetables in it. We also overheard a rumour that there would be another boxing match. Things like that made life more worth living. I got the buns to take to Jimmy. It was better not to trust anyone else to deliver them as you might have nothing for dinner or teatime. We had a look for lice and found none.

It was our turn to take the slop pails to the toilets. Quite a few of the sergeants had been got at about this as it was a disgrace, having to do your business in pails. Sergeant Bertram had approached the interpreter about this but he said he was still awaiting word. It was terrible for people to have to slop out every day, and sometimes it spilled onto your clothes or your body. Washing clothes was bad as at that time they were taking ages to dry. Jimmy and I were very concerned about cleanliness which you might think was daft, with us living in a hell hole, but you had to try to not get germs. We didn't know why we couldn't go to the toilet in the night as guards were there, unless they thought we would try to escape.

Someone saw Stephen speaking to Italians across the 3-foot trip wire and thought they were bartering. He saw a package changing hands and maybe it was a cash deal.

My socks were almost finished and I might have to throw them away soon, although I had done a lot of darning, taking pieces of wool discarded by other people. I would just have to go without unless something came my way. All my clothes were getting very thin and they had been patched time and time again. You would look around for pieces of material to fill up the holes.

A few more days went by and we saw the officer and interpreter come into the compound. The sergeants were at the head of all the groups and brought them all to attention as if on parade. The interpreter called one of them over, and then he shouted to all the groups that the toilets could be open again from that night. It took everyone by surprise and we were all talking among ourselves; then the sergeant gave one almighty yell and everyone stopped straight away. Nothing was said about parcels but at least there were no more slops to be carried.

If it were not for the parcels we would not have survived at all. It was a great shame the Italians could not give us extra rations but maybe they were short like the people in England.

it would have been much better if we could have had roll call inside every day, just standing by our beds, it was so monotonous hanging around all day just to be counted. This would have been so easy, especially when it was raining; perhaps it was their way of punishing people.

Sergeant Bertram came in that evening and said that the shop would open in two days' time and that maybe they would get everyone in our block to get served. And another thing: we would be getting our Red Cross parcels the next day. Everyone just put a lovely smile on his face. The sergeant added that there could be mail and parcels coming to our camp in a day or so: good news all round. He was going to pass the good news on to the other sergeants. Really, everyone was cock-a-hoop and said, 'Not before time.' We wondered if the Italians kept a check on how long we could last before we needed the parcels.

Next day we strolled round the compound to see if we could see anyone in the storeroom; then kept on walking until we could see the officer and the interpreter come in. After a few minutes these two came in, so we made our way over to our group. Sergeant Bertram was waiting for us and said, 'OK, lads, but try and get here a bit sooner because this officer hates to wait for stragglers coming in.' So once again it was a waiting game. We were just standing still as it would not be long before it was our turn when one of the groups on the other side was in a position to give us a signal that a few soldiers were beside the storeroom. We gave them the thumbs-up sign.

Just as we got to the top of the compound we saw the soldiers putting parcels in order for each block and the sergeants waiting to collect them. There would be four blocks ahead of us. We met Johnny and Jimmy gave him a couple of cigarettes and he thanked him saying his last smoke was yesterday. Even he said though that he would rather have the food parcels. In fact parcels were stopped until roll call was over. Then I got our parcel while Jimmy got the can ready for a cup of tea or coffee to go with something to tuck into. Skilly was much better with some thick biscuits to make it more filling; it was a pity we could not have more of them. Afterwards was a singsong and we made one hell of a noise as everyone had had a good meal.

When we went for our cognac there was a long queue every day; at that time our block was about halfway in it; each day you got nearer the front and after you reached the front you went back to the end. The Italians had worked out this system before we got to the camp so we just obeyed orders. We had just walked round the compound four times when we saw the officer and the interpreter coming into the camp and everyone stood to attention. They started counting at 10.15 and we thought it would be over by 12.15; they started quite well but all of a sudden they stopped counting for no reason at all. The two soldiers were having an argument about something so the officer came and had a word. It was finally sorted out but they proceeded very slowly indeed and it was going to make our bun supply late. At least it was not raining. But the two guards were still having a few words with each other until the officer told them to get on with the job and stopped with them.

Then I was on my way to where they dished out the buns and was just over halfway in the queue. Then I saw the sergeant coming out with a heap of parcels and letters, just as he was saying a few days ago, so everything in the garden was rosy. Some people were going to be happy or sad, but it was mostly good news.

Jimmy had our meal ready with a tin of soup and I could dip my bun into it; it was really nice and made you feel more satisfied.

I had a letter from my mother and a card from Stephen but three lines of this were blacked out and five lines of my mother's. But it was really nice to get them and to know that everyone was all right. There was still no news of Edie. I mentioned these people again to Jimmy, who had done this to me; he said I was in a terrible state with myself.

I said, 'Yes, Jimmy; if things had gone the way we wanted we should be married,' and I told him about going up to Scotland and everything going to plan until the Army changed it for us.

He said it was a real shame and he was annoyed at people doing things like that, sending a Dear John letter to a person in the front line. That was how people got killed, he said, because their mind is on other things.

That roll call they seemed to get on with it straight away – the officer must have had a word with them. Jimmy and I were just talking quietly when Sergeant Bertram gave one almighty holler, nearly frightening the life out of us. The reason was that they were counting the next group and he wanted everyone's attention. He said, 'I am sick of telling people to keep quiet on parade.' We could understand that he was trying to make a good impression with his group under control. But it really was murder, just standing there.

I asked Jimmy not to say anything about what we were discussing that afternoon. He said, 'I understand,' but then: 'Tommy, you got engaged in September last year. I cannot see why she would be going around with a married man.'

I said, 'I do not know, Jimmy, but we love each other and my heart tells me so, a person who wants to get married doesn't mess around. I will never know till I get home unless someone gives her my address.'

Jimmy said, 'Why don't you send her a card and tell her what the trouble is?'

'Jimmy, I cannot send a letter or card as my family live across the road. Also, my mother would ask the postman if I had sent one.' I went on, 'I really don't know what to do, I am at my wits' end about this.'

While we were walking around the next day, on rather a dark morning, we met Johnny, whose brother married my Aunt Eva. After telling me that the family were all right, he said:

'Do you remember that fellow whose parents were killed by a bomb on their farm? Somebody was in the toilets early this morning and they found him dead; they think he committed suicide. He was lying beside the water pipe and water was running all over the place and he might have drowned himself by putting the pipe into his mouth.'

It must have been a hellova fright for the lad to find. After roll call that morning the interpreter told the sergeant, who told us, that there would be a post mortem examination.

There was nothing special to do, maybe have a look at what the shop had got as our section would be in or standing by to go inside. We had no coupons in fact; these amounted to 3s. 4d.; we don't know where this money comes from, some said from our Government, some said it was our money that the Government owed us; or perhaps the Italian Government. There were grapes, apples, pears, oranges: no vegetables at all.

The sergeant came into our block and said he had just had word that there would be a boxing match some time the next week or in October; we would be told by the interpreter when. They had to see who could box and might have a bit of training. There would be different weights taking part. This would be a grand day but the sergeants would select different blocks as some had been to the last two; it would just be the luck of the draw, as some people were not too keen on going. It was another date to look forward to.

While we were at the toilets someone said they had heard there was going to be an issue of clothing soon. We asked where he had heard this but he said he had overheard one of the boxers but he would have his guts for garters if he knew. We said we would be careful about this news as we did not want to see this lad get a good belting. Jimmy said, 'If that was me I would have kept my mouth shut, because if it is right and this fellow finds out, God help him.'

The days were still quite warm but we would be coming up to bad weather as winter approached and the mornings were sometimes frosty. We were really pleased we were not still in tents as at the beginning of the year. It was a lot warmer inside the blocks though there was no heating and a lot of draughts. My clothes were very thin as I had not had any since I was taken prisoner at El Buda in the desert in November 1941. I was very cold on a dull day though when the sun was shining it was very good indeed. You would think the Army would send some kind of clothing, even the denim – 'fatigues' we used to call them – from our measurements when we were in England.

No wonder people were taken ill and some died of dysentery nearly every week as some men caught germs easily. There was a hospital in the camp run by our own orderlies who were trained by the Army. We had to be admitted by our own sergeants.

The sergeant came with letter forms. Jimmy said, 'If you get a card or a letter, why don't you write to Edie? You are going through hell, just to find out some news.'

I said, 'Maybe she has found someone better than me.'

He said, 'If you do not write you will never know.'

I said, 'Sorry, Jimmy, but I do not have the guts as I do not want her happiness wrecked by me and I will just have to go on loving her in my own way,'

'Tommy,' he said, 'you just torture yourself and it is a great shame to suffer from the work of an unknown person; they are definitely making your life very miserable.'

Later I wrote to my mother and asked what had happened to Edie; maybe she could shed light on this episode. When I told Jimmy he said, 'At least you may get some satisfaction.'

I gave the card to the sergeant and now would have to wait a few months. I hoped something would come of it.

Jimmy said, 'If that happened to me, I would write to the girl as she is the only person who knows the truth. '

I had a bad night but couldn't remember what it was about, with so many things on my mind. We wandered around the compound but could not think of anything to say; your mind sometimes went quite blank, wondering if you could say anything at all. We just hoped something would happen. Edie must have been thinking I was a wimp, no retracting what I had said and breaking off our engagement just like that. I was just daydreaming while the soldiers counted us on parade, wondering when the next parcels would arrive. We made a sandwich from the last food in our last one. I hoped we would get clothing soon as these were very thin indeed and when it was a cold day the wind went right through you.

We had just managed to have a bun sandwich when someone shouted that there was a priest coming down to our block, and then he came in with the interpreter. The priest had come from Bari. He had been sent a lot of medals from the Pope and every one had been blessed. He said that everyone in the camp was in his thoughts and he hoped that everyone would be home soon. He said that war was unpleasant for every country. This was really out of the blue and everyone was astounded at the medals from the Vatican. We all applauded the priest for coming to the camp and giving us some hope and the St Christopher medals. I hoped this would bring us some luck; we thanked him and he went away. At the roll call one of the sergeants thanked the officer for letting the priest come.

Meeting Johnny around the compound the talk was, as usual when we were short of food, of broth dinners, homemade bread, teacakes and many other things our mothers used to make: stottie cake – unleavened bread with plenty of currants in – it made your mouth water; milk, eggs, bacon, tomatoes, mushrooms and salads. Even talking about them was lovely. Jimmy and had a word with the sergeant to see if he had heard anything from the interpreter about extra rations. He said he had told the interpreter it was disgusting giving grown men this kind of food, and was told that it was very little more than the Italian soldiers got, so if this was true then the Allies must definitely making things hard for their Army, Navy and Air Force; civilians too must have been feeling the pinch.

It was a very depressing period drinking just hot water and eating dry buns. We had not had any mail for a while or any letter forms to write home. It was not a warm day, so it could be an awful afternoon, just standing around till roll call was over. Jimmy said, 'Never mind the cold, I just hope it does not rain.' We had not caught many illnesses as yet but with these clothes and with winter approaching it was going to be harder. It took a long time to pull yourself back if you were ill. There was a delay as the officer had to wait for the interpreter and when he did come the compound started clapping and the officer was not too pleased. Jimmy whispered that he needed a pee so we all bunched together so no one could see until he was finished. He thanked everyone who helped him in his time of need. It was raining by this time and it was going to be three and a half hours before they finished. The Italians had clothes plus overcoats and macs across their shoulders. We thought that the sergeants should speak to the officer who was in command of the camp, as this was ridiculous, making people go through this unnecessary ordeal. It was raining quite hard and we were going to be soaking.

These clothes would be hard to dry, just hanging them on the bedpost so we would have to sleep with nothing on and could be up half the night as it would be so cold. If you wanted the toilet you would have to put your wet clothes on to go. Everyone was jumping around just to keep warm. If we did not catch some kind of cold after this we must have been really tough. Even the officer was thinking everyone had had enough and he commanded the sergeants to dismiss all groups. He could have done this earlier and saved us a lot of distress.

In our block we took our clothes off and wrapped our palliasses around us. It was really wonderful, you could feel the warmth straight away. The clothes hanging on the bedposts were dripping like mad and later when we had our buns and hot water we would wring the water out as much as possible. Sergeant Bertram said that there would be a cigarette ration tomorrow but there was no news of Red Cross parcels. However they had had word from Bari about some mail on its way. He still had his wet clothes on and said he was looking forward to getting them off and having some hot water; Jimmy offered him some of ours as it had just boiled.

Next morning our clothes were still damp but I put mine on and went off to get the cognac and hot water. At least it had stopped raining. I felt terrible so I did a bit of running and then jumping on the spot just to keep myself warm. When I got back Jimmy had his palliasse wrapped round him and I did the same; there was no way we were going around the compound that morning: just let the Italian soldiers come and tell us when they were ready for roll call.

We hadn't been long back from the toilets when they came and shouted us to get out, so we said the sooner we got there the sooner it would be over and went straight to our group area. Everyone came to attention and the soldiers looked as if they had had a right telling off, also the interpreter as he was standing quite a way away from the officer. When they had arrived at our group we could stand easy so we were luckier than the next group who were still at attention. They seemed to be taking their time; other times they seemed to flow along. They just needed a kick up the backside. I had seen snails go faster; there must have been something on their mind. Maybe they were trying to get the officer to lose his rag and dismiss all troops like the day before. The officer should have given them a real ticking off or got someone else to take over. We were always praising them for being quick and now all of a sudden they didn't know what to do. The officer was getting really rattled and then shouted at them which he had never done before.

Within an hour the sergeant came in with packets of mail and one or two parcels. There were no cigarettes, just four cigars each. I had a card from Stephen, saying everyone was all right; and had a few drags at a cigar which was rather strong.

A few days later there were two new soldiers. No wonder the last ones were going slow; they had been sent to a new place or the Front, in Italy or Africa. These were slow, but you could expect that with new ones just learning.

Our clothes would not last much longer as they were just falling to pieces, even our shorts splitting round the seams; we would be going around naked if we did not get some soon. We had another word with the sergeant: we thought we were justified in asking for clothes even if only Army issue. We were wondering about the boxing match and if the shop would be open soon. It was a better day: a bit windy and cloudy but lovely when the sun was shining.

You wondered how much more the body could take after all we had gone through these last few months. God knew how much longer before we eventually got home: it could be a good few years. Now and again we could see bombers going northwards; if they did a lot of damage this might cut our rations like last time.

These new soldiers were very young, perhaps 17 years old or early twenties and must be a new consignment. They were progressing very well. I was thinking of Edie – we would have been engaged for just over a year if those rats had not spoiled it for us. I just kept thinking about her a lot as my love was only for her and I wished that we had got wed in Scotland. Every day my heart was just pining for her as she was such a wonderful person.

After our bun the sergeant came in and said, 'I have some news for you. The war in Africa is nearly over.' Everyone applauded this good news. He had spoken to the interpreter about clothes and he would talk to the office when he came on parade; at least this was a step in the right direction. Jimmy and I tried to roll cigarettes with pieces of the cigar, cut small and wrapped in newspaper with no print – plain paper was best. We managed to have a smoke each and it seemed much better somehow. When the sergeant left, everyone was smiling and very happy indeed. This was the best news we had heard in a long while. When we strolled around the compound everyone was talking to each other, something I had not seen for a long time. Johnny and his pals thought it very good news indeed, that we were progressing to victory. We had to wait a while to be served with our skilly but everyone in the queue was really delighted at the news. This is the kind of thing that lifted our spirits. Terry just burst into song and at first we just listened; then the next song we all joined in. We only hoped that the good news would get better though there was a lot more fighting to be done with more people being killed, wounded or taken prisoner.

One of us would have a chat to Sergeant Bertram after roll call to see where he got the news. He told us he might or might not; we could keep our mouths shut. He must be sick of us asking about our clothes and Red Cross parcels. You would think the Italians would have given us a supply of tea or coffee, unless they were short of both too. Jimmy had been whispering to the sergeant and after roll call he would be able to tell me the result in the compound or on the way to the shop.

But he didn't say anything on the way and there was a lot of produce; we were allowed a pound of grapes and two each of oranges, apples and pears. It did not take long as we had to take what they had. There were no vegetables at all. We got the equivalent of 3*s*. 4*d*. a month. We took the stuff down to our block and asked one of the lads, Len, who we could trust, to look after it. Jimmy still hadn't said anything and was still whispering to the sergeant at the afternoon roll call. Eventually when we were walking around he said that we might get an issue of clothing but the interpreter did not know when it would be. There was still no news of Red Cross parcels but a lot of mail came yesterday and so we might get some later. Apparently it was the interpreter who gave us the news about Africa, so we would have to keep quiet about that.

The food situation was getting really desperate. The Italian rations were really inadequate and we were more hungry than ever. There should have been more pressure on the officers though maybe the war in Africa was beginning to tell on their food supplies; with our Army and Navy controlling this part of the Mediterranean there could be havoc. We might get more news if more prisoners came into the camp.

We were still having two or three cigarettes a day from the cigars we got a few days before; they were a lot better than smoking the cigars themselves which just seemed to burn away quickly; maybe the newspaper made them burn more slowly.

The officer and the interpreter were talking during roll call, their hands going up and down. I wondered what this was about as it was unusual. Everybody's eyes were on the pair chatting away and hoping it was good news. It was getting really cold, clouds were starting to get black in the distance and we were all hoping it would not rain till after the roll call. Everyone was on edge wondering about the conversation. We were really desperate to go to the toilet, it could be the cold striking us as there was so little heat in our clothes. We would have to get a group of lads to shield us so we could relieve ourselves as otherwise we would have to do it in our trousers and then we would have to wash them and try to get them dry. So the lads made a ring facing outwards so they could see if anyone was coming in our direction. Jimmy said there was no way he could have held on and I said I was in the same predicament.

The interpreter called the senior sergeant over to him and they were talking and laughing, which was unusual; but I went straight for the queue for the buns which was the most important thing at the time as I had never felt so hungry for a long time. Then I ran to the block and had a couple of slices of apple and a few grapes in the bun. At least we had a little treat which others had not and it would be a while before we got any more fruit.

We made a cigarette each with fresh paper from the toilets; this was kept inside a cupboard and everyone could help themselves because there was a fresh supply every day. You looked through to see if you could spot a few blank sheets. I didn't feel too good, a bit sick, so I went back to the block and had a lie down.

When I got there Sergeant Bertram was there shouting out names to people. My name came up and he gave me a letter and a card. The card was from my mother; everyone was all right but there was no mention of Edie. I couldn't not believe this and spent a long time wondering why. Once again I would be playing war with myself about sending that card that dreadful day 6 May. Her birthday would have been 11 May and she would have been 18 years old. It made my blood boil. The card was from my brother Stephen and four lines were blacked out again. I kept telling him every time I wrote not to give away information that could involve the Government but he still did it every time.

This day on roll call was lovely weather but still no news of the Red Cross parcels. I thought it would be lovely just lying on a beach having ice cream and a plate of mussels and winkles. It had been my favourite when we were down at Whitley Bay for the day with my mother and father and brothers Stephen, Fred, Robert and John, just before the war. We would have a game of rounders, or sometimes football, depending on how many people were around. If it was a nice day it would be packed with people and children. We would just lie on the beach and sometimes have a cup of tea with some homemade cake and scones, stottie cake and sandwiches of ham or pease pudding. Sometimes there was a bit of stuffing with a smear of mustard. Just thinking of this made my mouth water.

Once we had been counted and could stand at ease your mind just took over, wondering what you would we doing back home. We loved to go for a walk, hand in hand, sometimes with a nice cuddle and kiss and just love each other very much. She used to say she was glad I was at Fenham Barracks because I could have been down south or in Scotland and we would hardly see each other. I was home nearly every other day and when I was on the tram it just could not go quickly enough to reach Forest Hall. It was really nice, just to reminisce.

I wondered why they had not had us out again as a working party; maybe they did not have the men to take us out. The roll call was still going on and I thought they must be as sick as us, counting for hours on end.

A few days later Jimmy asked me if I knew of any property for sale in Forest Hall so I told him I would get in touch with my mother and that if I got any news about it I would let him know. I said that there was a good place beside the Ritz cinema, just across the road where there were three shops. He was asking me if I would go into a partnership with him, taking a half share each of the building if it was up for sale. He said he would like a sweet and tobacconist shop and I said the other half would make a lovely ice cream parlour selling coffee and tea and maybe sandwiches or meals. We kept talking about it while we were strolling around the compound and he said we would just have to see if it was up for sale and we left it at that. I would ask my mother to keep a lookout when it did come up for sale. It was in an ideal spot, especially when the first house pictures came out or when young couples who had been to work could meet their boy- or girlfriends come in for an ice cream soda or whatever. Edie had worked in a shop since she was 15 but now that she was 18 she could be anywhere, in the forces or helping with the war effort.

His sister's letter said that everyone was all right; and I told him about my card from Stephen with the lines crossed out.

All of a sudden we saw people running towards the main gate. When we got there we saw a big lorry with a trailer, so we said, 'Red Cross parcels!' Jimmy said at last that Sergeant Bertram had told him that we might have a consignment soon but the two of them must have had as much of a surprise as we did. Jimmy said they were frightened to say anything in case it was a false alarm and they were quite right because in a camp like that rumours could spread like wildfire and it could cause trouble with some maniac. We were really pleased as this could be a good supply for two months or more and perhaps we could have another supply before Christmas. But now we knew that they were in the storeroom and our days of hunger were over. Never mind what was in them, everyone would be happy again with a spring in their step.

I sometimes wondered where my three other brothers were, Fred, Robert and John. My Dad was unemployed when I left. He used to work in the mines and might have gone back as he was an experienced miner. Fred might have joined him there; the other two were still at school.

Sergeant Bertram came in later with some cigarettes: ten for each of us. There was mail too, and Jimmy got a letter and a parcel but there was none for me. He was beaming. He could also look forward to the Red Cross parcels in a day or two; it took them quite a time to get organised and count them, to see if it would be one parcel between two, or four, or even eight. The cigarettes did tide us over while we were waiting: a nice smoke for a change instead of the Italian crap. Some people had died because they had not a tough constitution to help them; but my mother's cooking, her soups, broth and lovely Sunday dinners helped my body to control its health; and people were helped if they believed in themselves.

Jimmy was whispering to Sergeant Bertram about clothing and the boxing match so perhaps we might get something done. They must have been sick of us complaining; Jimmy said we just had to keep pressing to get things done. The interpreter had to get in touch with the senior officer in command of the camp who we rarely saw. Later he told us that the boxing match might be the next week or the one after and that he had mentioned the clothing problem again. Perhaps if we went round naked they would give us some cloth to wrap round us.

My only hope in relation to Edie was my mate Edward Blake and I decided that my next card would be to him, telling him to give my address to Edie.

One of the Italian soldiers showed us one of the parcels and it was an English one which had fourteen or sixteen items in but with not so much nourishment as the Canadian ones.

Each sergeant had to keep account of what position every one should have for the distribution of cognac, buns, skilly and parcels; it was a fair system. He also had to arrange who went to the shop each month.

Jimmy asked again about the arrangement to write to my mother and

I said as soon as I got a letter or card to send home; but on a card you could not put full details as you were limited for space to about eight or nine lines which is not very much. On a letter form you could write a lot more. Sometimes you had to do it in two halves so you had to end 'cont.', so they had an inkling in the next letter that there was more to say.

Jimmy's parcel was clothing: two sets of vests and underpants which was very good indeed; he would need them to keep himself warm. He told me I could send a letter home whenever I wanted so I wrote that I wanted to know if the shop opposite the Ritz cinema was still for sale, just to know one way or the other; and then I wrote to Edward Blake to ask him to give my address to Edie. I would just have to wait and see what he did this time but if I did not get any satisfaction I would not be writing to him for a long time. There is many a time I wished I had apologised at the beginning and waited for her letter to tell me what had happened from her end. I was grieving as if I had lost someone. She was quite young to be wed but she knew what she wanted the same as me, though I was older; but our feelings for each other were as if we were one person and those feelings would never die.

The rest of the day went as usual and I realised as they put out the lights that we had not had an air raid for a while; everyone would be wondering what had gone wrong.

The next day we were still waiting for the parcels. They were distributed by blocks and they need quite a few soldiers to distribute them. The sergeants were called up first so there was no cheating which could have caused havoc. It was really well organised by the Italians and our sergeants too would not stand any nonsense. We went to the toilets as usual and had a shave and a good wash; it was getting too cold to have a hose pipe bath as it was very cold water.

Back towards the compound and we could see that they had started dishing out the parcels and hoped they would get a group or two finished before roll call. When we met Johnny and his pals we discovered they had had theirs the previous night. We were due letters and cards sometime last week; they must have kept them so we would be more depressed – they did everything they could to hurt people, or perhaps they had been told by the Camp Commander who wouldn't give a damn about people's feelings. Perhaps the interpreter had been told to give us a bit of good news with no follow-up as it did seem a bit far-fetched; that was how rumours started.

That day it was sunny and a lot warmer so it was lovely standing outside but when it was raining it was hard for us getting soaking wet with nowhere to dry our clothes except on the grass or dirt on the ground. You could not approach the fence. At that moment I saw a lot of black clouds approaching and it started to spit with rain; maybe it would be just a shower as there was a break in the clouds to the west.

The clouds never came to much, and I went to stand in the queue to see if we would get our parcels while Jimmy went to have his meal; then we would swap over. We might get served then or have to come back after the next roll call. In fact we had to parade again and Sergeant Bertram was whispering to Jimmy so I wondered what was going on. it must have been something interesting as both of them were smiling. I gave Jimmy a nudge and he said, 'Not now, later maybe.' Somebody was saying that Ken who played the mouth organ might come over to our block tonight which would make it a good night indeed.

I was trying to remember an address to send a card to Edie. I knew the street and the area of Newcastle but not the number and it was a long street; it could give the postman quite a headache. I should rely on Ned Blake rather and hope that he gave her the Camp address. It was in God's hands and there seemed to be a wall of steel between us.

Our motto always seemed to be 'Wait'. That was what camp was like: waiting, sun drenched or drenched in rain and also cold. Jimmy was still not saying anything and it was bugging me not knowing what was going on; if he could only give me a sign of some sort.

We had been waiting for quite a time at the storeroom and our group was next. We saw the group before beaming like Cheshire cats and eventually the sergeant came to us and said we might be next but it was nearly skilly time and we would have to wait till the next day. We went away with our heads low but at least we had the singalong. It was a wonderful time with the mouth organ and Norman with the comb joined in as well, so we forgot our disappointment.

The next day we went along to the storeroom but Sergeant Bertram wasn't there which seemed funny. One or two groups had to go before us leaving us on stand-by. Eventually he came to us and said. 'Sorry. lads, but we'll have to wait till after roll call.' They gave out a few, and we said, 'Just where do we stand in this rota?'

It was a lovely day; in another two days we would be in October. This used to be my favourite time with my family; it would bring a lot of memories: laughing, and my brothers enjoying looking forward to Christmas. There would be very little cheer here if there were no parcels: just one cognac, two buns and skilly – not much to look forward to. Perhaps we would have a good meal that night; if it was Jimmy's choice I would just say yes and have mine the next day; better to agree over something than sulk. He came over to me and whispered we would be getting more cigarettes which was good news as we were down to our last one. If only we could get some good news about the war; there had not been any new prisoners in for ages.

I went to the gate while Jimmy went to get our buns and again Sergeant Bertram was not there. There were a few Italians moving around and stacking parcels for each group. The other group was served and we had to wait and see when the next one would go up but it did not look like us at all. If it kept on like this another roll call would be due. And then the officer came out and we had to go for roll call. After this Jimmy said he would go for the parcel while I got the buns and hot water ready.

We were wondering how the German and Italian POWs were doing at home, better than they treated us, I would bet. It was funny we had had no planes over lately; something must have happened. Everyone thought we must have been hoodwinked in the last report but it was great at the time and lifted our morale no end.

I went and had my bun and hot water and then went up to meet Jimmy so he could get his tea. When I arrived he was in the group waiting for their parcel. Sergeant Bertram told them to come to attention and marched them down to the main gate. Then we went to the toilets and I stood outside till he had finished and then he did the same for me and then we went to the block to see what we could have for tea.

He said we would open a tin of corned beef; he had his piece in his bun and I had mine in my hand. We had a cup of tea with a spoonful of sugar and a drop of milk. Jimmy whispered that the sergeant would be in shortly with some cigarettes which would be a surprise. Half an hour later he did come in with some mail which he delivered first. I received a letter and Jimmy had one too so what with parcels and cigarettes too everyone was happy. The card was from my cousin Eva in Birmingham, just saying she was sorry I had been taken prisoner. Later I wrote back to her but never got any more from her.

Two soldiers were dishing out the skilly who usually did the counting; it was funny seeing them there. We had to stand for quite a while so had a half cigarette each. It did not take long to get served as the two had a ladle each and we just formed two queues. After we had eaten Terry started to sing. Norman had the comb and Ken the mouth organ – he said he was going to ask his mother to send one of his own ones as he had a number at home. It would be grand when it arrived as we could have more lovely nights like these.

A few days later Jimmy was telling me that the boxing match was due the next week, if everyone was fit but we would just have to wait and see because low rations did take their toll. So things were going along nicely after the weeks of misery. At roll call Jimmy was trying to get in touch with the sergeant but he was not taking any notice as we were not at ease. He turned to Jimmy and whispered to him and Jimmy just stepped to one side and stood to attention.

Another thing we needed to ask about was for buckets to keep water in. There was no water installed in the blocks and every drop had to be carried to make tea or coffee and sometimes you would go thrice or more. And apart from the clothes we needed new mattresses and pillows as these were so thin that when you got up in the morning there were red marks on your body, just like tiger's stripes. You had to keep hammering and dripping away at them as sometimes they felt either deaf or dumb. We were not asking for a lot, just a bit of comfort. The cognac was getting a bit watery; maybe the soldiers were keeping some back for themselves.

We were just back at the block when the sergeant came in with letters and cards for us to write home. Jimmy and I had had ours the day before. We asked him again about the things that were troubling us and he said he would do his very best.

Chapter 11

A few days later I went to get my boots which should have been at the foot of the three-tier bed, only to find they had been taken during the night. These were New Zealand boots which had been given me after the boat was torpedoed in December 1941. They were size 11 and I was only size 10 but I did not mind the extra size as they were a lovely pair of boots. Maybe they had been stolen to be traded for food or money; I would never know. I just had to go down to the toilets in my bare feet and if it was raining I just had to borrow from someone in the block. Most of the time I just had to tear a piece from my shirt so I could clean my feet, or just go to bed with them dirty. Jimmy was very good at going to get the cognac but I still had to go on parade. Later I had a word with the sergeant to see if he could get a pair of boots or any footwear even if it was only a sack.

I would have to be careful going to the toilets and then back to the block as my feet were really sore.

We had Spam sandwiches with our tea when Jimmy came in with the buns, and half a cigarette. Jimmy asked me again if my card had been from my mother but I said no, from Stephen. He said he had had a word with Sergeant Bertram over the loss of my boots and he said he would try and get something for me if he could, and would see if I could stay indoors if the weather got nasty. He thought it odd that they should have been lost like that when they had been there every night since we came to the camp. Jimmy went for a walk but my feet were too sore so I just sat outside as it was still sunny. During roll call I thought I would ask if anybody could give me old socks or bits of cloth – no harm in trying to get something – as my feet were feeling the cold. Maybe I could get some shoes or boots from the Italians, or was that just wishful thinking? If I got half a chance I was going to sit down and rub some warmth into them as my toes were numb. Sergeant Bertram was not at all pleased at me sitting down though I thought he would understand the circumstances but no, he said that I was on parade and would at all times stand up. He told Jimmy that he would see me about this later. I said to myself, I wish it was his boots that were lost, and see what he would have done. I could hardly feel my feet by then.

Back in the block I wrapped them up in a sheet to try to get some warmth back into them. Jimmy said he did not know how I stood it out there. I said I was going to go to the next block and ask Sergeant Bertram if I could be counted inside until I could get something for my feet. Instead he came to see me and said he had asked the interpreter who would try to get something for me. He said that if the next day was also cold he would ask if I could be counted in the block but he could not promise anything.

The next day dawned sunny through the glass window but it was a bit colder than yesterday. I was sitting outside wishing they would make their mind up; if I had to go on roll call I would just have to, though it would be better to be indoors though indoors I would have missed the signal. I went over to the group area and the sergeant waved me towards him. I told him I had been trying to find something for my feet and that I had ripped a sheet. He gave me an awful look. I said, 'Sergeant, I am not standing like I did yesterday; it was quite a time before I got any feeling back.' But it was much better with the cloth around.

I said to Jimmy, 'I will get the buns as my feet are not as bad as yesterday.'

He said, 'If you want to.'

I said, 'Yes, because sometime I may not be able to get them and you cannot go every time.'

He said, 'I wouldn't mind because I might be in your situation sometime.'

I thought that was a nice attitude and I thanked him.

Jimmy whispered to me that maybe Stephen might get a pair of boots for some of our parcel. We could see what was being bartered at that time.

I just got a card to write home so I couldn't write much but asked her again about the property near the Ritz cinema.

Sergeant Bertram could only do so much as his hands were tied by the Italians' red tape; he had tried many times to get the things we wanted but had failed each time and could not get any satisfaction out of the interpreter for the officer. I asked if he could try and get me a pair of boots or shoes and he said he would try but played war with me for tearing up the sheet.

I said, 'You would do the same if you hadn't any boots.'

He said, 'Maybe.'

If only a new face came into the camp we might have got some news, information on the various fronts, in the desert or in Russia. There had not been any planes over bombing for quite a while; maybe they were getting a good supply of arms, tanks and ammunition to make a last push. Everyone in this camp must act as one big happy family, we had a part to play; we got the blues once in a while but had to keep our spirits up at all times.

I was standing during roll call just shifting from one foot to the other and trying to rub some heat into them before I had to walk anywhere. When I did walk it took some time as I could not hurry up. I just hobbled to the block; Jimmy went ahead of me and started to make the tea. When I got there Jimmy had nearly everything ready, just waiting for the can to boil. This would be our fourth cup out of these tea leaves. He went later to get our skilly and then we had a singsong until lights out.

This was going to be the last meal out of the parcel, There was a bit of dried tea which might last a week and maybe the milk as well but the sugar would go within a few days. Sergeant Bertram came into the block and said, 'You ripped the sheets and you want me to get new ones, and palliasses. If they see yours torn they may not give us new ones.'

I said, 'What's done is done, I cannot put it back, and my feet ache with cold. It would be better if I stayed in the block and didn't go on parade. It is really cold out there and will get worse.'

'You cannot stay on the block,' he said, 'until I get permission from the officer. You two have given me a lot to do.'

'Not only me and Jimmy,' I answered. 'All the block is asking about these things; we have been let down time and time again.'

Roll call again and I started to massage my feet which were freezing with standing still. If I kept on like this I was going to end up with a dreadful cold or even frostbite. I was getting cramp and then pins and needles even though my feet were wrapped in the cloth. The people who took my boots should be thrashed. Better still, take their shoes away from them and see how they liked it. We might have a look to see what was in the shop later as most folk did sometimes, wishing it was you going through as there were sometimes different items such as apples, pears, grapes, plums, oranges and very rarely, vegetables. Jimmy said that Sergeant Bertram felt awful about having me come on parade like that, and I said it was a disgrace that I should have to. Well, I was just a prisoner of war and nobody cared at all.

It was very boring being counted. Perhaps they were frightened we would run away, but where to? The camp perimeter had lots of guards and dogs on duty all day and night; we did not know the language, we did not know anywhere to hide, and on our clothes were big red patches so we would be very easily recognised.

It was starting to rain and we were wondering if they would call it a day. My feet were just beginning to get warm as I massaged them, one at a time, but if it kept raining my clothes were going to get very wet and it would be hard to travel to the toilets during the night in just my bare feet and try to dry them with the cloth. I would not be able to see any sharp objects around and might get cut toes and soles, unless I tied on the sheet I cut, which might help a little. I was glad the parade was nearly over as my feet had gone into a cramp. Jimmy went ahead and when I got to the block Jimmy had the can boiling and had the buns done as well. That was the last of the cheese but there was some margarine left so we wouldn't have to have dry buns the next day.

The sergeant came in and said there was no chance of getting boots or shoes at that moment, but he had some cloths to wear for the time being. I suppose it was better than nothing. They never said anything about buckets to keep our water in or new palliasses, pillows and sheets.

The cloths made a great difference on parade and I felt a lot warmer the next day, but the ground was still wet though the sun was coming through, which would help a lot. The interpreter and the officer were talking for some time, and we were wondering if something was happening. They were smiling at each other. We were wondering too if they would release more of the parcels. Perhaps they were waiting for a letter or phone call. While I was rubbing my feet Jimmy came over to whisper that they might be doing the parcels that afternoon, but not to take it for granted. The cloths were really wet with all that standing.

I decided to see the sergeant again and show him the cloths all soaking wet; if they didn't do something I was going to report sick. He said he would try to get some boots or shoes or let me stay indoors. He had seen my feet before but still made me go to roll call each day.

I wished I could get a card from Edward Blake. He was the only hope I have of getting in touch with Edie. How I wished I had never received that letter which gave me all this grief.

Jimmy and I were still expecting a card or letter so that we could think about our business at Forest Hall if it was still empty, as it had been a while before, but my mother was unreliable. I would also have liked to hear about Edie. Soon it would be November and I would have been a prisoner for a year. It seemed a long time since my capture, but at that time it seemed as if the war would go on for ever. No one could predict when it would finish or even what would happen next month.

Jimmy had been great to me, going for buns and cognac and skilly; he must have got sick of it, but he said that is why mates in the Army help each other. The sergeant came after roll call and told me he had had another word with the interpreter who went to the officer who said he might do something for me but he did not know what.

A few days later there were guards at the storeroom and so we could look forward to more parcels which would be very welcome as we were down to dry buns and hot water again. I waited for the signal from Jimmy about joining my group; he waved his arms aloft which meant to join them; if I was to go into the block he would put his arms down by his sides. I just started moving my feet from heel to toe and they got quite warm; I wished I had thought of it earlier. We still had not heard about the boxing match but at least we were going to get a parcel. At that moment, the sky became very dark and we all hoped the rain would keep off as that would delay things throughout the camp. If they didn't hurry up they too were going to get wet and all we had on was ragged shirts and trousers. We were glad this was the last roll call for the day, but the ones getting their parcels would get a real soaking. It came on heavy rain and we were all shivering. Jimmy said he would go and get the skilly and that he would gauge the time to go instead of going at once. The parade was dismissed early and everyone ran to their blocks.

The cup of hot water was really welcome. Just then Jimmy shouted that the rain had stopped and went off, wet through. Everyone was stripping and getting into bed to get warm. God only knew when our clothes would dry.

A couple of days later and we still had not got our parcels. It was a fine day though with some dark clouds in the west. The interpreter called the main sergeant to him and told him what to say to us. He called out that someone had tried to escape last night but had got caught; and that every parcel would be opened and shared between four people; including the parcels that had already been shared out so some people would be some articles short. Who knew when we would get another consignment and it looked as if we were in for a tough time. The sergeant went to his area which was the one next to us, and he was very upset about the whole thing. Everyone suffered when someone tried to escape; it would have been good if he had got away but getting caught made it hard for himself and others as well. But there was nothing to be done but grin and bear it.

Everyone was disgusted at the news but at least opening all the tins meant that we could have a few days' meals before going back to Italian rations and we would have milk and sugar and tea for a fortnight. The parcels would certainly be delayed however; this was an unlucky period in our lives.

The sun was shining at last and a north wind was blowing the black clouds away and perhaps our clothes would get dry, even if they were on our backs. There was nothing else we could do. If we got colds there was no one to help us, no doctor. The sergeant was sick at what we kept telling him, but who could we turn to for guidance? There were no officers in our camp, just a senior sergeant and maybe a staff sergeant.

When Jimmy came in I had the kettle boiling for us and was just pouring the water into the cups. He told me they were carrying on with the parcels but were opening all the tins. There were four groups waiting. Sergeant Bertram came in with cards, letters and two or three parcels and started by shouting out the names for the parcels. Jimmy had a parcel and so did Ken who played the mouth organ. I had a letter and a card. He said that he was rather busy at the moment, and if we had anything to say, to see him after roll call.

We did have some things to say, and it was about a good idea concerning the Red Cross in Switzerland; perhaps we could get in touch with them and ask for clothing. Perhaps the sergeant could mention his clothes in all his letters, and maybe he would get a hint, by marking capital letters in some way.

I didn't mention that there was a bugler who played every morning, really different to our Reveille and the Last Post in evening and then the lights went out.

I could hardly feel my feet that parade. The cloths had no heat at all as they were just like a bundle of rags. Sometimes during the night I would hit a stone and my foot would be bruised for a few days. Even the small ones could give you a nasty cut. It was disgraceful having to put up with this. I bet our Italian prisoners were lapping it up in lovely warm places, even if only a fire in the middle of the hut. When we were guarding them in Genefa near the Suez Canal we did give them a hard time and the sergeant in charge of us really gave us hell for doing this, though when he was not looking we still gave them a little dig. Little did we know that we ourselves would end up in a prisoner of war camp.

I was looking forward to reading my mail and seeing if there was any news. The last news of the war we had had from new prisoners said that we had a lot of ships of all kinds being sunk in the Mediterranean, the Atlantic and the Far East, and some in the North Sea.

I read the card and it was from Ned Blake. He said that he would not give Edie my address because I had told him not to; but I had written this other letter saying that he could! That was most distressing. Then I read my mother's letter. She said that everyone was all right. but the last two lines were blacked out and there was still no mention of the property unless she had not received my letter yet.

After the skilly, the next thing we heard was Terry, Norman on the comb and Ken with the mouth organ playing and it was so beautiful – really different from the other one with different tone and we had indeed a marvellous night until lights out. They seemed to follow each other as if they had played together for years and it really did lift our spirits.

People sang along and some whistled like me; I did have a little sing if I knew the words, especially the old ones by Gene Audry and some cowboy singers.

The next day in the toilets I discovered that my foot was cut; I had no bandages, just clean water and salt to soak it. My cloths had to be washed as they were very dirty and I had to put them on wet. Again I was rocking my feet heel to toe to keep the circulation in them. Jimmy went over to the sergeant and he was whispering; I thought this was funny as they seemed not to say anything until we were actually being counted, so it must have been important. When Jimmy got back to his place he gave me a nod, so at least he was going to tell me something.

I was pondering what to do about Edie as Ned had been my last hope. I was thinking about her and wondering about me, how I was coping. I hoped I would get a letter to tell me I was wrong to doubt her. Just then Jimmy came and told me we might get a cigarette issue that day and a chance of a Red Cross parcel. He told me to go and get the buns and have my hot water while he waited to see if there was a parcel; and then we would exchange. I went to the toilets and looked at my foot and it was bleeding but all I could do was wash it and the raggy cloth and then put it back on.

The sergeant asked me why I was limping so I told him about my cut toe. He said that after the next roll call he was going to talk to the interpreter to try to get some bandages for shoes; he said he was really sorry I had to put up with this. I thanked him. Later Jimmy said that he had had a pair of socks in his parcel and that I could have them if they fitted. I could put the socks on then wrap cloths around them and that would keep my legs warm as well. I thought that was very generous of him.

I relieved Jimmy at the main gate and the time went on to 7 o'clock. The sergeant said, 'Just keep still and as soon as this group comes out we will go straight to the storeroom area. Be on your best behaviour and we'll get through a lot sooner. By the way, I had had a talk to the officer about you having no boots and he said he would try his best and let us know tomorrow.'

Jimmy was waiting for me and we went back to the block with the parcel. We asked Len and Joe to share with us and we divided everything possible into four portions. These were the two lads, Len and Joe, we trusted with our buns. First though we had a lovely cup of English tea with milk and sugar and a few biscuits. We also had an issue of twenty cigarettes for each man which was more than we expected and we each had a whole one as it was quite a while since we had had any English ones. The last ones were from India and were full of saltpetre, but we should not grumble when we were getting them for nothing. After skilly Ken started to play old songs and war songs then the others joined in. It was a great night again and we just whistled and sang with them till the bugler played lights out.

In the morning people still seemed in a happy mood. I was in the wash house with my cloth off washing my left foot when someone knocked me over. The chap said, 'I am really sorry.' It was a Kiwi and his mate was with him, and said, 'Snowy, it was nice to receive apologies from that chap,' and I said it was very kind to give me a hand up.

On roll call, I was dreaming about the times we went to the Palace, and before then we used to go to a flower girl who kept carnations for Edie and Ned and me. We had white ones; she always had a pink one. I wondered if they would be having a white Christmas in England but for most families it would not be nice just having their loved ones far away in different places in that war. I had told Jimmy I would get the buns as he must have been getting tired of always doing it for me. I was barefoot as the rags were useless.

If I got a chance that afternoon I would go down to the wash house and have a shower with the hose pipe. We tried to keep ourselves as clean as possible. Just dreaming again, how nice it would be to lie in a bath and have a soak with plenty of soap and then go to the pub and have a nice cool drink or go to a cinema and see a good film; or just have a Wall's ice cream. Or have a nice stroll up a country lane. In fact there was too much of a queue for the hose pipe; but I met that Kiwi Snowy again. I had three cuts on my right foot and one on my heel which was really nasty. It was bleeding and I just kept bathing it with cold water. I would have to walk on my toes to keep the dirt out. Jimmy said he didn't know how I had been walking.

Len, the lad we were sharing with said, 'What size shoe do you take? You can try mine, these are a ten.'

I did have a try and with my feet being so sore I could feel pain when I walked, but it would be nice to use them even just to go to the toilet. It was really nice just walking to the toilet in boots and while I was there I gave my feet another wash; they had stopped bleeding. It was especially bliss during the night, not having to look where I put my feet. I was not going to take liberties with them though and would just wait for Len to offer them. Snowy the Kiwi saw them and said it was nice to see me with a pair of boots, but I told him I just had a loan of them. Jimmy said that I seemed to have an infection on my heel.

The sergeant came in with letter forms and again I wrote to Ned and to my mother asking him the same questions about Edie. That evening we had cheese with our buns and everyone got an equal share, spreading it on their buns with a spoon. There was an equal share and no animosity. The sergeant came with two pieces of cloth with me and looked at my feet; he said I should be excused roll call until my heel healed. I told him that someone was lending me shoes and he thought that was very good of him.

It was especially useful to have the loan of the boots at this time as I had diarrhoea

I had the new cloths from Sergeant Bertram and while the others were at roll call I kept bathing my heel and trying to squeeze out the pus. I took my time on the way back, trying to throw as many stones as possible out of my way. Nobody was back so I started to put the can on to boil. To light the charcoal you had to roll paper into a long strip and keep it there until the charcoal took light. It was better to use wood, and sometimes people took bits from their beds; sometimes the Italian guards threw some in, but it often landed between the two wires and we would have been shot getting it. Sometimes carpenters came to do jobs in different compounds and there were bits left over.

That night the Welsh lad, Terry, played tunes from the First World War and songs of Vera Lynn and Gracie Fields; and then went on to cowboy songs like Gene Audry. This weekend would be 1 November. Jimmy and I talked of what we did when we were young. I lived in a small mining village where most of the people worked in various pits. I was the oldest at home and the only one at work as my brothers were at school; the youngest only three years old. My mother had her hands full with the five of us plus my Dad was not working. He went out to get coal from the pit heaps, just so we had a good fire. Even on the coldest days he would wrap himself up and spend a good few hours at this and if he got say three bags full he would sell one of them to buy a few cigarettes and give my mother some money, just a few shillings to put food on the table. Jimmy said he knew what our family were going through as his dad worked in the pits in the Midlands and worked very hard just to make ends meet.

While Jimmy was out at roll call I lay on my bunk and must have dozed a bit. As I got up I saw this lad Ron across the way making different expressions; his face was very taut. I shouted over, 'What is the matter, Ron?' but he just could not answer so I went over. He was having a fit. I just let him lie there, hoping he would not swallow his tongue, and took the little spoon with me just in case. He lay for a while and then just came out of the fit. Now I knew why he did not go to roll call. Later I tried to talk to him but he had something wrong with his speech and just mumbled. The Cockney lad Stephen was the one who always looked after his place, and he had spoon fed him and mixed his bun in soup. Sometimes I bartered his cigarettes for him in the compound as he did not smoke.

Each day I would bathed my feet and tried to get the pus out of the wounds; sometimes they would bleed but this seemed the right treatment. The cut on my left foot was about two inches long, and deep. Despite my care, it seemed to be getting worse again. I met Snowy the Kiwi who was asking after me.

Jimmy said that the sergeant was going to come to see me and he advised me to show him my foot so that I might get off roll call for another few days. When the sergeant arrived he had a bundle of cards and parcels and the last card was for me from my brother Stephen.

I showed the sergeant my foot and told him I was bathing it three times a day but he said it still looked awful. He said there was no way I could stand on parade like that, bleeding and oozing pus and red around the wound. I asked him if he could perhaps get some salt, which had worked so well in Greece and he said he would try. When I walked to the toilets I either hopped, which was very tiring, or walked on my toes. It was a pity we had hadn't had Canadian tins of milk most recently as they were large and I could have boiled my cloths in them and used hot water to bathe my feet. The English tins were rather small. I was frightened the sore might ulcerate.

We had finished all of our parcels now, the last of the watery tea and sugar and we would be back on Italian rations. Jimmy said, 'Let's not get downhearted, we have to let these Italians know what we are made of.' It was a good job we had a great singer, Terry, and Ken the mouth organ player to help us through. Some of the blocks had nothing like that but someone was saying they were trying to have a story night, like the live shows they had in theatres. I had been to one or two shows when I worked at the pithead; we went once by bus to Newcastle Theatre Royal to see a show about the pit men in Wales, *The Corn is Green*, which was very enjoyable. At first I thought I would not understand the story line but it got better and better and was very interesting. Later they made a film of it and it was even better because they were real actors. The other time was a very tragic show but at least it was a night out.

The Italian officer wanted me back on parade. I said that my foot was worse, not better, but it was out of the sergeant's hands. I said I should really have a doctor to look at it, but meanwhile I would hobble out on parade when Jimmy gave the signal. The sergeant had his orders but I did not know how long I could stand. I would just have to wait and see what the next day brought. Everyone was disappointed about this decision from the officer.

The next day was windy but the sun was shining and at least that was not too bad. When I saw Jimmy's signal I hobbled along as best I could as my foot was really throbbing. I didn't know how long I could stand this parade, let alone the next one. I could feel the cold coming up through the cloths. I could not even stamp my feet to keep them warm though the right one was perfectly all right. I did hope that the weather was going to be better than at Brindisi at the beginning of the year. I would so much have liked to go home for Christmas and everyone was in the same mind.

The sergeant said that he could not get any boots or shoes or clothing of any description but brought me four more cloths. He had another look at my feet and said, 'It is really bad. I will have another word to see if you can stay in the block,' so I thanked him. He added that he wished he could get in touch with the Red Cross and tell them how these officers were treating prisoners of war. He said that the young lad with the fits, Ron, really should be repatriated as he was really ill and should be in hospital. 'You should see a doctor about your wound but these people do not want to know.'

I went to roll call when Jimmy gave me the nod and though I was stamping my right foot and once bent down to remove the cloth as I had cramp, the sergeant never said anything. The pain was so bad I was crying, tears falling down my cheeks, and it seemed to get worse. I wished I could go and clean it up which would give me a bit of peace. They could count me in my block any time; I couldn't possibly escape like this anyway. in my state. Where could I run to? I would stick out like a sore thumb. Some days you just got fed up with everything. If only we could have a little good news, just something to keep our morale up. It was really monotonous, just standing around day in day out. There were black clouds to the north and the wind seemed to have increased in the last half hour.

The interpreter was called by the officer and they were talking and laughing away quite a while; everyone would love to have known what it was about. We were amazed at them laughing; it was not for us a laughing matter, standing around. Just then I started to feel dizzy and gave Jimmy a shout. As he came over I went down to the ground and just lay there. Even Sergeant Bertram came over.

'Are you all right, Tommy?'

I said, 'I don't feel too good at all.'

The sergeant said, 'Can you stand, as the ground is not very warm.'

I tried to get up but just managed to kneel and he told me to keep like that till roll call was over. Jimmy stayed beside me, saying, 'This is ridiculous, those brutes should get you a doctor or at least leave you in the block.'

The sergeant said, 'You cannot leave the parade, just hang on as best you can. There are only about four more groups to do.'

A couple of the lads took hold of my arms to try to steady me as I was not very good at all, and really cold. The sergeant said that there were only two more groups to do. He said, 'I don't think the prisoners in England will get this kind of treatment; since we have been taken prisoner, they have not been very kind and there has been nothing but trouble. We are let down on everything we ask for.'

The lads kept hold of me but I just wanted to lie down; the pain was terrible. When it finally finished he told them to take me over to the toilets to deal with my feet. I said that if only I could get some hot water and salt; I could boil the water if I had a Klim tin. Jimmy told him that I had done their wounds effectively in this way when we were in Greece.

At the toilet, with being so cold, I wet myself, which was really embarrassing but the lads said they would have done the same. Joe took the cloths off my left foot and gave me a hand to get it into the basin while Len kept hold of me in case I toppled over. They said they did not know why I didn't collapse earlier as it looked terrible. I told them I just needed a tin to make hot water dressings and my problem, and he said, 'No problem, mate, I have one in the block; my mate doesn't like milk or sugar in his tea so I always have spare sugar and milk and I always use the English parcels first.'

I said, 'I cannot thank you enough for your help.'

True to his word, he brought the tin round straight away; it was lovely and clean. I straight away got the blower from the corner. This seemed to give me a new lease of life because I could do something to help myself. I thought Jimmy would understand, and Len and Joe who we shared with. I gave little blasts with the bellows until the charcoal took hold, then put on the water can and blasted it until it boiled. I took a piece of cloth off my foot and put it into the can with the spoon handle, waited a while then put it against my foot. It was bliss. I apologised for holding up the tea making but they said it did not matter so long as the treatment was going well. Jimmy took off his shirt and showed the others how I had helped him with his wound and those of the others. While he was telling them the story I put the cloth on again – it was such a relief and I felt a great deal better. A bit of pus came out and this time it did not bleed. Jimmy then made the tea and gave me some.

'Thank you all for being so understanding,' I said.

'Look, it could have been us in that situation, we really feel for you, you must have been in terrible pain to collapse like that. How does it feel now?'

'I just cannot get over what hot water can do; if I'd had that tin earlier I would not be in this situation.'

Sergeant Bertram came on to see how I was. He said, 'By, you look better.'

I told him what I had done; I was about to repeat the process so he said he would burn the charcoal for me, then he would be able to see my foot. While we were doing this Terry started to sing and Ken on the mouth organ and Norman on the comb joined in and he said, 'You lads are lucky, we have no entertainment.'

I said, 'Why don't you bring one or two lads along, there will be an hour or so before lights out.'

The sergeant said, 'I had a talk about you collapsing on the parade ground and you did it twice. I said you were in torture with pain and was there any salt. He said he would try to get some, but what for? I said it was for your foot and suggested a doctor but he just laughed at me. I said it was no laughing matter: what if it gets infected and then gangrene and he loses part of his foot, what would you do about that? I just left it at that – the Italian interpreter is very young and rather stupid. The sooner he gets sent to the front the better; he may get some sense knocked into him,'

He told me not to come on parade the next day but just to work on the foot.

A few days later I still had not gone on parade and with the boiling water to kill all germs, the foot was a lot better and I could walk on it. Len was very generous, offering his boots to me quite often to go to the toilets. I asked the sergeant if he could get me any more cloths. I was off parade for nearly a week and it certainly did my feet good.

The sergeant said it would be great to hear from someone about the progress of the war in the desert and now, at the end of 1942, people in many countries would be wondering when it was going to end. Everyone was just hoping they would survive this ordeal. On my first parade back I could stand without pain and massage the feet from the cold when they had finished counting our group. The weather was still quite good but I did not know what would happen if it rained unless they let me stay indoors then. It was anyway really good to be outside in the fresh air after the stuffy block. It seemed a lifetime since we were captured and in fact it was a whole year.

There was still no sign of parcels. We were meant to get them once a fortnight apparently; and we should have received a certain number of calories per day but we did not get half that and that was why we were so hungry. Jimmy signalled that he would go for the buns and I waved agreement. Some of the lads in Signals could communicate properly to each other and it was wonderful watching them but they were trained to do it. I did wish they could teach us; it would be great fun.

We were still wearing same clothes we had been captured in, a whole year later, and they were very thin; the rain and wind went straight through us. It's no wonder we were laid up with illnesses and we had never seen a doctor in the compound in all that while.

When I got back to the block after the second roll call that day the sergeant was reading out names from the post and I had one from Stephen. There was still some blacked out and maybe he was trying to tell me something but I could make out that everyone was all right. As far as I was concerned he should still have been working for the NAAFI as he had done before the war started, in the Hexham area. He would never tell me anything. We all had to keep quiet anyway when the war started in case of Fifth Columnists; they used to say on notice boards: 'Beware, someone can hear you, even if you whisper.' He told me about my cousin John and his family and Aunt Martha, a lovely caring woman, always with a helping hand. There was not even a mention of Edie; he had not mentioned her name at all on any of his letters.

I asked if Sergeant Bertram had any word about cloths for my feet; and we asked again about clothing and Red Cross parcels but there was no word about either. We might get letter-forms and cards to send home the next week. Jimmy hoped my letter was from my mother.

The next roll call there were a different two guards who came through the gate. One was tall and lanky and one small and they were going to start late. Then came also a new officer, very young indeed, about twenty perhaps; the last one must have been sent to the front at last, and he was a real pain. As everyone came to attention the interpreter said his name and everyone just stood while the guards started counting. The sergeant straight away nodded to Jimmy and was smiles all over his face. Jimmy gave me a double nod, as if to say, 'I'll tell you later.' I fell to thinking about Edie which made me even more determined to keep alive. I had fought all the way till then, trying my hardest and with God's will, to help me through this ordeal. I loved her with all my heart and wished I could tell her so. Never would I take anyone's advice again but would trust my own instinct. I wondered how my younger brothers were getting on; my mother had said everyone was all right but you were never sure. Robert would be at school and John would have started in August, after the summer holidays.

That was a very long roll call and finished at 5.35 but they had a very long talk with the officer afterwards and there was something wrong as the officer was not pleased at all. Jimmy went for a couple of trips around the compound while I did my feet, and I was glad that Len and Joe agreed to go with Jimmy as I was housebound. That night at the singsong Johnny and his mate Bob from the next block came in, saying how lucky we were. One of the lads sitting beside us said, 'Why don't you have turns to come in each night; you could always leave about quarter of an hour before lights out. We could have six people every night.' They went away saying they would ask the others and thanking us for an enjoyable evening.

One of the chaps below me asked why I was shaking the bunk beds. I said I didn't know, that I woke up with my body sweating, but could not put my finger on it. He said this was not the first time it had happened but I couldn't remember anything like this and offered to swap beds but he refused and we left it like that.

The next day Jimmy had the news that we would be getting some letter forms to send home and I thought that wonderful news. I asked him if he had a chance to ask Sergeant Bertram if there was a chance of any more cloths. The letter forms arrived next day, together with a bit of post. The sergeant said he would stay for a while as this was his last block and we asked again about clothes as our things were falling off our our backs. The sergeant said he was sick of asking these people as we were not the only ones with this problem: 'I have tried to tell them all of us prisoners are in a sorrowful state but they take no notice at all. I am sorry, now I must go and have a bite to eat before I go on parade shortly, but it has been nice listening to you lads.' He added that he would be over that evening with a few of his lads to the entertainment, and we said they would all be welcome.

Dawn broke and Len and Joe went for our cognac. When I got back from the toilet I saw everybody with a big smile on their faces, and Jimmy said there was a big lorry and trailer beside the store room. I said, 'This is wonderful news for everyone,' and Sergeant Bertram said it was quite out of the blue, and that by the way, the shop would be open for two blocks, if they had the stock, half a block going there at a time. We were well down the pecking order for parcels and our turn would be in three or four days time.

During roll call I thought how I wished Ned Blake would send me a card saying he would give Edie my camp address. I had put myself in an awkward position, not remembering the number and street of her Uncle Tom and Aunt Fran which could be a bolthole as they could give her my letters and then I would be able to correspond again. I had been there many a time. A year ago everything was going along beautifully.

I hoped that Sergeant Bertram would come into the block and have a good night with us, just swapping tales, not asking questions as I thought he did a great job and he was very much appreciated. He could relax with us with a cup of hot water; it would have been nice to give him a cup of tea and a biscuit. I was nice though to see happy smiling faces again with the thought of the Red Cross parcels awaiting us.

Just as I was thinking there would be no boxing matches until next spring with the warmer weather, I found out that they had a show in the next compound where there were some amateur players who worked in theatres. It would be nice if we could go over there if people were interested; it would put in an afternoon or evening; it was probably like the kind of show they did at home in England.

That day I discovered three more cuts on my feet, so dealt with them first. Meanwhile Jimmy said there were now two lorries and trailers and that they were getting unloaded; they were Canadian parcels. We all said that was lovely and then he added that Sergeant Bertram was bringing an issue of cigarettes for everybody. We all gave a loud shout, 'Hooray! Hooray!' and everyone had a lovely smile on his face. He brought also a bundle of letters and a few parcels and he had four cloths for me. Things were looking up for us, not before time. My letter was from my mother who said that everyone at home was all right and that my father had been getting a job, and that cousin John had been over for the weekend; that she would be glad when I was home. Stephen's card just hoped I was keeping all right, hoping to see me soon; 'Keep your chin up and we will have a ball when you get back.' Both communications had a lot blacked out. No mention of the place in Forest Hall or of Edie, but my mother sent her kindest regards to Jimmy and also to Johnny Ward.

Sergeant Bertram came back during our singing and stayed for a while and we each had a cigarette – they were Capstan Full Strength and it was a long time since we had seen any of them. The bugle blew and the lights went out straight away with us still getting into our bunks; then sirens started blowing and we heard planes going northwards. Just so long as they didn't drop any bombs on us … then the noise faded away.

Everyone in the camp said they would abide by the rules as the Italian Commander had said that if we did not every parcel would be opened like last time. Now it was to be a normal issue, one parcel between two. If anyone tried to escape it would make life hell for everyone but we had to put up with it because if they did get away, good luck to them. But more likely they would be caught and put into a dark room somewhere in the camp.

In a few days it would be the anniversary of the capture of us lads of the Royal Northumberland Fusiliers, in the 1st Battalion. It was a platoon and a half who were captured, though we lost some of them on the boat when it was torpedoed on 9 December 1941. At least we had survived up to now and hoped we just carried on doing so.

I was still concerned as to what Stephen was trying to tell me in his blacked out lines; maybe something had happened that I just could not put my finger on. I could not understand why he had not mentioned his girlfriend unless they had finished with each other because he was always one for going around with different ones. And I could not understand why he had not mentioned Edie because before, he was always praising her, just as my mother did.

We got our Red Cross parcels that afternoon and at last could have a nice cup of coffee with sugar and milk. We decided to have a Spam sandwich for dinner and tea the next day, together with a cigarette. My feet were improving very much; being looked after each day had done them a lot of good.

Here we were in December and I had had heard that we were to have double rations on Christmas Day. It was such a pity I could not send Edie a Christmas card with my camp address on it, without suspicions of my family as I had a feeling they had something to do with this silence. Edie was the only one who really knew about the whole situation.

Christmas came but we only got single rations as usual. The parcels had run out so it was going to be bleak and we would be glad to reach New Year's Day and a new start to a year. It would be good if there was a continuous supply; of parcels, another lorry load arriving just as the last was done instead of living off Italian rations. There was still no sign of clothing or shoes. The parcels didn't arrive until the very end of January and with the delay for distribution it was going to be February before we got them. This time they were English but it did not matter where they were from; they were most welcome.

At parade one day early in February the officer came through and instead of waiting for the interpreter, he said in English, 'I want the parade to come to attention.' Everyone was taken by surprise. He said that he had been to England before the war with his parents and had lived in the south of England, Everyone was quite pleased; this meant that the sergeants could talk to him instead of through the interpreter. We all came to attention and the guards started counting but it still took over four and a half hours, and standing all this time was not good for my feet.

I had a card from my brother which again had two lines blacked out. He said that everyone was well but I still didn't know what was going on; once again I was in the dark. I thought there must have been something going on and it was really getting me down because I blamed myself for jumping the gun in the first place. I shouldn't have relied on other people telling me what was right and wrong. But every day was one step nearer to seeing Edie and this was what kept me going day in day out, always wishing someone could help me along the way.

The sergeant spoke to the officer and it was much better as he understood my plight and said it was a long time for a person to suffer like that. He told the sergeant he would look into it straight away.

I missed walking round the compound and meeting Johnny Ward and his pals, but Jimmy kept me informed about them and as they are the next group to us, he gave a wave now and again which I appreciated very much. The roll call was taken again by the English speaking officer and after the four hours, when we were dismissed, we saw him giving the two guards a real rollicking and they left with their tails hanging down. The officer had a good chuckle. So he was going to stamp on slack counting as it was not right that they were not pulling their weight.

Ron, the young sick lad, told me he was going to be repatriated to England together with one or two more from this camp and more from other camps. Things seemed to be moving at last. Our meals that day were salmon sandwiches which were very nice indeed; whatever Jimmy said about the meals I just agreed without argument as it saved a lot of time.

The next parade started a lot sooner than we expected so the roasting must have got through to them. The officer came through and commanded all sergeants to come to attention and all the groups responded as one; I think he was quite pleased. We were quite different to the Italian soldiers who were quite sloppy with drill. They seemed to go slow at the beginning of the count then the officer gave them one glance and they speeded up all of a sudden. This was four hours, though the one after that was only three and three quarters, a bit of an improvement.

We were just having a meal of cheese spread when Sergeant Bertram came in. In his hands were a pair of clogs: 'These are for you,' he said.

I said, 'Sergeant, I cannot thank you enough for what you have done.'

He said he had had a word with the officer who said that the interpreter had never said anything about my problem to the other officers. I was really thrilled and tried them on – a perfect fit with just one cloth on. I said to Jimmy that he could lie back for a bit while I did the running around but he said, 'No, we will still take turns.'

'Not yet,' I said, 'as you have been doing everything, It is my turn now.'

Before the sergeant went away he said, 'Tomorrow they are issuing clothing to certain blocks. They don't have much to hand, but will try to give some out; at least it is a start. This officer should have been here sooner, he certainly has got things moving.'

Jimmy suggested a stroll round the compound and I said that would be great, and maybe to see Johnny and his pals. We went round three times and then I said I would go for the skilly to give him a break. It was wonderful to be able to get around with the clogs on; no more picking up stones to throw away from my path. Next morning it was me that went for the cognac and it did seem funny, but Jimmy had been doing it since October, a long time, in all weathers and without once complaining. I got served and walked back with Len; I thanked him very much for lending me his boots all that time. He said he was pleased to help and that he could not have gone through what I had done, with my feet cut to ribbons time and time again. I said it was the fault of the interpreter in not telling the officers of my plight; as soon as this man came on he did something straight away.

Chapter 12

There was an issue of shirts trousers and coats, but only a few people got them; their names were drawn from a hat. Everyone was surprised to see them as they were the very first since we arrived at the camp.

After a few circuits of the compound it was time for roll call and we all came to attention with pride, just to let the Italians know we meant business. The guards seemed to get better every day; this was just under three and a half hours and the officer was delighted. That evening the sergeant came and put cigarettes on everyone's bunk and said that the parcels would be distributed the next day. Everyone gave him a good hand clap. He added that there would be cards and letters to send home, and got another clap. 'Things are looking up for a change,' he said. 'Everyone tonight will sing their hearts out.'

The music that night was indeed really beautiful and there were quite a lot of people outside joining in singing and whistling. Terry was in good form that evening but all too soon it was Lights Out; but everyone went to bed happy.

I realised next day that I had gone a bit white with my months inside the block, on my arms and legs and the top half of my body. When the sun got really hot again, I looked forward to getting a bit sunburnt: just half an hour a day sunbathing till I got brown again. Another change in the early routine was that we seemed to get smarter every day at roll call; we didn't know why but it was since the English speaking officer came. I think he appreciated it; perhaps for everything he had done for us we were giving something back.

We were looking forward to having a cigarette made of the dried tea leaves, but they were still wet at tea time. Then Jimmy said, 'But we have cigarettes, don't you remember, all of you, the sergeant put twenty on each bunk.'

I said, 'I remember, I put them behind my pillow,' and Jimmy and the other two lads, Len and Joe, started looking for theirs. It was really nice to have an English cigarette, but fancy not remembering. There had been a lot going on: parcels, forms to write home and we were told that there were letters and cards from England for some of us that evening. We would have to hope that everything was all right for everyone but sometimes there was tragedy for someone in the camp.

There was talk again of another boxing match, but we only really found out when we saw the boxers going around with the people in charge of their fitness.

Two groups were standing by to get their parcels: one group was getting theirs and another getting ready but this could be the last tonight; never mind, we were moving up the list. While waiting for the skilly we just hoped the weather would hold as there were very black clouds coming up from the north. Then they started to serve our group, twenty on each side and the rain held off. We went straight to the toilets and then down it came so we just hurried as fast as we could, pleased it was the last errand of the day.

I had a letter from my mother but she still did not mention Edie, still silence about her, so I was wondering if it was my family that was causing the trouble, unless I was clutching at straws. Never mind, I had to get on with my life.

Jimmy said he would come and stand with me in the line for Red Cross parcels; I said 'All right, there is nothing worse than standing on your own, not knowing what to say to other people, as some people are funny, with taking-in stories which are very far-fetched.' Jimmy had been in the same position. But if he was with me and told stories, his different episodes were true, not fairy tales. We thought it would be that evening after roll call. So Sergeant Bertram got us ready to enter the storeroom and we marched in good style, just to let these Italian soldiers know we were the best marching soldiers in the world. Everybody did the same – just to let them see what we could do; even if we were prisoners. It did give our morale a great boost. Jimmy eventually went in to get the parcel while I got the skilly; our group was the last to go in but the Italian soldiers did help a lot.

The lad Len who had lent me the boots had had a letter from his parents saying that his father was not very well, which really worried him. It is especially hard being away from home and unable to do anything.

'I do hope he gets well soon,' I said, 'and do keep me up to date with his progress.'

That day we had a nice cup of tea with milk and sugar and a bun with sardines and they were lovely, a real change; you got different tins in English parcels. We each had half a cigarette and put the stubs into a tin we had found in the compound which came in very handy indeed. We were talking to Stephen who said Ron was going to be repatriated soon. That was good news as he was in a bad way and we hoped he made it back to England; there were quite a few going from the camp. As we were going up to the compound I met Snowy and he said, 'At last you've got something for your feet.'

I said, 'I am really pleased with them; my feet are lovely and warm,' and we just kept on talking for a while.

Then we met Johnny and his pals, and it was quite a while since I had seen them. He said that my Aunt Eva and his brother Bill were asking after me, and he had told them that he had not seen me because someone had stolen my boots.

Jimmy went for the skilly that day and got caught in a heavy shower of rain, even though he had tried to time his turn exactly and was not too long outside. When they came back they took off their wet clothes and I gave Jimmy my dry shirt and wrapped myself in a blanket. Jimmy wrapped his own blanket round his lower half and wrung out his clothes and hung them on the bed post.

Jimmy's clothes were still wet a few days later but he had to put on his wet trousers and stand on parade for hour after hour. It was really dreadful and the sergeant said it was not on, but what could he do? There were many more people there with wet clothes, and the wind blowing around made it worse. The two guards came through the main gate and a few minutes later the officer came through as well but again we were three and three quarter hours. The wind went right through you. We wondered if the soldiers did it on purpose, to keep us out in the cold, but they were after all in the same boat as us, though they had better clothing.

Tea was buns spread with margarine and cheese and after that we had a cigarette, rolled with stubs and the dry tea leaves. It was best to use them before they got too dry as then they sometimes went mouldy and were wasted.

Jimmy said he would try to dry his clothes with the blower that we used to heat water. I said, 'Good luck if you can do it.' He said the only way was to put his clothes on and stand by it while the water boiled, like using an iron. I said that I would try to find some bits of wood while I was out around the compound, unless he was to take some more wood from his bunk. I met Johnny and his pals while I was out and they were asking for Jimmy. I said he was trying to get his clothes dry but did not say how as it might not be a success.

The sergeant said we might get clothing within the next few days, not to mention letters and cards to send home tonight; and that our two blocks might be going to the shop next month, April. This is what the officer had been telling him.

Jimmy said that his drying efforts had been partly successful and that his shirt was still damp but better than wet. This seemed effective but was going to take an awful lot of wood. I told him to take a lath out of his bed and put two others across the space, which is what I had done last time. I might get just one more out of mine and that would be the last. One of us stood outside just in case an Italian saw us breaking a lath and we gave him a hand, as you had to be quick. We had some paper rolled ready to put on the wood; we lit it and I just kept blowing the bellows till it became red. Meanwhile we had our bun with cheese. Later would be the skilly which was at least warm but had no bite in it at all, just water, bits of macaroni, pieces of carrots, horse meat and a taste of tomato purée and olive oil. It lasted a few minutes and then was gone. You didn't need a spoon, you just drank it out of the aluminium dixie.

That evening Terry was in good form – you could hear him quite a way off and as you approached the block it was even better as everyone was singing and some whistling; they seemed to be enjoying themselves. The sergeant and four lads from his block were standing by Jimmy's bunk. Everyone applauded loudly. Our visitors had to go quite soon as they wanted to get back before lights out; it was very dark until your eyes accustomed themselves to the conditions.

At the toilet block one day I met Snowy. He said, 'If you ever get back to England, and you and your family would like to come to New Zealand, you would all be welcome. I can trust you to be a good man.'

Well, I said, 'I will have to think about it but it is a good offer.'

He said, 'We have thousands of sheep on our land.'

Then he said, 'Cheerio for now,' and we went our separate ways.

I was still going to get the cognac, the buns and the skilly and Jimmy was saying that he should do at least one of these jobs; but I said that I would think about it. It was not too bad at all if there was sunshine. He went to get the buns that day while I got the blower going. We agreed to take turns each day standing in a line for the Red Cross parcels which was more tedious as you had to stand still, not like the moving lines for the rations. There were more rumours about clothing but it didn't in fact turn up. Maybe there was not enough to go round, or maybe the Italians did not bring them.

The news of the parcels was that they were one between four, but that was better than nothing and was something to look forward to. We would be next in turn for the shop the next month, and there were apples, pears, grapes and oranges. We expected our parcel in about three days, though if the parades went on a long time this did not leave much time for issuing parcels. We arranged to share with Joe and Len. Everyone would get a turn in dishing out food: perhaps Jimmy first, then his mate, then me, then himself, so it was quite fair. Sometimes it was difficult if there were say five sardines in a tin but we would take the smallest ones first so it was easier to divide the big one at the end. The same with the sugar and powered milk; everyone would have a half spoon each

We were still waiting for our parcels a few days later. There were a couple of groups waiting by the store room but we didn't recognise them and after a visit to the main gate area Jimmy told us there were four groups. But then the two wallies came through the main gate and then the officer. Roll call that morning was three and a half hours; we couldn't believe it. The best they ever did so maybe the officer playing war with them had played off.

After this I said I would put the tin on to boil while one of the other lads, Joe or Len, went to see if it was our turn soon. Jimmy and the other lad were getting their buns. But the burner was not working at all so I took it outside to see what was wrong with it. The bottom tin had come away leaving a nasty gap. I would have to wait for one of the others as it needed two people, with a nail and piece of wood as a hammer. One had to hold the piece of cloth in place while the other put the nail through the two, As the nail went through it left a bit of tin which you flattened against the cloth. I was meant to have relieved the lad at the main gate so I went there and told him what had happened. He said he thought something had gone wrong as we two were usually good at relieving people.

Another sergeant was at the gate – he was the one whose job it seemed to be to keep count of who went through each time. Just then I spotted Sergeant Bertram, who said that we were about eighth and I told him one group had come out and one gone in since then which made us seventh. They were much quicker when it was one parcel between four, so that made us sixth, probably after the next roll call. In fact when we got our parcel April had begun, but it was nice to think of a few days with extra food. Jimmy searched for some wood while he was collecting the cognac but with no luck so maybe one of the other lads would give up a lath from his bed to keep the home fires burning. We had corned beef sandwiches and really enjoyed them with our cup of tea.

When we arrived at the group area the sergeant was waiting to talk to us. He said that that night the Italians were giving the sergeants an issue of clothing and that there were letters and some parcels from England. The guards appeared twenty minutes late and it was four hours and ten minutes this time; the officer dismissed the parade and once again called the two of them over and gave them a right ear bashing. They were not very pleased especially as this took place in front of the parade again.

It was important to go for our skilly at the right time with our group, between seven and eight o'clock, or we did not get any. I was on my way when the sergeant came in with the issue of clothes; the names were drawn out of a hat, omitting those who had got some last time. Jimmy and I did not get any. I had a letter from my mother however and a card from my mate Ned Blake. My mother said that her mother had died during the Salvation Army meeting. She had lived at Houghton-le-Spring in County Durham and the last time I saw her was in February 1941 when I was on leave. She never mentioned her age. It was sad to have bad news in a letter, but everyone else was all right. She never said anything about Edie. I managed to read Ned's card before lights out and as usual he had gone against what I had told him to do, to tell Edie my camp address, and refused again.

A few days later I met Johnny while walking about and he said he had been ill for a few days with the runs. I didn't ask how it had happened; anything could have set it off and he did indeed look very white. He carried on with us until it was time to go to our group areas, just a nice slow stroll. Later, as we were going past the toilets we saw a Red Cross official with the officers making their way towards our block so they must have been going for Ron, to repatriate him. Maybe we would get more information from Stephen. He would be glad to be going as he needed medication and he would not get any in this place. He could hardly walk and had to be supported by two Italian officers. As they made their way to the main gate everyone gave him a very loud clap and told him they hoped he would not be long getting home to England. We were very pleased for him.

Over my sardine for tea which was really nice and tasty I reread Ned's card. I just could not believe it; I always thought he was a good mate but he was not any more; mates always helped you especially in situations like this.

Two days afterwards my stomach was rolling as if I had cramp and I only just made it to the toilets. Before our stroll Jimmy said they had seen a trailer just outside the storeroom and could not believe it but there were people telling others in other compounds that Red Cross parcels had arrived again. They would signal like a big square and then a cross, one down and one across, so that the man in the next compound could inform his mates and then pass the message on to the compound after that. Jimmy passed on the news as he was just fifty or a hundred yards away from the lorry on the other side of the wire. The soldiers were still on unloading it but nobody cared as at least they knew they were there.

Len was in the queue for the buns. We were talking about when we were young. He said he had very strict parents and had to be in at a certain time each night; I said my parents were the same and even when courting my girl friend I had to be in at 10.30 as I had to be up at 6.15 to start work at 7.30 at the pit head. I could understand my mother's point of view as I was terrible at getting up, and there was always tomorrow to see Edie and many tomorrows until I left for abroad. Joe said he was nearly twenty-one and he had the same problem with his parents. He had no girl friend then, only later when he went into the Army but he said he wrote to her whenever he could. I said, 'You are a very lucky man,' but I did not tell him my sad story. We got served then and then I really had to rush to the toilet as my stomach was rolling around again.

Jimmy had the tin boiling and said we had about two days worth of tea left. We had a tin of soup and managed to get four cups between us. These cups were not very big, about the size of the small cup your parents put out for special guests who come for a visit, but the soup was very wholesome, much better than the skilly.

Johnny and his mates asked if they could come round to our block some evening as we always seemed to enjoy ourselves and we said if it was not their turn to get the skilly why not come that evening, They said someone else would get the skilly and they could go back about 8.45 and drink it before lights out; it did not matter if it was hot or cold, it would still go down. One of the lads he brought, Martin, was a canny singer though not in the class of our Welsh lad, Terry, but he could get by just the same and our block applauded him just as much. They said, 'Thank you very much for letting us come to your block,' and we said, 'Any time,' but they said they would always ask if it was convenient.

We got a letter and a card to send home and I decided to send one to my parents and one to my brother Stephen. I wanted to ask again about the place at the Ritz at Forest Hall as Jimmy kept on asking me if I had heard.

The sun was shining which was good as it did warm your body up a lot. We thought we would get the old tea leaves dried more quickly so we took them with us next time we went for a stroll. We put them on clean paper and took turns watching them drying in the sun. Sometimes in the block it could take a day or two to dry and sometimes they went mouldy; this was much better. On the way to the toilets we had another look beside the storeroom and could not believe it: there was another lorry and trailer just a bit away from the area where the soldiers were putting the other parcels for issue. This was presumably why the earlier ones had been delayed, as they must have known about this consignment. Everyone was really happy and some were sending signals to the next compound. The sergeant said that there might be an issue of twenty cigarettes each and maybe a batch of mail either then or the next day and that the officer had thought there would be another issue of clothing shortly.

We got our cigarettes and Jimmy and I had one each but saved the stubs for later. There was a guard on the lorry and trailer just in case someone tried to break in; it was for our good as well as theirs as it was very tempting. The sergeant came in after the singsong with parcels, cards and letters, so everyone went quite still to hear the names called out. Jimmy got a letter and then I got a card from home with not much in it, mostly about my mother's mother who had died. My mother went over with my Auntie Jenny from Walker as company as my Dad could not go as he had to go to work that day. He had not been long at work and I thought he was afraid he might lose his job if he took time off. He had been out of work for a very long time. Then we went back to whistling and singing before going for the skilly. On the way we saw parcels being dished out but those were the last for that night and we would have to wait two or three days.

We got an English parcel and there were sixteen things in it: soup, tea, tinned milk, ¼ lb butter, ½ lb sugar, tin of 6 pieces of bacon, wafer biscuits 2x2 inches in size, sardines, corned beef, 4 pieces of cheese, meat extract to spread on the biscuits, a small tin of jam, egg powder, 4 small sausages and two other things I just forget; maybe salt and pepper in small containers. That could last a week, or more if you were penny pinching.

Another day it was our turn to go to the fruit shop with 3s. 4d. in Italian lira to spend; this was one month's money. One and a half blocks were to be allowed to go during the time it was open, maybe about midday. I was to go for the buns while Jimmy stood in the queue with my money though I hoped I would get there in time. He was going to say I was ill to get my share. Meanwhile it was roll call and it was fair weather though we had had one or two showers and were a bit damp, but could probably dry our clothes by holding them up to the breeze. There was quite a queue for the buns and Jimmy must have left by then for the fruit shop.

By the time we joined Jimmy and the other lad they had already been served and in fact when we got back from the toilets Jimmy had the blower going for our cup of tea and also had biscuits spread with meat extract waiting for us. They tasted lovely and we hadn't had that for quite a while – all the parcels were different. In the evening we had soup and fruit as well. I cleaned the grapes with cold water and then started eating them; there was about half a pound and I ate the lot while listening to the lads playing and people whistling and singing. When we came back with the skilly Terry was singing something he had sung before with Welsh and English words and it had lovely words indeed. When he finished everyone clapped and he started again and we all had a wonderful evening.

Chapter 13

In the night I had to go to the toilet in a hurry as my stomach was rumbling and I only just made it. I had diarrhoea and it was just like water. I stayed there for quite a while so I was glad I had put on my shorts and a shirt. I felt rather sick as well. It must have been the grapes. I just waited there, as I was terrified I would not make it back to the block; every time I made my way back it started again. Another chap came in, running as fast as possible. Again I had a pain. I felt so weak and it seemed to go on and on. By this time daylight was breaking. The other lad said he had been eating grapes; and within twenty minutes another lad came to the toilet with the same story. We talked about different things from home; he also came from a mining village with one or two pits and I told him about our area with six pits within a few miles of each other.

He went back to the block and I started again, this time with a little blood, and this got me very worried. I only wished I could get to bed and lie down. The others both said they felt really awful too. Jimmy came looking for me to ask about getting the cognac and I told him that there was no way I could go for it and that I had been there since before the sun came up. He said he would have a word with Sergeant Bertram that I could not make it for the parade; I told him that every time I got up to come back it started off again and I felt weak as a kitten. I took one step outside the door and once again had to rush back and again there was blood on the paper. Another lad rushed in. I was getting very sick and the pains in my stomach were crucifying me. I did not know which way to turn.

Sergeant Bertram suggested I should go to the camp hospital taking a parcel with me. He would have to see the officer sometime today, after roll call. He would say there were quite a few down with this but the others would have to get in touch with their own sergeants. When he came back it was getting late but he had made the arrangements. He said I must stop a week there. I had to wait for an escort of two guards to take me; it was situated at the very top of the camp.

When we got there it was nice and clean with two-bunk beds and the toilets not far away. We settled down for about half an hour and then it started up again so I rushed to the toilet as quickly as possible and only just made it; my stomach was heaving and I felt sick. I did not know where to put myself. Mark, the lad I'd been talking to, said that he was losing blood too and was going to talk to the orderly and see if there was any way to stop it. But the orderly said they had nothing; we were all in a state being in a place like this. Two more chaps came in and they had all been eating the grapes. We could not get away from the toilet and some could not make it in time; and nobody came to clean it up. I took my trousers off as I knew they could not wash them if they could not even clean the floor. I had to use part of my shirt to clean myself using as little pieces as possible as I could have nothing left at all if I took big pieces. I thought there was going to be very little sleep that night.

Next day I was run off my feet all night trying to get to the toilet like many other people, but I could not make it and it just ran away from me just like water. I was still losing blood, not a lot but still worrying. The floor was ankle deep and we hoped by morning they would come and clear the place up. Once again I had to use part of my shirt to clean myself because the paper was very hard. We tried to use a bucket but it was overflowing with paper and cloths. I would lie down again and just feel my stomach rumbling again. The toilets were overflowing too. There were quite a few from our block and some from the other one. No one seemed to care for us though they were happy to welcome our parcels and we just had to manage the best way we could. I really wished I had not come to this hospital block. I seemed to get weaker by the hour. We were told we had to stay till Saturday but I wished it was here then.

More people were coming in and they were shocked at the conditions there. Eventually some of the orderlies brought us cups of cognac, just warm but at least it stayed down. The place which had been so spotless was now a shambles, with excrement three or four inches deep in places.

The smell was terrible. This was only the second day: what would it be like if we got any more people in? I felt a little better though some of the lads that came in with us were very ill. I had a little sleep for an hour; we were all exhausted. We were all in bare feet as it was easier to clean them than shoes or boots or my clogs. We had to wash our hands all the time which took more cloth to dry them.

At midday they brought sandwiches with our bun ration but no tea or drink of any kind and within half an hour I was again rushing to the toilets with quite a few of the others. It was quite a while before I could get back to my bunk. I thought I was a bit better after a sleep but again within ten minutes I was back again, making a mess on the way and could do nothing about it. The orderlies all had very high wellingtons so they were nice and dry but they still did not do anything about the mess, walking about just like having a paddle at the seaside.

Mark was very ill indeed and the orderly said he did not think he would see daylight; his whole body had given up. Some people fight, he said, and some just cannot fight this disease; it took people in different ways. As he was seeing to the dying man he was eating his bun; he said it was a shame to waste it. One of the lads asked if we would get any good food at all in this camp hospital.

'It all depends,' the orderly replied.

'It depends on what? A little for us and a lot for you?' and we all said, 'You have hit the nail on the head.'

Later the orderly came back and looked at Mark again and said he was fading fast, and just then the death throes started. It was a shame as he was a nice lad and his family were going to miss him.

The next night I was up and down all night with stomach cramps. The floor was getting much worse and a few more people came in – there must have been thirty-five by then. They still brought us very small meals, very little of it items from parcels. The orderlies were in very good shape however. Three people had died. We still got no tea or coffee and the cognac was the first drink since the morning the day before. No doctors came to see us, nor any officer; it was all left to the orderlies who only seemed to appear when someone was on his way out. Not even our sergeants knew that this was going on. We all had dysentery very badly.

I was feeling a bit better and had not had to run for the toilets for some time so tried to get some sleep. Another chap died and another was in a bad way. I woke up in time for tea which was buns with a little butter and some spreading cheese. We wondered if these chaps had any qualifications as they did not seem to have any idea of what they were doing. We had some skilly and I hoped it would not just go straight through me.

That night I was still going to the toilet about eight or ten times in the night and I got very little sleep. I knew I had lost a lot of weight as I could feel my ribcage. I must have started off about nine stone and now I would be lucky if I was seven stone. The food we were receiving was just about Italian rations, just tiny morsels, like what we would receive on the block. Another lad died in the night and it was terrible hearing his screams. It was a crying shame. We just hoped someone would believe our stories later.

The cognac was lukewarm again and I really could have done with some burnt toast but we would not get that here. The mess on the floor was now up to the bottom of my calf. I had only half a shirt left. When I got out of there it would take a few cold showers to get the smell off me. Quite a few people didn't even attempt to get down to the toilets, just doing it in the corner of the room. I thought that the next day would be Friday but we were not sure of time as very few people had watches; just as well as you could never trust people not to steal them. I had lost mine the day I was captured.

I was still bleeding a bit which was worrying as if you lost blood you could not put it back on the meals at this 'Hotel Hilton'. My weight too was just sliding off me and it would take a good while to put it back on again. An orderly was sitting with one chap and trying to persuade him to eat some soup but he was just refusing so he must have been in a bad way. I managed to get my bun down which might help to stem the dysentery, I thought, but no. Two lads dies just before dawn. That day I thought I was a little better and really hungry. I didn't think I would ever eat a grape again but when I got my bun I just ate a very little piece at a time, better than rushing it. My bowels had been quiet for an hour and I hope they would stay that way and maybe I could get back to my block the next day. As dark clouds fade a away there is always a silver lining to follow; this was something you wrote to your parents about. I would not tell them about this illness as they had enough to worry about, like where the next bomb might fall.

Bun time came round again but the orderlies still were making no effort to clear up the mess; we thought they should be reported to our sergeants who could tell the Italian officers who could condemn this place. The bun came with jam, but we could see what was happening to our parcels: into the orderlies' stomachs; they were living a life of luxury.

During that night another two lads took ill; they had come in two days ago. You never knew where the illness was going to strike. The orderlies were sitting with them: a bad sign. Sometimes I felt that my ex-girlfriend was praying hard for me; we were so close to each other that sometimes I felt I got messages by telepathy. I still wished I had got her pregnant before I left that night; it would have been nobody's business but ours, though there would have been a stigma in people's minds. My dad would not have felt like that as he thought a lot of her and when I missed the last tram he would always walk her home in the black-out because you never knew who was lurking around; there were lots of soldiers from different areas. It gave me peace of mind. Sometimes her older sister would come down and would catch us up and again I would be pleased someone was with her.

Now I had no shirt left – I gave the last piece to a lad across from me. He said he might be out the next day, Sunday and wished he could get out that night as he couldn't stand the stench.

Later one of the orderlies came and said I would leave after I had had my bun and that they would give us three tins from our parcels to keep us a day or so before we received our next issue the next week. How did he know about parcels next week? There was one tin of corned beef, one of soup and one of sardines. Away I went and I just stayed outside for a while, just pleased to be in the sunshine. As I was going away the orderly shouted me back.

'What do you want?' I said.

'I have an army jacket here,' he said, 'it is off one of the lads that died during the night.'

I was very pleased to have the jacket.

'You are very cold,' he said, 'how do you feel at this moment?'

I told him I was all right and that I was going to make my way to my block, and thanked him for the jacket.

The Italian guard was waiting for me and gestured that he wanted to take a picture of me. I asked why but he did not say anything and I shouted at him. Again he said nothing. He put his hand to his mouth and I knew he was not able to speak. He took my photo, just above the waist. He made a 'Wait a minute' gesture with his hand. The photo was given to an Italian officer to give to me a few days later. I thought I would send it home but I would have to get permission from Sergeant Bertram. The guard took me to the block and I thanked him as best I could.

I got a welcome from the block and within a short time the lads started playing and singing.

Jimmy said, 'By, you lost some weight.'

I said, 'It was a nightmare being in there; it is so hard to explain.'

Jimmy said he would go and get our skilly and I said, 'If you don't mind.'

'Mind, I am so pleased you are back after being told so many people did not make it.'

I said, 'You are right. If you don't mind, can I go with you?'

'Do you feel like it?'

'I cannot really tell what I feel at the moment.'

'I think the best thing is for you to go and lie down; you can use my bunk for a while as you will not have the strength to get to the top one.'

I did what he said and lay down and must have dozed off. Jimmy gave me a nudge when he came back and said, 'Have this and then you can lie down.' I went out like a light and though it was not long till lights out, I did not hear the bugle call.

Chapter 14

I was still waiting to see Sergeant Bertram, to see if I could have a few days in the block after all I had been through that last week. Jimmy had again taken over getting the rations, but when I was better I would try to take over again like last time. While I was away Jimmy had kept an eye on all my personal things like my letters from home, and my photograph of Edie that she sent when I was in Tobruk. I did not go to the morning roll call as I was still rather weak. Jimmy gave me a letter and a card to send home. I still could not tell Jimmy what had happened in the camp hospital as I wanted to tell Sergeant Bertram first so that he could give the Italian officer full details. Those people should never ever run a hospital ward again. In fact they should have closed it immediately.

I had my own rations for a couple of days then it was back to the Italian ones. I think the block got a bit of a shock when they saw the people who arrived back from the hospital. Two other lads came back that day, just about dinner time and asked me how I felt. 'Dreadful,' I replied. They were the same, very weak, and were going to see the sergeant.

'Why don't we all go together?' I suggested and they said, 'Why not? It would be better if all three spoke to him.'

Jimmy made me a sandwich with my corned beef and we had a cup of tea. The singing that evening was very good, it was lovely to hear them again. Len asked me how I felt as I had lost a lot of weight and looked really ghastly. I said I was really under the weather but then I had to go to the toilet so he said he would come with me for company, which was really kind of him. I said I had been really ill.

Once there, I asked him if he minded waiting while I got a good wash down. I took off everything I had which was not much and he said,

'You are just skin and bones.' I told him that I could not tell him what had happened as I had to see the sergeant first.

When I arrived back the sergeant was waiting to see me and the other two lads and I asked if we could talk in the passage. I told him that when we arrived the place was spotless, the floors clean and toilets but after that the arrangements were very poor indeed. We had got very little of our parcels, just a bit of meat extract on our buns twice a day, then jam, nothing like soup. We told him that they only looked after people who were dying, and didn't always even get our skilly. We told him about the faeces on the floor getting deeper and deeper. We thought that the place should be closed down until they got someone with qualifications. We asked him if he could see the officer about this; and also ask if we could miss roll call as we had been very ill indeed.

I had a very good sleep while they were on parade. Jimmy woke me up with a cup of tea and I really played war with me for giving me his rations but he said it was not his but the other lads; what was a cup of tea between friends. They just put their hands over their ears. I did indeed enjoy the cup of tea.

I and the other two lads from the hospital thought we would try to get a parcel extra just between the three of us as we were frightened of going back to the camp hospital. Jimmy thought it was worth a try. Meanwhile the cognac was really lovely to drink, and another consignment of parcels arrived during the night. I decided to go to the toilets by myself on a very slow walk and though it seemed ages until I got there I was rather pleased as it was a lot easier than the last time. I was so tired when I got back that I must have dozed off and once more was woken by Jimmy with a nice cup of tea; the tea had been given by Len.

Later the sergeant came into the block to say they were going to issue a parcel between two people which was good news; everybody applauded him, just to say thanks. He asked me how I was getting on and I said I didn't feel too good but better than before and had been trying hard, but there was no way I could stand on parade.

I kept having a rest and this seemed to make me better; Jimmy said I was making up for the sleep I lost in the hospital; I must have missed quite a bit there. They said as long as they had food they would share it with me and they knew I would do the same in their place.

As each day passed I seemed to get more strength. After a few days it was Edie's nineteenth birthday. They started issuing parcels and we might get ours then or the next day. We still had tea, some sugar and the milk might last till the next day, and still having a smoke with the dried tea leaves, just twice a day and just small cigarettes, about three or four drags, as you tried to eke them out as much as possible. Jimmy continued to go for the cognac and buns as he wanted me to take my time and not rush things; I had had a serious illness.

Later that week it was a lovely day with the sun shining and I thought I would go out into the sunshine later. I was very white; you would never think that I had been abroad. Just half an hour would do me as I did not want to get sunstroke. Jimmy and Joe went to stand by the main gate so that they could relieve each other; we might get our parcels that day. If your group was not ready, a group that was ready would go ahead of you; and the Italians were not too keen on people being late as it knocked their system out and everybody got a roasting by the sergeants. If you got your parcel you had to hurry down to the block as they were not allowed on parade. If anyone pinched anything out of someone else's parcel they would get a good beating but up till then we had not heard of this happening. Everyone was in the same boat; besides, we wanted to let the Italian people know that we were civilised soldiers. Jimmy never came back so I presumed he had gone on parade; later he said that we were the fourth group in the afternoon.

Meanwhile I wrote letters to my mother and father and one to Fred, Bob and John. I asked my mother again about the property by the Ritz picture hall as she had not mentioned it at all in her last few letters. It might be sold but at least she could tell me one way or the other. Jimmy came in for his dinner and said that they had miscalculated the number of groups ahead of us, and we would be put into the evening batch. Jimmy was the only one who can claim our parcel, as each one had to say his name and they marked it off on the sheet. Well, they all came into the block with parcels and straight away we had a nice cup of tea with some biscuits, just plain but very enjoyable.

A couple of days later I decided that I would see the sergeant about going on parade on Monday, which would be the third week in May. The food parcel might help me a good deal, and I would try to get some more sunshine before then. I was sick of seeing the same four walls week in, week out, and would have to get on with my life. It was great to have lovely food again. Shortly after, Sergeant Bertram came in with ten cigarettes for each of us.

We were hearing a lot of rumours about our troops landing in Sicily but we did not take any heed because you always got let down. Your hopes were up one minute, dashed the next.

By the next Monday everything was going along fine so I asked if Jimmy if I could go along for the cognac, but he said, 'No, not yet, we will see how you perform this morning.' I made the beds while he was gone and felt very good, better than I had since I came out of the hospital; it could be the good looking after by Jimmy, Joe and Len. They had been wonderful to me; also the sleep might have helped. I really wanted to go on parade, it was such a lovely day, sun shining and very hot. I took a slow walk and then just sat on the grass till Jimmy caught up with me. Johnnie Ward came up and asked how I was. He said that he had written to his brother and told them that I was ill, so I told him that I had not mentioned my illness to my parents. The only thing I could do was to ask the sergeant if I could send my photograph to them as they would be worried sick. That is the only card I could pull to convince them that I was all right. I went back to the block then as the sergeant gave the signal to go. I was actually quite pleased to go back and lie down by then as it had taken it out of me and I thought Jimmy was quite right to make me take it easy, Maybe next week could be my target. I got the blower going while they were out and we had soup for dinner – I mean real soup, full of meat and vegetables. A bun made it really filling. In the afternoon I made the three of them cheese buns and handed them a cup of tea each. They said, 'What is this for?' I said it was a thank you for looking after me when I was sick. They thought it was a lovely surprise.

I started thinking of dear Edie, wondering where she would be; I had thought of her a lot the last few days. Although we were parted she would always be the one for me as she was such a lovely honest person and I loved her so much. I still kissed her photo whenever I could without anybody seeing me as I did not want to be a laughing stock in the block. At least while I had her photo she was still beside me and I would carry it with me wherever I went. The music in the evenings was very lovely and romantic at times, playing songs from when I was courting her or writing her letters on the ship. I had a sad evening with these memories, reminiscing the days when we went to the Empire and the Palace and most of all the last tram to Forest Hall.

I decided I would walk just a little further each day until I was doing a full circuit of the compound. We had been looked after quite well these last few weeks and maybe I would be able to increase my weight. The blocks seemed to be coming in a lot sooner this week; maybe they had someone who could count quickly.

I didn't say earlier about the time we only had a parcel between sixteen people; they wrote all the articles on pieces of paper and we each took one. I ended up with the smallest item, a small tin of meat extract, but it lasted me two days.

I saw Snowy who said, 'I have not seen you for ages.' I told him I took ill on the Friday after eating grapes from the shop and on the Monday had gone in to the camp hospital. I told him of the dreadful conditions there and he was appalled. I told him I was getting better each day and trying to go on parade the next Monday.

I sunbathed from time to time, just ten minutes at a time so as not to get burnt; I would count up to two hundred and then put my jacket back on – I still had no shirt. I was getting a little browner on my legs and arms though my body was still slightly white. When the lads came in I had fallen asleep on my bunk so the meal was not ready, but they were fine and said we would all muck in with the meal and making the tea. While we were eating, Jimmy said the sergeant was coming round to see me and also that he had something to tell the block.

I told the sergeant that I would like to send my photograph to my parents and he said he would have to get permission. I showed him the photo and he asked if he could take it with him, to show the officer the size. Then he called everyone in the block.

According to the Italian officer the English had landed in Sicily. We were all pleased with this news and thought that was why we had been getting better treatment lately with extra parcels. This news would spread like wildfire through the camp. Jimmy had heard this news while out walking but did not know whether to believe it. We told him no, this time it was right. He said it was a pity they didn't try both sides of Italy but perhaps they didn't have the troops; now it was going to be a waiting game to see what the Italians were going to do with us.

The next day I tried to go three-quarters of the way round; I was much stronger and was putting on weight. I made a mark with the heel of my clog where I got up to and would try to do the same the next day. I thought I would tell Jimmy I would try to get back to my own bunk, too. I did a few more sessions at sunbathing, just counting to two hundred with my jacket off.

That evening they were singing 'Run Rabbit Run' and 'Over the Rainbow' and other songs from theatres and some from films. It was good just to hear them again.

Then came Monday morning, the start of a new month and another start for me. I was going to try to get all round the compound; and I was glad I was going on parade. I knew that meant standing for a long time but if I could not make it I would just drop to the ground until they counted us. I persevered with my walking and achieved my goal. Jimmy, Joe and Len were also pleased with my progress. I saw Sergeant Bertram who said it was nice to see me back on the parade ground. I told him what I would do if I felt tired and he said that was quite all right, just as long as I was on my feet when they started counting. I told him I would do my best to stand as long as I could and he said, 'That is good enough for me.' Later I saw him smile at me, he must have been pleased that I was still standing but I found I was a bit wobbly and sat down for a bit. I think if I had had to stand another ten minutes I would have collapsed. Jimmy gave me a sign to ask if I was all right and I just gave him a thumbs-up sign.

I was carrying Edie's photo in my pocket as I was frightened someone might try to take it away; you could never take chances in these places. I had made a hole in my pillowcase for it. The guards were very slow that day and I was needing the toilet badly. As they were leaving down I went and the sergeant gave me a look; I just put my thumb up and he turned away. It was a great relief; I did not want to make a mess of my trousers. I knew they were holey but I just wanted them dry. They were very late with the roll call, probably the worst yet and when the sergeants said fall out even the officer was not too pleased about things. That afternoon there were two new young guards and we thought perhaps the old ones had been sent off to the front line. We all came to attention together, just to show these young ones how smart we could be. They started at 3.30 and seemed to be doing fine. They seemed very keen and were marvellous. I went down and lay on my side for a bit, wishing they would give us some more clothes as I could feel the wind blowing through my trousers, though it was also dry and sunny. Jimmy was giving me hand signals as to when to stand up when they were going to reach our group. I thought I had done really well for my first day. The guards finished at 6.30 when we were called to attention and dismissed.

Another load of parcels came in the night and we knew there were plenty in the storeroom, so it didn't matter that there was very little left from our last one. The guards were even quicker next morning, starting at 10.30 and ending around 12.45; the officer was obviously pleased with their effort. That afternoon when we had come to attention the officer said he had something to say: that the troops in Sicily were fighting hard with the Germans. Everyone was cock-a-hoop at this and someone shouted, 'When are they coming here?' He just laughed and told everyone to be patient, then everyone applauded and roll call was delayed for a while, but after this good news I did not think anyone would complain.

I went to get the skilly that evening and when I got back there was a letter for me and twenty cigarettes and news that the issue of parcels would start after cognac. My letter said that my youngest brother John was not at all well and might go into hospital for checkups though they didn't say what for. No word about the property by the Ritz. We got our parcels a few days later.

During the second week of June the shop was to be open for fruit, but nobody would be getting grapes after the last time. Maybe we would get apples or oranges. But that day the two guards came through the main gate followed by the officer who said, 'I want you all to come to attention.' Everyone was astounded as he said then, 'I have to tell you that next week everyone will be going to a different camp.' He added also that there would be a boxing match sometime this week. Everyone was cheering about everything he had said, but were all wondering where we would end up. At least there were plenty of parcels to keep us going unless they did not unload the lorry but sent it away to some other camp. There would only be a morning roll call on the day of the boxing match, and after that the whole camp had to be emptied so there would not be any shop for anyone. At the end of the parade the sergeants on parade saluted the officer, and our sergeant made everyone in our group salute him and the other groups followed suit. Then he thanked everyone.

We all went away wondering what was going to happen. The officer sent two more guards to help with the distribution of buns, so that was a lot quicker. Now we would get our dinner in peace, not worrying about the next roll call, we could just relax in the sun. We wondered if they would increase the skilly ration or if they were actually short of vegetables. It was amazing to be treated like human beings for a change. At least we would all get away from this horrible camp; everybody we talked to seemed quite happy about moving. We wondered why. Perhaps our troops had taken Sicily but that might just be wishful thinking. When we moved that would be the second time missing.

The sergeant came in later and had a talk – he said this was all quite out of the blue; he just could not believe what the officer was saying. He thought things would progress a lot more quickly now as the higher rank officer would go away and leave the English speaking one in charge. If we had any news we were to go and tell him straight away.

'Well,' Jimmy said, 'looks like we're winning the war in this area. Maybe they will start to invade France. It will be a matter of time before everything comes to a head. We will know next week where we are going. At least we will be travelling light. We must find out about the boxing match – what weights they will be fighting at and when it is to be held; it will be something to look forward to and a good way to say farewell.'

We had a full tin of corned beef as it was a long time since we could do this, and Jimmy said it was no good thinking about tomorrow, we had to look after today and we would manage whatever the Italians gave us as there were only a few days left. The singing that night was very good indeed; everyone was singing their hearts out and people were even coming to the door and asking for a favourite song, maybe to remember their sweetheart or wife. The skilly was again served by four guards so Jimmy was back quite quickly, saying, 'Why didn't they do this before instead of us standing in the rain for an hour getting soaked to the skin?'

What a day to remember. A little later the Italian bugler was playing the Last Post and after that we heard planes going overhead and they just kept on going.

A few days later the sergeant told us that the boxing match would be held at 3 o'clock in the same compound as before, the next day. There were to be all different weights and all the protagonists were ex Army battalion champs, or maybe Navy or Merchant Navy; one could never tell who was who in a camp as at Brindisi there were even two submariners and they must have been here as well as we all moved together.

With one roll call a day and with four guards serving food it was just great. The sergeant said we all had to travel as light as possible and to be ready to move at any moment. We were to use up all our Red Cross supplies, and not even to leave tea or coffee around: to brew up five or six times a day if necessary. The morning roll call only took three hours, not too bad. That day Jimmy was waiting for us with a surprise; he had buttered the buns and we had soup and a tin of sardines between us, but we still had left cheese, jam, Spam and bacon.

At roll call the officer said that one or two compounds would be going that day to another camp and then one or two more each day, or more, depending on transport; then he hoped that everyone would enjoy the boxing match; and then he dismissed us. Later we saw a guard with wire cutters cutting the outer wire – he made quite a large hole so that people could go through to other compounds. We saw a guard in a wooden guard box and saw some of the lads in front of us tip it over with the guard inside and start stamping on it; this went on for quite a while.

When we got to the arena there was such a large crowd we wouldn't be able to see unless someone sat down. The sergeants told everyone to sit down and some did and some didn't. 'Come on, lads, be fair, everyone would like to see the boxing,' they said, and eventually everybody did sit down.

The first bout was flyweight, three two-minute rounds. Everyone gave them a great welcome and the ref started the round, saying first, 'Any funny business and you are disqualified,' so they made a clean fight and fought hard. The second round had hardly started when the lad with the blue ribbon knocked down the lad with the red one. Everyone clapped and shouted. There were six bouts altogether: some won on points; there were two knock-outs and a draw. It was a good contest and everyone went away happy, making for the gaps in the wire.

When we got to the gap we heard cries for help. It was the guard still trapped in his guard box. We tried to lift it as best we could, we managed to get a plank and lifted it a bit, then levered it up with the plank. There were six of us but it was still very heavy. We managed eventually to get it up so he could get out. He was really frightened, just a young lad, about seventeen and he just ran away.

The sergeant brought twenty cigarettes each and some more mail; and said we might be moving Tuesday or Wednesday. He said that my photograph had been sent home to my parents and I thanked him very much for his help. My letter told me that they had kept John in hospital but I was not to worry as he was going to be all right.

We walked round the compound a couple of times and then made our way to the parade area. The officer said, 'I have some news for you. Your troops landed in mainland Italy yesterday and there is fierce fighting going on. For this reason three blocks will be travelling tomorrow, so would you all rise at Reveille, when the bugler plays, as no one knows when you will be called to go to your transport to take you to the station at Bari. I do not know your destination but the sergeant will be informed at the station. Take very light packages as you will be given something before you board it to eat on the train.'

The sergeant called us to attention and the sergeant made everyone salute and then we gave him a cheer for the help he had given us since he came to be in charge. He said there would be no parade that day and said goodbye to everyone and dismissed us.

Our singing could be heard as far as the toilets; everybody was having a good time and people were coming to ask for their own favourite songs of yesteryear: 'Roll out the Barrel,' 'Run Rabbit Run,' and many more songs even from the first world war. The last song was always 'Now is the Hour' from New Zealand; it was a love song and a lovely way to finish the evening. We went for our last skilly there and the Italian soldiers came and shook hands with us all; they were thinking of our troops at the foot of their land and knowing that for them the war would be soon over for them.

'Well,' Jimmy said to me, 'this will be the last night we sleep here and by, we have travelled a lot of miles together. I wonder how many more we will travel.'

At least we would not have to take any more laths from the bunks. We would always remember the blower we made which was our lifeline.

This was Wednesday and we had to be up early. It did not take long to get ready. We decided to have someone posted at the door to tell us when the sergeant approached the block, to be relieved every quarter of an hour. I only had to pack my photo of Edie and the letters from my family and friends. Someone shouted from the toilets that there were lorries lining up outside the main gates. The sergeant lined us up in ranks of three and the other two blocks did the same and we just waited. We were determined to be as smart as we could going up to the main gate for the last time, so the sergeant could be proud of us. The Italian guards must have been amazed, everyone keeping step and it was a big parade.

The sergeant said twenty-five men to a truck so we all got aboard and the flaps were drawn so the Italian people could not see us. It was quite a while before we came to the station where there were four coaches and an engine pointing north. When we came to a crossing we seemed to point east and quite a while later someone spotted Rome. We lifted the blind and saw the Colosseum. Everyone wanted to have a look but the guard pulled the blind down. We had two dry buns and no drink at all though the coach was warm and no windows could be opened. They were very old stock and must have been used for fourth class people as the seating was very poor with no springs.

Eventually the sergeant came and told us we were going to a camp somewhere near Rimini on the east coast. We were still rolling on but could be there in the next hour. Jimmy and I had a seat together. There were lots of Italian soldiers in different parts of the train and on seats by the doors; they all had sidearms and were mostly corporals and sergeants.

Chapter 15

When we arrived we were to get off only a few at a time. The sergeant said, 'Come on, lads, let's show them what the English soldier can do without discipline, even without me giving orders, as you did this morning. I was really pleased then. Can you do the same and show these Italian soldiers that you can still march, even if you are all in poor health. It is the spirit of your English training that you have not forgotten that makes it a lot easier for me.'

So we did what we had that morning, got three men in a rank all down the line and the sergeant just gave us a nod as he had that morning and we marched to the new camp. When we arrived we just marked time until he gave us a nod again, then closed ranks as best we could and turned round. He gave a nod and we stood easy; and then he dismissed us with his only command.

He said, 'I am really pleased with everyone the way that was done. I think the Italians got an example of good old Army training.' It was really appreciation of him.

The interpreter was calling our names to go into the blocks. It was funny but Jimmy and I, Len and Joe were in the same one; we could not believe it; and on our bunks was a parcel between two people. Jimmy was on a top bunk and I was on a bottom one next to him. it was now about 4.30 and we had nothing to drink so we were all very thirsty indeed.

This place looked quite pleasant with a large football field in the middle with the blocks all around; but the wire was very high and there were plenty of sentry boxes on stilts and a machine gun on every one. We had new palliasses and a new pillow so we would sleep well. The only thing we had not got was Terry. The lad next to me, Raymond, came from Shropshire; we seemed to hit it off straight away.

Another dawn at a new camp. We would have to wait and see what the routine was here; maybe Raymond could help. He said you had to wait till your sergeant informed you which group to go to. By the time he came the guards had gone and we still had had nothing to drink, no cognac at all. They said that the morning roll call would be at 9.30 and the afternoon one at 2.00. We went to examine the toilets: they were a bit further away than before but a lot nicer and smelled very well; still a hole in concrete section with two footmarks though and just a hole for the urinal which was good really as no one could catch any disease from it.

We four together were still in our group but had a new sergeant as Sergeant Bertram was in the other block. They started the parade exactly on time and it took three hours. We all went for our buns as we did not know if they would give them to one person for another and we got served very soon. We were not allowed indoors with a blower but had to build a fire outside and in a corner was plenty of wood to burn. You could take about two pieces; this was written up inside on a noticeboard in English. They were pieces of lath, very easy to break as we just put them against a wall and smashed them with our feet; easy for me in clogs. We had to make our fires where other people had them and sometimes you might catch someone who had just finished. We had to borrow their Klim tin. The afternoon parade finished at 5.30 and we only had till 6.30 to build fires; that was the rule at this camp.

It seemed strange not to have any music in our block but we had a stroll around the compound until the skilly was due, and again it did not take long for three of them to dish it out.

A few days passed and we heard there was going to be a football match that day and roll call would be later. Raymond and I went to the touchline early to get a good view. We had a piece of cloth as protection against the sun and I had my jacket around my shoulders. A good crowd started to gather and said to us, 'You are not two pouffs?' 'You must be joking,' we replied and we all had a good laugh. All of sudden onto the pitch came a lovely lady so she could start the match. She kicked the ball just like women do, not very far. We thought the guard must have taken a fancy to her. It was a fun match; twenty-two players on the field but some kicked the ball into their own goal area and one of them scored; the next minute he put the ball in the middle and went straight to the other end and scored again; It was a hilarious afternoon with both teams having a lot of fun even changing shirts.

At the end with the score 2–2 the Italian guards got hold of the lady and took her through the main gate. We were told to keep quiet while the roll call was on and they were finished by 6.30. Just as we were going again the Italians brought the lady into the compound and she started taking her clothes off; it was a bloke in drag. Everybody had been taken in; we even thought the Italian guard was quids in with her. It was the biggest laugh of the day.

We were well into July now and there was a rumour that some people were going to get moved away from here. We would have to see. This camp was a lot better than Bari, more efficient. Lorries and trailers arrived during the night with parcels; we thought they might have been the ones we left at Bari. The sergeant told us that he thought we were going to get a cigarette issue too. That evening in came Sergeant Bertram with a bundle of letters and cards to send home and he also gave each man a packet of twenty cigarettes. We had to get the letters written by eight o'clock as he had to give them to a guard in the morning to get away to Britain. I wrote to my parents and to my younger brothers; I had not heard from my brother Stephen for a long while.

I wished I could write to Edie to tell her I had been moved to a new camp at Rimini. I did not know the address of her Uncle Tom and Aunt Fran because when we visited them the young girl, Joan, would just stand in the doorway and give a shout. We used to babysit her and her sister when Edie's Uncle Tom was home from the Navy.

Next day we met Johnnie who said that he loved this place and would be happy to stay here till the end of the war. We agreed that Bari was a dump.

The sergeant was waiting for us to say that that night we would have some mail waiting for us from England and that we would have an issue of parcels in a few days time. We all talked about the real fun day we had the day before and that was the best laugh for a long time; it had the camp in stitches.

The news that our lads were fighting in the south of Italy put a spring in our step and did wonders for our morale; we felt that we were getting nearer home. We were always early for roll call and the sergeant was quite pleased; the people who had been here all the time just seemed to take their time and we put them in the shade. They were the ones who were complaining about not finishing soon – what could they expect? The guards were very good at counting but still didn't finish till 6 o'clock.

I had a card from my mother to say that everyone was all right and that John was out of hospital but no answers to any of my questions.

Here everyone had to go for their own cognac and meals unless they were sick in bed, when the sergeant could tell his mate to get it for him. After we had collected that, the four of us and Raymond, we made our way to the group area and discovered our sergeant waiting for us. He had something to say.

'I just had word that so many people could be going to another camp from here; and it could be the new arrivals, or mixed, nobody knows for sure; that's just what I've been told by the interpreter. It might be round about the end of this month, unless the lads are pushing like hell, or they may have made a landing near to us, as things are a lot faster now, perhaps they have better communications than we did.'

I was at the toilets with Raymond and his two friends. We spotted that another man had been circumcised and as we talked afterwards he said,

'I am a Jew although I am English. I was born in England and I was conscripted by the government and I've always been afraid that someone would spot me here and turn me in,' but we said that we would keep it to ourselves; no way would we tell the Italian police or *carabineri*. 'It would be a shame if someone gave you away after fighting for our country.'

'It is my country as well.'

We shook hands with him and said that his secret was safe with us. I didn't even tell Jimmy.

That afternoon the roll call lasted about three hours and afterwards Jimmy and one of the lads went ready to collect the parcels from the storeroom and we others got permission from the sergeant to collect two cups of skilly as the others were getting the parcels. The Italian soldiers were rushing through the distribution so they could be finished for the night and perhaps seeing their girls or wives. Our skilly was just warm by then, but we had our parcels and they had sixteen items in.

We were all wishing that we could stay at this camp as it was very well run, not like the one at Bari. But early the next week the officer told us through the interpreter that some people would be going the next week and the sergeants would be informed later who it was to be; where to would be told on the date of departure. We had a distribution of letters to send home and I thought I could write something like 'Uncle Joe is going away,' to let them know I was on the move again. It was worth a try anyway.

We were strolling round the compound when Raymond said, 'Stop!' We all stopped and going along towards the gate was the Jewish lad we had been talking to. With him were Italian soldiers and civilian people and outside was a civilian car. Someone must have turned him in. We told Jimmy the whole story and Jimmy said we were right to have kept it a secret, 'but perhaps someone overheard him telling you.' Who knows what must have happened to him.

Two days later Sergeant Bertram was calling names of people who would go tomorrow or the next day and mine was among them. There were twelve all told from this block. Jimmy asked me what I had put on my form as occupation when I got captured and I said, 'I said I was a clerk and also worked on farms; I didn't say anything about the pit heap or working down the pit,' which I did but it was just taking girders on a cage top. So this was my last few days here. I supposed that if we were going north it was that bit nearer to England. The sergeant came over and said, 'I am sorry you are going; you have come a long way with us all; all I can say is "See you in England some time".' He grasped my hand with both of his and added, 'Good luck, Tommy, wherever you go, and I do hope you make it.'

I thanked him for everything he had done and he said, 'That's all right, it is a sergeant's job to look after people like you.'

Jimmy and the lads all said they were sorry I was going on my own; all the lads who were taken prisoner with me would be left behind. It was the luck of the draw; maybe what God wanted. This would be my third time missing.

There was not much wood left to make tea as the pile had not been topped up and I felt that there they were worrying about wood while I was worrying about where I was going to go the next day. We had our buns with sardines which make lovely sandwiches and Jimmy was wondering what I was going to do about food. I said, 'Jimmy, you will have the rest of the parcel to yourself as I will get buns on the train, if that's the way I am travelling.'

They went out for a walk, but I said I would stay in in case the sergeant came in, though in fact he didn't so it would be the day after that I was going. I wondered what it would be like going off on my own; but still, I have a tongue and a lot to say to people. Jimmy said it would not be the same for him, not having me around, as we had been together for a long time; I said that it was easier for him as he had Len and Joe, and Johnnie and his pals, but he still said it would not be the same. All we could say was, 'See you in England when all this is over.'

The sergeant came in the next day and said I would be leaving early the next morning and I should be up with Reveille and ready to leave after cognac. I was to leave the camp by truck and then leave Rimini station before 11 o'clock. He did not know how many would be leaving with me, but not many.

I helped Jimmy get a last dinner together and we made plans for after the war in England. That night I woke up to go to the toilet and then I could not get back to sleep; I tried time and again but to no avail; and then the bugler was blowing Reveille. I got up and got ready and Jimmy and the lads also got up, saying they wanted to spend as much time as possible with me. We had our cognac and then just waited. In the meantime the sergeant came into the block and said, 'Before you go I have twenty cigarettes and a Red Cross parcel each.'

'That is good news,' I said, 'but how am I going to open a tin on the train? And how am I even going to make a cup of tea; I don't know how long I'll be on this train.'

'You may get buns, like we did from Bari.'

'I do hope so as it would be a long boring journey without something to eat.'

It was nearly 7.30 and everyone came with me towards the main gate; the other lads leaving were also accompanied by their friends. I shook hands with everyone and said, 'I Hope to see you in England soon.' I had Edie's photo in my hand, just to comfort me. The tears welled up but at 8.45 what could I do but go? I clung to my parcel like a lifeline and also had a cigarette handy but the guards had orders for us not to smoke at all.

It was quite a while before we arrived at the station at Rimini as the traffic was very slow. We got out of the lorry and formed into threes. The Italian sergeant shouted orders but we just stood; he shouted again and we still did not understand; so he stood beside us and started marching; a good quick march and we whistled 'It's a Long Way to Tipperary' as we went along. When he put up a hand to stop us we all came as one to a halt, amazing a lot of Italian civilians: us being prisoners with a lot of red patches on our trousers and shirts or jackets.

We got into a compartment with just enough room for thirty people and we each were given two buns. It was a third class carriage but better than the truck. There were other carriages with civilians in and we were at the back. There were two engines, one pulling and one pushing. No one saw us as the blinds were drawn, but we saw at one station about twenty Italian officers with rifles or revolvers. As we got hungry we ate our buns, which were very dry with nothing to drink and it was very warm. We stopped at quite a number of stations but not for very long at a time. The scenery became hilly and we could see mountains in the far distance. As we went through the mountains it was quite frightening looking at the drops and we would be glad to reach our destination. Then the engine at the back seemed to part us from the rest of the train and we went on a way and then alighted at a small platform

Trucks were waiting to take us to our destination. We passed a board that said 'Bolzano'. The trucks then drove very slowly on bumpy roads and then we heard the brakes and we were there. We were taken to a billet with three-tier bunks, almost new. The toilets were in a small building next door. After that long journey it did not take us long to fall asleep.

Chapter 16

This was 1 August 1943 and it was my first day at the fruit farm outside Bolsano. I slept like a log but the next day we were wondering what was to happen next. I could have done with a nice cup of tea as we had had nothing to drink since yesterday morning. We could not open the tins from our Red Cross parcels either.

About 8 o'clock a woman came into our billet and said we could have milk and bread, and. a maid brought us two slices of bread each and a glass of milk which went down a treat. She could not speak any English and used sign language. The first woman who did speak English took us round the farm were there were apples, pears, plums, peaches, and black and green grapes, hanging from trellises right above your head. She took us to the apple orchard, gave us ladders to climb and showed us how to pick apples without harming them. We then put them into an apron around our waist and fastened with a belt so we had both hands free. Some of us did that and some did cut the grass which was pretty high and we had a scythe each. After we had done this for a while she came back with a jug of milk and six glasses. With the grass being so tall we had accidentally cut some young trees and she played merry hell with us for doing that and called us saboteurs. We said we sometimes did not see these small trees until too late, so once again she told us how to cut away the grass a bit at a time. She stood and watched us for a while to see if we were doing it properly.

Later she served us with sandwiches and jugs of milk; the bread was dry with cheese. After we had it they went away to give the other lads theirs. We continued with our grass cutting and now we seemed to be doing better and she was pleased; later she brought bags for us to put the clippings in. We told her about our problems opening tins and she said she would take them away to be opened and we were happy about that.

We sat down for a rest as we were quite exhausted. The sun was beating down and it was a long time since we had done anything like this and our legs and arms were aching. The maid came with jugs of milk and it was lovely and cold and really delicious. We asked her the time with gestures and she put up four fingers and a half. We then saw Italian guards in the background; they must have been patrolling the area in case we made a break for it. But this place was like manna from heaven; we would not mind staying there till the end of the war. We did not really need Red Cross parcels as we had everything we needed: plenty of fruit, bread not too bad with cheese or salami and we were living like lords.

When the woman came back she said it was six o'clock and time to finish. She said we could have some small potatoes and gave us some water to boil but not to drink. She said we could build fires, but only in four places. With this I planned on eating a whole tin of corned beef as it would go off if I kept it but I was quite full after eating and drinking milk. so thought I might have the second half later.

The next day we got up and were given bread and cheese and milk at 7.30 a.m. We were to start on the next two sections. As we passed the green grapes I picked two or three, still wary after what had happened at Bari, and put them beside an apple tree for later, but the birds had them instead. It was another very hot day. At our break time we had more milk and again at 12.30 with sandwiches of cheese and tomato; at this rate I would be putting weight back on.

My trousers were really falling apart; the pieces I had sewn were falling away and if I could not stop this they were going to be able to see all I had. When the women came I lay down and asked her if she could help me. She said at six o'clock she would bring some thread and a piece of cloth and a needle. Later I sewed up my trousers as best I could but it was very dark in the billet so I had to do it outside before the light faded. I just tacked some of it for the time being. For tea she gave us potatoes and one or two carrots and said to take any fruit we wanted, but not too many grapes as they might make us ill. I went along and got a peach and a pear but it took all my time to eat one, they were so large. The peach really quenched my thirst. I had the pear later as it was hot in the billet.

The woman was apparently Austrian, and she spoke Italian and English as well as German. The maid was German. The next day the grass was really high and although we were very careful we cut down a few of the small trees; sometimes you were too late as the scythes were very sharp. Sometimes you hit a stone or a brick and work was very slow. At 4.30 the maid came out with something to drink which turned out to be red wine; there was not much and I must have drunk the lot. I was not used to drinking and I got a fuzzy head. When the woman came out she asked if I had drunk it all and said it had been for the six of us. She told me to lie down and not do any more work that day and to do an hour and a half extra the next day. I decided to get up early and do an hour of it in the morning. That evening we had potatoes, tomatoes and lettuce with some bread, together with half a pint of milk each.

I realised that I couldn't get up early to work as I had no scythe but the woman said I could do half an hour each night. The grass in that section was about four feet high and it was slow progress. When I needed the toilet a guard had to go with me and that was another few minutes away from that section. At 6 o'clock the guards took the other lads away and left me on my own so I took my time until he shouted. I put the scythe on my shoulder – it was not heavy, just awkward – and away we went. The others were just finishing with the fire so I had a few potatoes with sardines and tomatoes and made a nice cup of tea as I still had tea, sugar, milk, butter, jam and cheese left.

A few days later I had finished doing my extra hours and we were nearly at the end of mowing the sections. As I was working I thought that we would not get letters or cards to send home from here and that my parents would again be wondering what was happening. It was as bad for them as for us. There were very few trees in the way in this section so we finished a lot sooner than we expected so we sat down till she came. Then she took us to the far end of the orchard amongst apple trees and gave us aprons to put the apples in. However she put me and another lad onto picking up all the apples that had dropped from the trees into special barrels marked in English and Italian 'Not to be eaten'. We found some with a few bite marks in so someone was doing a great job, spoiling a few apples a day. The time just flew by. If we needed the toilet we mostly just went behind a tree as it saved time and sometimes you could not find a guard to take you.

So that was a week over already and when you think what I had been through, this was like paradise. We had everything we wanted there, though we still moaned. Perhaps it was because our bodies were not used to working. But there was no roll call, and two people brought us food each day: not much but pretty regular. We always thanked them very much and I hoped they appreciated our politeness. That day there was salami, with cheese and tomato, and we were again filling barrels from windfalls. This job meant stooping all the time but Norman said, 'Let's try it this way: I will kneel and fill your apron then you can do the same for me. This method helped a great deal. While one was emptying his apron the other could get a few ready.

The woman came and said, 'I am going to put four men onto lifting these barrels; if you think they are too heavy just transfer some apples into an empty barrel as I do not want to injure anyone; it is no good to me if someone is laid up with a bad back. You will put them on a truck to be taken away. Two men will go with it to unload the barrels.'

We could have been there for days filling barrels with windfalls; I don't think she had had anyone there for months. The day flew by till teatime and the two guards and two women came towards us with milk and sandwiches. There was salami and three slices of bread each. We sat for a while after eating them but I did not want to get too close to Martin, not after what happened at Rimini.

I said, 'Right, we will concentrate on this area between the two barrels, but before we start we will move two others near here and fill them up halfway.' Then the guards were there to tell us to stop work at six o'clock, and on my way back I picked a bunch of black grapes, a pear and a peach to save time later. I was nearly out of sugar and tea and there was no milk at all so I was going to ask the maid or the woman if I could have some for tea – just yes or no.

A few days later there were still another couple of sections to do but she was to give us three more people so it shouldn't take long and we might get a whole section done that day if we all worked together. Some people were put onto grapes and she showed them how to cut them off the vines with a small knife; one cut and the other laid the bunches in a box. We showed the lads who came to help us our method. One said, 'This is donkey work,' and I replied, 'Yes, it may be, but better than the camp I came from in Bari.' I said, 'How long were you at the camp at Rimini?'

'Just over a year. I got captured in 1942, just outside Derna in Libya.'

This Martin was a right old moaner; I did not think he had done any work in his life, or he had had an easy job. When the lorry came, the other lad, Norman, went over and said they had to load it; he said, 'Why don't you do it, mate, you were detailed by the woman,' and there was an argument.

Then the woman and the maid came with a tray of sandwiches and milk. She heard Martin shouting and said, 'Right, no dinner for you, just go and pick apples in the next section by yourself.' And if he did not do any work he would not get his evening meal either. We said amongst ourselves, 'He had only himself to blame. He is a real worky ticket – here we have a lovely billet, good food, plenty of fresh air and fruit.'

The other lads said that even at the front Martin was lazy, moaning and groaning; we all said that one was best left alone. Then we loaded the truck; Sam brought them to me and it all worked a treat; by the time one was on board the other was ready. When the truck was nearly half full the guard came with the lads that went with the truck and away they went. Apparently the driver always stopped off for half an hour at his house in the village. The soldiers thought that one day he would get caught and the woman would take it out on them; but we thought not as she had always been fair. When she brought our food, she said she had been over to Martin and he was sound asleep so she just left him there.

In fact when the truck eventually came back she gave the driver a real rollicking and sent him packing; he just left the truck where it was. The three of us continued but there was still a long way to go. Near the middle of the section the apples seemed to get thicker and we came across more of the ones that had been eaten to put in the reject pile.

Martin, who had been causing all the trouble, came over and said where were his meals, nobody had been over to give him anything. We told him that the woman had been over with his tea but had found him asleep so she gave his milk and sandwiches to us, thank you mate. When the woman came she told him that there would be no tea for him, and no fruit at all: no work, no food. The rest of us got potatoes, tomatoes, cucumber and two slices of bread as we had no Red Cross parcels left.

We had a bath and a mirror in the toilet so we could shave but we got no money at all so we were going to ask if we could have some blades or the sort of razor you sharpen on a strop. She told us that we would be picking apples off the trees as there was an order to go out into the hills in a few days time. She said we four, Martin, Sam, Richard and I, would go with the truck; I don't know why she was telling us unless it was because she knew she could trust us. Those apples were beautiful. We just half filled the barrels so they would be easier to lift and would fill them up when the truck came. Later we took just one bite out of one and threw it away, and then tried to see who could throw the furthest. We went on picking saying we would try again later, but to be careful not to get caught as that woman pulled no punches. Luckily we were working when she came to us with our sandwiches.

Martin, the lad who was moaning had had no breakfast and perhaps he had learned his lesson as he was working a bit harder according to the people he was working with. We climbed up the apple trees and just kept picking as we all thought, what sort of punishment would she give us for throwing apples about. Later she told us we had done very well and that we could go with the truck the next day; and the day after another four people could go. It was quite a long way to the mountains.

So the next day we got up early and the maid came with our breakfasts, two sandwiches with salami, sliced tomatoes and lovely cold milk, and she gave us a package for our dinner. The two guards took us to the barrels of apples, so we would be ready to load them. One guard got in the front and one in the back with us and we pulled away towards the farmhouse. The woman went in and brought out sandwiches and milk for us. Then we started our long drive, climbing up and then dropping into a beautiful valley. The guard with us kept dropping off to sleep and we whispered that we should take his rifle as we must be very near the Swiss border, but just as we decided to try it he woke up. We whispered it was not worth it; we would find it difficult not speaking the language. After that the guards stayed awake; maybe they felt something was up.

We could see a small village and arrived at a factory full of women who were eyeing us up. These robust lasses just got hold of a barrel and walked into the factory and as there must have been twenty of them altogether, it did not take long to empty the truck. One went into the office and came out with some cold water; she said it came from a spring in the mountains. I had never tasted any water like it and the others said the same.

They brought some milk and told us we could have our dinner so we opened our packages and inside were four lovely chicken sandwiches. Then we had to start back as it would be a harder journey as the mist came down from nowhere and one might have to stop until the wind blew it away. But we only had to stop once though it was a real pea-soup fog and you couldn't see a thing through it. I saw a hut near the road where perhaps you could shelter for the night if you were caught. But it only lasted three quarters of an hour. We all nodded off on the way after our early start. When we arrived our legs were stiff with cramp and pain shot down them so we just walked round slowly to get our circulation back.

After more chicken sandwiches and salad which we ate with great enjoyment for we were really hungry, we thanked them and went to the billet; and within half an hour I was asleep.

Here we were into our third week and once again cutting grass with a scythe. If we were thirsty we went and picked a pear and I never tasted one like them, lovely and soft and the juice just trickling down your chin. We had to look out for small trees again and be careful of our fingers as the scythes were very sharp. I seemed to be putting on weight again with the regular meals and the exercise and the weather helped as well: just like being on holiday. I was wondering however what my parents would be thinking as they had had no word. Nothing much happened for the rest of that week as we went on under the pear trees.

At the beginning of the fourth week the woman said, 'Your troops are doing very well. Rome is an open city now and things are moving. But that is all I know.'

This was good news, the best for a long time. So we sat for a while, but then just got on with the grass clearing and there it was easier as it was only about two feet high. Some trees we saw had been damaged with fungus. Then it got taller again and our job became more difficult but still it was a surprise when we saw the guard coming and it was 6 o'clock.

The months were just rolling by – here it was at the beginning of September. This time we were apple picking. It did not take long to fill a barrel when a lot of men were working on it and we had to wait for the truck. The woman came along and saw us sitting waiting, but she said the truck had broken down and it was not our fault. She said that she had some more news for us. Italy had surrendered to the British forces and King Emmanuel was taking over from Mussolini. Now it was up to the British to accept the terms the Italians gave them. So we lay on our bunks wondering if this meant we would be going home. Perhaps we would stay here until they came to pick us up; the Italians at least knew we were there. It was quite a long time before she and the maid came with our sandwiches but she said then that there was no new development but that from that moment we were all finished working there and that we could be free in a day or so. She said she would still keep on giving us food as we had been so good working and she had been very pleased in every way.

Now it was 31 August 1943. The woman in charge would still not let us go to work; she said as far as she was concerned she would let us go but she could not until she heard from the authorities. We still got our food and she said we could have fruit, except if we wanted apples she would send the maid for them, and not more than two each as it was quite a long way. The pears, peaches and grapes were all handy. She also brought a dozen razors for us all and some blades. When we came to think about it, it must have been quite expensive for her to feed us all, thirty men.

On 1 September she said that everyone in Italy and Austria and Germany was waiting for the decision of the King of Italy and Britain to come to some agreement. It was very hot so we did not stay outside for long as I remembered the day I got sunburnt. It was always wise to cover up when we went outside. The news then was that Italy had surrendered unconditionally and from 3 September we would be free; that had come on the news on the wireless.

I picked some lovely peaches and we all got pears and grapes – some went over the top with their collection and wasted them. I hoped one day they would go hungry and think of the day they just wasted good food and dropped it and squashed it under their boots. That day nobody came with supper and we wondered what was happening.

On 3 September we still had no news. According to the woman, they were still waiting for confirmation and it seemed like stalemate. We had the lovely sandwiches and milk for breakfast. The woman said at dinnertime that we were free men but that she advised us not to go off the farm as she was not responsible for our safety; we were still under the military and would keep the guards for our protection and that she would still feed us all.

Most of the lads went towards the wall facing the village and there were people, young and old, who had not seen an English soldier before. The girls were giggling and laughing at us because we must have looked a state in our old and wornout clothes. I was just a ragamuffin – jacket, clogs, worn-out trousers, no socks or shirt. Some lads tried to make dates with the girls but I just went back to the billet, sat on the stairs and tried to get some more sunshine on my body. When the women brought our food there were only about fifteen of us there and the women were waiting for the glasses to take back; when some of the lads came in late she said, 'Next time you are late we will take it all back as we have not time to sit around like you lot; I still have a farm to run.' Again we thanked her for everything; this time the sandwiches were chicken and sliced tomato.

I could see the village girls taking a lot of notice of our lads, but I went away and thought of the good times Edie and I had had with my mate Ned Blake: not a good mate in my eyes any more. We used to go to the Green Market to get fruit and we would get carnations: one pink and two white with silver paper wrapped round the stem of each. We would go to the Palace Theatre and I would hold Edie's hand except when I had to take it away to clap. Sometimes there was a singer or a good comedy show; sometimes there were four or five harmonicas making lovely music. As I walked I could almost imagine she was beside me.

The women brought us an extra sandwich at tea time and said that we would not be getting supper; we only got that when we were working.

On 5 September we were sitting and talking about various holidays we had had such as Butlin's and we were enjoying the sunshine. It was getting close to dinner time when someone spotted a white horse and somebody riding it; it looked like a German officer and behind him some German soldiers and some Italian soldiers. As they got nearer we realised that the Italians were prisoners now; they were the ones who had been guarding us. They waited outside the billet until a truck arrived and the German soldiers made them unload it. Inside were treble bunks and the Germans made then move all our double bunks close together so they could get them in as well. This major with a row of medals across his chest, including the Iron Cross, spoke some English and told us that we had been taken by the German Army as prisoners of war and would be taken to Germany in a few days time.

That was our twenty-four hours of freedom over. He seemed a right old so-and-so and treated his soldiers like muck; they had to come to attention and salute 'Heil Hitler'. The women brought our food and the officer said she would now have to feed the Italian prisoners as well. When the officer went away he left six German guards to look after us. They stopped us going for fruit so we just ate our supper.

It was going to be terrible in the billet with the extra people. The Italians were all working like beavers trying to get their bunks fixed, carrying all the laths; you need about sixteen of them to take the weight and if you did not get it right you could have a nasty fall, right on top of the person beneath. The woman took one of the Italian soldiers to help her; they were allowed to roam around as we were not.

On 6 September the German officer was in charge of everything; what he said went, and his soldiers were like lapdogs, jumping up and saluting. Maybe they were young lads who had not seen any action yet. In the toilet the lads were in stitches when they saw an Italian with his hair in rollers, watching him take them out; his hair was down to his shoulders. It was quite a while before we got our breakfast as the German soldiers had to be fed first. The officer was all smiles to us and said,

'Good morning.' We said, 'Good morning,' back and he was not pleased and put a scolding face on. He made us go inside and followed us in. He said that tomorrow or the next day we would all go on a march; he did not say where.

The woman brought only one sandwich each and said she was sorry but she had had to feed all the Germans and we said that it was not her fault and we were still grateful. She was going to go to the village or Bolsano to get more food. We took off our jackets and sat in the sun; the German soldiers must have been really hot lying around in their uniforms. We had no food that evening which would not hurt us but it was a shame we could not have any fruit which would have filled the gap; those lads who were biting fruit and throwing it away would know now what it was to go hungry.

The German guards must have stopped outside all night; they must have thought we were going to run away, but where could we go to? We did not know the area and there were a lot of pitfalls out there. The toilet was packed; you had to wait your turn and the Italians were incredible, taking lots of time or just pushing in; they were a pain in the neck, having been there just a few days and thinking they could take over.

We were left waiting in the morning of 7 September and felt like unwanted people; they seemed to think we were war criminals but we were prisoners of war and should be treated as such by them. The woman apologised when she brought our breakfast, saying she would have liked to feed us first as we had worked very hard for her. We were really hungry and enjoyed the salami sandwiches with sliced cucumber and tomatoes and the lovely cold glass of milk. I went to the toilet and just made it in time as I had diarrhoea and my mind went back straight away to what had happened at Bari. I lay down as my stomach was in some pain; maybe it was some bug I had picked up. We had to spend the day cleaning the billet which did not take long and later the women brought us egg sandwiches with lettuce and cucumber. I had thought I would not eat anything but in fact I enjoyed mine very much.

Around 1.30 we saw the German officer coming towards us. The guards came into the billet and told us to form groups of three and to take any personal belongings with us. I only had the photos of my mother and Edie; better to travel light as we did not know how long we would be marching along the road.

The officer gave a command in English then a command in German and the soldiers put their rifles on their shoulders and marched off. We passed the farmhouse and then about half a mile to the main road then the same distance along it. Then he told us to turn round and go back again to the billet. Everyone was amused at what he was doing, unless he was trying us out to see how far we could march. We think he might have got a shock at how well we performed as we tried to be as smart as possible.

The next day we were wondering whether we would be marching again. I went to the toilets but again had to wait till there was one vacant then I would be in and out in a jiffy; when the Italians went in they forgot to come out; I would have liked to know what they were doing. A couple of the lads went out to see what was going on at the farmhouse. One of them said he had been asking around and that I was the oldest prisoner there, having been captured in November 1941. After breakfast we went on another march in the same direction, through the village. Someone started whistling 'Colonel Bogie' and everyone joined in which made our marching a lot better. We were really out in the country and the officer did not stop us. We changed the song now and again and there were some I did not recognise. Some were first world war songs that everyone knew. All of a sudden the officer stopped us and said about turn; and the Italians crashed into us as they did not understand the command so he made them go to the back of us. Then we whistled our way back and there we were back in the billet. We had gone quite a long way, perhaps two miles out and two miles back, and were really jiggered.

There was no tea that evening; we gave up expecting it at about 7.45. The next day the woman apologised and said that the officer had said we were going away so she had not prepared anything. She said she did not know why they had stopped us eating fruit but that she would have a word with the officer about it and that she knew we had only taken what was necessary. If he said it was all right she would send the maid up with a note.

We wondered what would happen that day, but one of the lads said,

'It does not matter what this Major does to us, he will not break our spirits. Our Army is in this country and that is good enough for me.' Quite a few of the lads agreed with him.

One lad said that he understood I had been taken prisoner in November 1941. He said that he had been taken at Gaslala and put in a pen in Derna.

'That is where we were taken the next day,' I said, 'and we slept, or tried to sleep, with soaking wet ground sheets at a place called Acroma.'

'I was taken just before then, as that was our next objective, to fall back and hold, but Jerry overran us in the morning.'

Just then there was movement. The German officer mounted his white horse and came towards us. We went inside and told the others, and I decided I would go to the toilet as God knew when our next stop was. We formed up in threes and off we went with sandwiches wrapped in paper. This time it was about three miles before we were told to turn round. We wondered how long this was going to go on. The maid came with a note saying we could not have any fruit, which was a shame as there was lots of food to which we could help ourselves. There was no supper so it was early to bed again. One of the Italian soldiers jumped onto his bed and then came a bang – someone must have taken the laths out of his bed. He was the one with the rollers in his hair.

The next day was much the same except the march was about four miles each way. We were marching quite as well as if we were on a proper march and we thought that the people would see us and know we were not downhearted. This time we whistled 'Lilli Marlene', and even the Germans joined in so at least we had something in common. We were certainly feeling the strain of these last few days of marching as we had had very little to eat. The first world war songs put new spirit into us, with 'Colonel Bogie'.

The next day after the usual morning routine the Major said something in German and two of his soldiers went to the trees and brought us pears and peaches in their pockets and we ended up with two pears and a peach each. We were surprised, and thought this really must be our last day there. We went on the usual route to the village and put a lot of effort into our marching, pushing out our arms as far as we could. The officer seemed pleased and made his horse prance along to our whistling and everyone seemed to be enjoying himself. After the third mile I took out a pear from my pocket as it was getting very hot and it quenched my thirst well. At about the fifth mile the Major stopped and made us turn around; we just could not believe it. The woman had not expected us back and so there was no supper so I was glad I had saved an extra sandwich and the fruit helped a great deal.

The next day the performance was much the same. We were each given two pears and two peaches and the woman gave us extra sandwiches and stood waving us goodbye, perhaps for the last time. In the village some people started to clap us on our way. We had a break at the third mile and I ate a peach; it was a canny sized one and very juicy. This was better than water as you always drink too much and need the toilet. We came to a gap in the hedgerow and the officer got off his horse and went though and we all followed and there was plenty of cover for us to do our business; he said we all had to go as he would not stop again. After the fifth mile back we turned again. We were really tired and might not get back before dark and he was really trying to push us but suddenly the front ones began to slow down. He shouted at them but they took no notice. He could shout but he could not make our legs go faster. The sun went down over the mountains and it was pitch black and we stepped up a bit. We had to grope our way round when we finally reached the billet.

The 13 September was the same only this time we marched seven miles each way. Everyone was disappointed at not finally going to Germany. The officer must have thought we were fit men, but we were not because of the treatment we had had; had it not been for the Red Cross parcels the majority would have been dead by then. This time it was so dark when we got back that we fell into a lot of trees but luckily no one was hurt.

The day after that we started out quite early and without any breakfast; the women were waiting at the farmhouse however to give us a glass of milk and sandwiches for the day and we had peaches and pears and grapes in our pockets. We all said thank you for looking after us so well. My thoughts of Edie kept me going as we marched. We needed a toilet break and if he did not halt us soon we would have to do it ourselves with a whisper along to the people at the front. We had decided that someone at the front would collapse and that would stop the march. So that's what happened, and people gathered round and while they were seeing to him we could relieve ourselves as we had at Bari. The German kept shouting at us but we just said we have a man down; then he got up and shook his head and said he was all right and we started the march again. We kept right on into the tenth mile and about 2 kilometres from Bolzano. All of a sudden he said 'Halt!' and we all jumped straight into the hedge, only just in time. We sat on the side of the road and had a sandwich and quite a long break. I could have just gone to sleep.

All of a sudden he was telling everybody that today we were going to Germany and that we just had to march the last couple of kilometres to Bolzano and then could have time to ourselves. As we approached the town we could see houses and then railway lines going south and north; we certainly would not be going south. Someone had heard that the Brenner Pass was blocked as it had been bombed but we would have to wait and see. We went across the bridge and around to the left and there were saw lots of British and Italian prisoners and other nationalities, and there was scarcely a place to sit. Some people made a space for us.

'Here you are, mate, you all look shattered.'

'We are,' I said.

'How far have you come?'

We said, 'Twelve miles and only two stops but we made it three as we got one of the lads to collapse.'

The other lad said that there had been a landing at Salerno in the south of Italy.

Then we saw the train coming towards us and we could not believe it: it was cattle trucks, some big and others smaller. We were going to be treated like cattle.

Chapter 17

They started to load us into the wagons. On the top of the trucks were soldiers with machine guns and there were plenty on the ground as well. They rounded up the people like cattle, pushing and shoving them inside and locking them. I was with a few people who were at the farm and a lot of strangers. There was a long roll of salami which had to last two days with no water at all; luckily I had a pear and a peach to fall back on but I would try to keep them for later. The cattle truck was dry with a small hole in the corner for people to relieve themselves. It was going to be one hell of a smell, but at least there was fresh air coming through the gaps.

It was dark by the time they pulled away as there was very little twilight there. Whistles started blowing and we could hear the engine pulling away. Someone said, 'Where were you taken prisoner?'

I said, 'At El Duda, sometime in November 1941.'

'What regiment are you in?'

I said, 'What do you want to know for? I am not saying anything at all; do not ask me any more questions.'

'I just wanted to know.'

I said, 'I am really sorry, I don't want to get attached to anybody as I have had a bad time leaving my mates in another camp,' and there I left it, though he was not too pleased about it. In this sort of situation you did not know who these people were; they could be planted to get information, even if you were prisoners. Sergeant Bertram had said to be careful how you gave a person's name which could be used.

We went through the Brenner Pass into Austria and it slowed down there. We could just see flat wagons with tanks on board and we slowed down so they could pass. It became very cold indeed and was going to be a windy night. I had a piece of pear which kept my mouth from getting dry; and my last sandwich.

During the night we stopped many times to let ammunition, tanks, armoured cars pass to go south to Italy or wherever they were fighting. When we stopped it was never at a station but always in marshalling yards so nobody saw us except these soldiers who were out in great force. I had some of the German sausage for my breakfast which was hard to digest. The floor was getting wet and we would have to squat on our heels like pit men. We could hold on to an iron bar which ran right across the truck about two feet off the roof. Above us was a German soldier with a machine gun, or something like a Bren.

We moved on into the country. Some people had diarrhoea and the place was beginning to smell. We had stopped in a siding and there was a mass of troops all around the train, all armed with rifles. The signal was at red and there was no sign of movement. After two hours we moved on and picked up speed; we could hear the German soldier stamping his feet so he must have been cold up there. Then we reached the main line and the train started to go like the clappers, as if trying to make up lost time. We whizzed past villages and the countryside and then found we were slowing down again.

We still had no water and here we were facing our second night. I managed to get a little sleep. We stopped many times during the night and it was very cold indeed, the wind just cutting through you. We lay beside each other and tried to keep warm as best we could. Having very little clothing did not help. I had my last piece of German sausage for breakfast. The floor was getting worse – when the train went on a slant to the right at least the urine and the diarrhoea went down the hole but the more solid faeces could not. They promised us food every two days, but this had not happened. We had now been on the train two and three quarter days with no water.

It was seven o'clock and the train was still going on; the Germans could not be trusted, just like the Italians: tomorrow never comes. There was very little light left; then all of a sudden the train started to slow down and we saw troops right round it; then it pulled away into a siding. We were there past midnight and then there were many more stops during the night. Now it was 17 September 1943. Everyone was hoping we would get some food sometime that day. Every time the train stopped it did it by slamming on the brakes so we were knocked off balance.

You always tried to save yourself by putting your hands out and usually into some urine. Of course you could not wash your hands so you tried to wipe them on the slats; but your hands were still smelly. I did my best by spitting on them but my mouth was dry from the lack of water. Sometimes you ended up with wood splinters in your hand.

The train was going fast, as if the driver was in a race. We rested as well as we could but there was not much room with forty-five of us on board; and everyone was talking about food. Well after dinner time this day we stopped in a marshalling yard and troops started to open the doors. When they reached us they handed out German sausage and one of them said in English that it was two days' rations. Someone shouted out that this was the first since we had left Italy but he did not say anything and just kept dishing out the sausages. I just had a small piece then as I did not want to be sick and our stomachs had shrunk anyway. There was still no sign of water. It was some time before we moved off and now we must have had a proper driver as it just kept going nice and steady.

After what would have been teatime, a storm started up – just what we needed. It pelted down with rain and came through the slats so we had more water on the floor. But at least we could get a drink – we cupped our hands to try and get some in and just kept licking their hands. I tried to wash my hands first as there might be germs on them and you had to take precautions at all times. Then I had a drink and it was luxury after all that time. It was raining very heavily and sometimes a gust of wind would catch the rain and it would come through the slats with a vengeance. Then we stopped in a siding and I tried to get some sleep.

We were there for over four hours and as we moved off some were soaking with the rain but at least we had had a drink. Some of us tried to move around to keep warm and we could not lie down as the floor was soaking. Everybody would be pleased when it was daylight and we could see where we were going. Some people had no coats at all, just shirts and shorts full of holes. At least I had a good jacket and I had some sausage left as I had saved some of mine. The rain was easing off and we had a drink just in case it stopped, and washed our hands. Some had been to the corner which was now loaded but what did the Germans care? They were treating us just like cattle and were keeping their distance as we must have smelled terrible. At least they were getting wet; it served them right.

Suddenly the troops were dispersed and the train started to move and it was gathering speed. We passed a lot of villages and diverted round a large town so the German people would not see us in our state. Again we went onto a slip line and came to a stop and were amazed to see baskets of food arriving. They started distribution and each end of the train and we were happy at this. I went to the corner then and had to use part of my trousers to wipe myself; I managed to get my hands washed and have a drink while it was still drizzling though it took some time.

That night was very nasty as the rain started heavily again. We had now been travelling for some days and it was 19 September. It was very dark out there, not a glimmer of dawn breaking. The train started to slow down and we wondered if this could be the last stop; we saw a light in the sky and it was the moon coming through the clouds. We stopped in a marshalling yard and again there was a mass of troops with rifles and machine guns; they looked like young ones this time. I put my hands through the slats to wash them and to get some rainwater to drink; God always works in mysterious ways; no one gave us water to drink so he provided us with some. After that the train seemed to be going at a good speed as if trying to make up time and I tried to find a space to have some sleep and dropped off soundly.

When I woke up another lad asked if he could have my place; I said, 'Of course,' and he was sound asleep by the time I got back from the corner. It was good to take turns. This was the seventh night on the train. In the morning I had my last piece of sausage and asked the lad with the watch what the time was. I said he must be sick of me asking, but he said, 'Not at all, it gives me something to do as I am very bored with travelling.'

'I think everyone is bored sick,' I said. 'If only we knew where we were going it would be great.'

It was now 2.30 and we were on a branch line to somewhere; there were villages and farms. The train was steaming along just as if it was on a main line. It slowed down at last and through the slats were could see a large camp and people there looking at us. People started getting out of the trucks and going towards the main gate; well, at least we should be getting food of some kind. When they got to us my legs were like jelly. We formed into threes and marched us through the gates, but the Italians were put into a compound away from this one.

Chapter 18

We were put into different blocks, wherever there were spaces, and I ended up with the chap I had met first on the train; there was something strange about him but I could not put my finger on it. One of the lads on the other side asked where I had come from.

'Italy,' I said, 'on the east coast at Brindisi, then Bari, Rimini, and Bolzano.'

'You've been around.'

''Do we get any food?'

'I'm sorry,' he replied, 'we have had ours; we get no breakfast, just dinner and teatime. You get three potatoes each time, not fit for pig swill; the tea you get when we run short of parcels is terrible and the coffee not very nice. Which way did you come?'

'Through the Brenner Pass in these cattle trucks.'

'When did you leave them?'

'Seven nights and six days ago. What do you call this place?'

'It's called Moosburg. It's not a bad camp and we get parcels though sometimes you have to wait a week or so.'

Then I told him about Brindisi and the Italian food we had to live on but then just wanted to lie down and have a sleep. I was in a top bunk with a blanket a pillow and a palliasse. Across the room were lines of washing. I had a good sleep, the best since the farm in Italy. For dinner there was just three potatoes but we might get a parcel between two. The lad with the watch was sharing with his mate and I was left with the strange inquisitive one.

A lad said, 'Do you fancy a cup of tea?'

'Yes, if you can spare it. That will be the first for over a month.'

'Never,' he said. 'How was that?'

'Well, the place we were at did not have parcels at all; in fact we did not need them as we had all the food we could eat plus as much fruit as we wanted.'

'You lucky beggars.'

'Yes, but the last eight or nine days when the Germans took over were very different. They made us march every day and finally we marched to Bolzano and boarded the cattle trucks. Where have you been?'

'Oh, a few places, all of them in Germany, but this is the best so far.'

The time was now 12.30; I couldn't believe it but he said I had woken late that morning; I must have been all in. Just then two lads came in with a German guard and a big pot; inside were boiled potatoes. They dished out three each and the lad had been right; they were not fit for pig swill and by the time you had torn out the bad bits there was very little left. I said, 'Right, if they can eat them so can I, and as I have had nothing since yesterday I will end up in a hole somewhere if I do not eat them. Beggars cannot be choosers.'

The lad again said, 'Here's a cup of tea,' and I thanked him very much. He said, 'This is what comradeship is about, helping each other. When I told him I felt tired, he suggested a lie down and asked how long I had been on the cattle truck. I told him all about it and about the people who had dysentery and he thought they might have been taken to the camp hospital.

'The Red Cross sometimes send pills, not always, but at least they will get looked after properly as these lads are medically trained by the Army and have Red Cross emblems on their shoulders. They have been with us all the time.'

A German guard came in with a list and an interpreter and we four newcomers had to follow him. Outside were a few people and he told us that we were to be issued with a parcel, one between two. We stood in a queue but it did not take long and we would be able to have a good English meal for a change. Later we were given two potatoes and a loaf of bread between eight; an independent person cut it up so there could be no bickering. I was stuck with this lad; so I cut up a tin of corned beef and gave him first choice, then I took the rest. I got hold of the knife as the bread was a bit thick and I cut it in two so I could put a good slice of corned beef on each. We made a cup of tea, borrowing the other lad's gear.

I went to the toilet and everything was all right and good after the days on the cattle truck. On the second morning I slept till ten o'clock and had another good wash as I smelled terrible. I had washed my clothes the day before and when I had gone for the parcels a lad from another block said, 'Hang on and I'll get you a pair of trousers as one of the lads died last week; but he did not die in them as he was in the camp hospital.' I said I would be very glad of them as I had been wearing these since I was captured in the desert in 1941.

'By, that's a long time.'

'I cannot thank you enough.'

'That's all right because they were too long for anyone in our block.'

I put them on straight away and they fitted round the waist lovely but just a bit too long so I turned them up. Someone gave me thread and a needle and it did not take long to tack them up.

The odd lad and I had had a cup of tea yesterday and he put two spoonfuls of sugar in his cup whereas I had one, but this I did not mind. At dinner time he had opened a tin of Spam and cut in in two but also had first pick and so I said than in future any sharing would be done by someone else. He did not know what to say; he thought he would get one over me. I took most of the bad bits out of the potatoes and threw them away; I had to be careful having had dysentery twice.

Much later a chap came in and said, 'I have the latest news.' He said that in Italy everything was going fine, and from there, different places in Germany and France were being bombed. The nice lad said that the clothes lines were for the radio but they could only use it at certain times of the day as there were always people around trying to catch us out. They called the guards 'goons'. a word I had never heard before.

The other lad said he wanted some more from the parcel, but I said no, that we would have to save some for other days as otherwise we would be on German rations; he saw it my way eventually but it took a lot of persuading. Two lads came in with our potatoes for tea; they were on a rota and the guard came with them and took the bowls back. I had a biscuit and then was going to have an early night but some people next to me were playing Monopoly which had been sent out by some organisation. It was the first time I had seen it and seemed to be a very exciting game. I watched them for a while before going up to my bunk.

After a few days I knew the routine. I got someone else to divide our food and with a piece of black bread I saved for my breakfast I had some butter and jam. We had two roll calls a day which lasted just over an hour each, a lot better than in Italy. There was very little therefore to do but have a stroll round the compound which was quite big as we were right out in the countryside. It was well fortified with a machine gun post at each end and in the middle of each side; the fence was quite high with rolls of barbed wire all along and at night there were dogs patrolling to make sure nobody escaped. Each day there was news time and we heard about developments on the various fronts. The Russian front was at a standstill but in Italy we were doing very well, pushing on towards Rome.

When we got our potatoes they were not too bad and I got the other lad to open a tin of sardines for us and we split each fish down the middle to put beside them.

Just then the interpreter came in and said that the next day an officer would come and give the names of people who were to go to another camp, and they were to take as little as possible with them. He went on to the next room until the whole billet was told. Mail and parcels came and I just sat on the side of my bunk with my feet dangling and it was not long before I was in bed for the night.

The next day was lovely and sunny. I slept well and in the morning made tea with the lad's gear which was a tin with an element inside so you could plug it into a bulb socket and it boiled the water in quick time. I went for a stroll round the compound, remembering the walks I had with Jimmy Hurst in Italy, but I did not want to get involved with anyone else. Then it was time for roll call; we formed into groups of five and the interpreter said that before the roll call he was going to call out the names of people who would be moving on. He started calling names and some I had heard before as they were in the truck I had been in; and eventually he called my name. I shouted, 'Here,' and he went on reading them. He said that all those whose names had been called had to go to the main gate that afternoon. We saw the cattle trucks again and by 2.30 we were all aboard.

Another nightmare to go through. We were given a roll of sausage out of a basket; they counted us and then the engine pulled away.

A lot of trains were passing us laden with guns and tanks, perhaps for the Russian front. We passed a small station where people were waiting for their local train and they must have thought we were cattle heading for the abbatoir. Again there was no water and it looked as if this journey was to be like the last one. At least it was warmer now and I had long trousers which would feel better.

We kept moving, sometimes stopping in a siding or moving along a branch line, and then there were a lot of trains and we must be going through a marshalling yard on the outskirts of a town. At least we were moving and that was better than standing still. I decided to find a place to put my head down as it was lovely and dry at the moment. If we could get two days without a wet floor that would be good.

On the second night, 30 September, I woke up through the night to go to the corner and found we were travelling again fast so we must have been on a main line. Dawn was breaking and it was looking like a nice day. I went back to the area I was sleeping in and just flopped down and lay there; the train thundered on and sometimes made a clicking noise as we went over crossings. I decided to eat my sausage lying down as it was more comfortable than standing. Suddenly we seemed to go onto another branch line but there was no one in sight. I had another sleep and when I woke up it was afternoon, a lovely day with just a gentle breeze. I spat on my hands and tried to clean them and I had a few splinters in my hand from rubbing them on the laths; but I still carried my needle and thread and would get them out at the next stop. In the evening we ran into a marshalling yard and again there were soldiers all around There were baskets of food all round and they were running around with torches with a cross cut in the glass, the way ours at home were. Eventually we got served and everyone sat down and ate their food, leaving a bit for the next day.

As I ate my last piece of sausage the next day I was talking to Harry, the lad next to me. He said, 'How do you get premonitions?'

'I can't answer the question, sorry.'

Harry was very worried about his wife as he had just found out that he was a father. He had been caught at the foot of Italy and had left England in December 1942. He had only been married a couple of months before he was given orders to join his regiment. He had received a letter from his wife a few days before but was taken by truck to the station the next day. He had been put on a cattle truck, to northern Italy, then to Moosburg early this year. He sent his card and letter then. He said it was good talking to someone, though I didn't say anything out of the ordinary.

'How long have you been a prisoner?' Harry asked, so I told him, and that this was my third time missing.

'You must be joking,' he said.

'This is very real,' I answered, but he could not believe it.

I looked out and saw some lovely country outside. We had no idea whereabouts we were but it felt like dinnertime. I saw a lad looking at his watch and he said it was just gone 1.30. Later the train stopped and Harry and I decided to have something to eat as it was apparently 5.30; the lad with the watch said he would shout out the time from time to time so it would stop people asking every five minutes. The floor of the truck was still dry as no one had diarrhoea and other stuff the person tried to push the hole with his boot and then cleaned his boot on the bottom of the truck. It was much better than last time but it might not last. At seven o'clock the train started moving again and at 9.20 I settled down for the night.

Next day was much the same. Harry and I talked about different things: about his marriage. He asked if I was married and I said I had been too young and my girlfriend was only seventeen though now she must be twenty. He said that he and his wife just made it; he was twenty-three and she just turned twenty-one years old. I told him that we had been going to get married in Scotland but I had been put on a ship; and he said, 'What a shame.'

The lad with the watch said it was 11.30 and shortly after that the train slowed down and we were in a marshalling yard. We looked out for the baskets and there were plenty of them so everyone would something to eat for the next few days.

I asked, 'Did you have a son or a daughter?'

'A son,' he said.

I took hold of his hands and shook them and wished him a happy life with his family when he got home, and he thanked me.

Again there was no sign of water. We all knew we should have it though sometimes we went ages in the desert without it, sometimes putting tablets in it to try to make it drinkable but it didn't work; even the tea was made with salty water. I got my ration and the troops started putting the baskets tidily away and we hoped we would get moving, but no; they were just standing around in quite a nice day.

Harry said, 'Have you had any letters from her?'

'No, I am afraid I have not.'

'Do you know why?'

I said, 'At this moment I want to keep this to myself, because I am afraid I may have lost her. I have so much to sort out when I get home.'

'That is a shame, when the two of you were going to get married.'

'Something happened along the way,' I said. 'Well, all right, I will tell you,' and went on to recite the story of the Dear John letter.

Harry said to me, 'Whoever did that should be ashamed of themselves; playing about with people's lives. That must be heartbreaking.'

I did not tell him any more but he said he thought I must be an unlucky person. I said to myself that he did not know the half of it.

He asked me a few more questions but I said, no more, that was final.

He said that he was really sorry if he had upset me, and I said I would like to say more but it was very upsetting, and we left it at that.

The next morning we had been on the train for five days and four nights. It was getting very boring in the truck but at least the floor was dry. The engine was quite big and there was one also on the back of the train. We wondered if this would save time, particularly if there was no turntable in the marshalling yard. We looked out of the left hand slats for a change, and my companion said how nice it would have been if we were on holiday.

'I do miss my wife very much,' said Harry. 'Had you known your girlfriend long?'

'I met her on my twentieth birthday and she was just sixteen in May 1941.'

'You did not know her long.'

'If you love someone it does not matter if it is an hour, a day or years, I knew what I wanted and I want to marry her as soon as I get home, which I hope is not long. And I hope you and I get back in one piece.'

Having a chat along the way really made the time pass more quickly. Harry asked me about my travels in captivity and I recited the places but did not really want to talk about it. I discovered he came from Norfolk where he had worked on a farm. We both thought of how lovely would be a cup of tea, with or without sugar. I told him about my escape from the ship when we were torpedoed.

Eventually the train started again and I fell fast asleep, rocked by the movement, but the lad woke me again later saying it was past dinner time. He said he had had his but thought I would like to get up before the floor got wet in our area. I showed him how to sit on our heels like my father did down the pit: you just put your bottom on the heel of your boot and it was quite comfortable. As the sun went down and we were resting against the side of the truck I was telling him how I could hardly write and do sums; this was because I was left handed but they made me use my right; they made me do work over and over again and sometimes made me cry. I was nearly ten before I could do up my shoes and when I went to the Modern school I was still getting into trouble for using my left hand. I started work in August 1934 when I was fourteen and worked on the screens at the pit head for 5s. 6½d. a week; the next job was on the railway at Percy Main Depot, three or four miles away when I was the only person working in our household, so I decided on the pit.

On 5 October we had been on the train for six nights and were into the seventh day. We had not been given any food for a long while. Now I told my companion about the ship from Greece when we had waited to sail with no food for a very long time. And these people on the train were complaining about no food for a few hours.

'Is that why you always try to keep food as long as you can? Now I understand.'

The train kept going and that afternoon we started down a single line and then saw lots of trees and a few houses; and then all of a sudden we saw a camp and a large one at that; within a few minutes the train pulled up and we saw different nationalities in different compounds. The troops started to open the doors and the German troops made us form into threes and march in through the gates though it was ages till we got out.

Chapter 19

The compound we were taken to was empty and the rooms had three-tier bunks so I grabbed a bottom one and Harry, the lad from Norfolk, was two bunks away from me. All we were waiting for was food of some sort and some water. Then some lads came with steel pots with boiled potatoes which they dished out just like the last camp and then another one came with a tray of black bread and gave us a loaf between eight people. He lent us a knife to cut it.

He told us that we were in Sagan, just south of Berlin, and that this compound was emptied two days ago and the people had been sent away on working parties to a factory by the Polish border. He told us we would be getting parcels, one between two people; so that would be good and we had forms to sit on and a table to eat at, though it was rather cold; still, much better than lying on a cattle truck floor.

Next day it was cold but bright and I had kept a piece of black bread for my breakfast. I tried to get to the toilets for a good wash, but everyone was in the same mind so I thought I would have a stroll before trying again later. The compound was quite long but in parts very narrow and I enjoyed it on my own thinking about Edie. When I got back to the billet they said there was to be a parade shortly so after Harry and I had been to the toilet we made our way to the top of the compound where we had to find our room sections. Just before we were dismissed by the officer we were told there would be letters or cards to send home later that day; and that parcels would be issued room by room that day or the next. All rooms had to be kept clean and would be inspected and one man had to be selected to be in charge of the room. I nominated Harry as I thought he would be good at this. He said, 'All right, and if I do not like it I will call on someone else.' We were told there would be another roll call at four o'clock and away he went.

We had our boiled potatoes for dinner and Harry said he would try to get some paper and a pencil so he could make a rota so that no one would do a job twice. While I was walking around afterwards I saw that the first billet were getting their parcels: a lot quicker than the Italians. I found the toilets empty so had a good wash in cold water and dried myself with my jacket. In the billet Harry said that I would be getting the food parcels tomorrow and told me that parade would be in ten minutes. He said he was exempt from roll calls but that he would come up later and talk to the interpreter to see if he could get some paper and pen not to mention a knife so we could cut our own bread.

After a few days like this we had received our parcel and also letters and cards to send home. At least they would know we were in Poland now even though they would take a few weeks to get there. I asked Harry to share with me but he had already found someone so I had to share with someone else. This lad complained as I put jam and butter on the bread I had saved but I said that was his fault, not keeping any bread, but said he could have a biscuit or two and I would have mine later. At dinner time we opened a tin of sardines and I mixed my half with the potatoes but he had his separately; he asked if he could try mine and said that it really did taste better like that with the oil as well. We made a cup of tea in someone else's contraption; it was a tin you put water in and then plugged into the wall: a long wire like an element. I still had the cup I had in Italy for my tea. We were issued with twenty cigarettes each too; the first draw nearly took my breath away as it was the first since I left Italy.

Roll calls lasted about an hour and a quarter: much better than the Italians at counting. Harry eventually got his pencil and paper but not a knife.

The next date to record was 22 October 1943 and there had been the same routine every day in this camp which was called a Stalag, Sagan 8C. We had now finished all our Red Cross rations and were back to German food. Before the roll call the officer spoke to the interpreter who told us that names would be called out for work parties the next day. There would be thirty names and they would travel in three covered trucks. Harry was called and much later so was I. Harry said later that he was amazed as he had heard about this as a rumour and now it had come true; mostly rumours were wrong. I did hope it was not to the mines but he said we were going to a factory. At that point the lads came round with the usual rations. The lad with the boiling contraption said he would boil anyone's water but they had to bring their own. I borrowed a tin to carry water in but brought back enough for four people so we could have some water to drink when it cooled down; better not to drink it from the tap.

We were told that any mail that arrived at the camp would be sent on to the factory and that we would receive letters and cards to send home. But there was no talk of Red Cross parcels.

I got up early the next day and had a nice wash-down and used my jacket to dry myself. I waved it around to try to dry it as it might be cold on the truck. The lad with the boiler heated some water for me and he said it could be my last drink for a while; so I thanked him and he said, 'No bother, mate, this is what comrades do and we are all in the same boat.' I had my piece of bread with my warm water.

The trucks were very warm indeed so I just took off my jacket and sat on it. When we hit the main road we sailed along, lovely and smooth; we stopped a good many times, perhaps because of traffic but we kept going and arrived in the late afternoon.

We all got off the truck and were led to our billets. There were double bunks this time in a middle sized room and within half an hour we were given food: the equivalent of two slices of black bread each and three boiled potatoes: a lot of black bits in them but we were so hungry we ate the lot. Later we were given a cup of tea; whatever it was made from it was terrible, but we just nipped our noses and took it. Then we sorted ourselves out and I managed a bottom bunk; and the toilet was just along the block which was handy. We were given a blanket, a pillow and a palliasse. This was an unknown place.

The interpreter then said that we would be woken at 5.15 to start at six o'clock and would work through to six o'clock at night, but that on Saturday and Sunday we would be doing eighteen hours. The meal would be at at 12 o'clock at night when there would be soup and there would be potatoes and bread during the day. There would also be night shifts of twelve hours. If we did not wake up for our meals we would not get them.

I was detailed with another lad to go where they were offloading sugar beet. You had to use your hands to take all the sugar beet away till there was a hole so you could use the prong fork with steel balls on each prong, as when you started with the wagon, with snow and ice on them, they just slid across the sugar beet, and you had to do it with each wagon. They were old fashioned wooden carts drawn by just one horse and the driver was Dutch. I used a fork with a steel ball bearing on each prong to prevent the beet getting damaged. I had to throw the beet to two lads who had to take the leaves off and they put these leaves on the outside of a grid while the beet itself went through a hole in the middle to be chopped. It was very hard at first but easier once you got a hold of it. Sweat was pouring off me but the driver just sat there, smoking his pipe. When I did get to the bottom it was all ridges of wood, which made it worse as you did not know how far they were apart.

The next cart to come in had a French driver and he too sat smoking as though he had not a care in the world; this cart had sides on and it was hard to get at the sugar beet. All the carts seemed as old as the hills and the next one to come was driven by a Pole. 'Engländer?' he said. 'Yes,' I answered, and we left it at that. This cart was not so full and it was easier but there were four more waiting. It was a bit cold but I still took my jacket off as it was in the way and I was hot.

I was thinking it must be dinner time but nobody had a watch. The next truck had a driver who spoke English and he said that Krupps ammunition factory was just a mile and a half from there. Eventually we saw a bunch of lads coming towards us and they were the relief. The lad who took over from me asked if we had had any break and I said 'No'; he said we would get some food when we got in.

I was on this job all week, doing twelve hours each day; then on the weekend it was eighteen hours with two half hour breaks. It was very tiring and every cart was different. On Monday I was put to cutting sugar beet tops. You had to be very careful as the knives were very sharp and with one mistake you could lose a finger or two. You didn't get anything to eat until you were finished and the tea was horrible, made from some kind of herb, and the coffee from acorns.

People said that the nearest town was Breslau and that Squadron Leader Bader, the chap with the tin legs, was somewhere here; they got information from a driver, some of whom spoke some English.

In the third week I was working on a machine non stop from start to finish doing the night shift; it was the stuff left from the roots after the sugar had been taken out and the stuff I was bagging was for animal feed; it was very light and sometimes when it came fast off the machine you dropped the bag. They were 56 lbs in weight. I had to take them off and two lads were tying them and they were going as fast as me. Within a few yards was a Polish guard with a face like a horse and you had to watch him as he had struck a lad the day before for minor things. We were sailing along nicely, going like the clappers; you did not even have time to wipe your nose. At 11.30 you had a break of half an hour or maybe only ten minutes as the guards were shouting at you to get back to work. You just got one bowl of soup which was all potatoes but better than Italian skilly.

At one point a bag fell to the ground and the guard gave me a slap with the flat part of the rifle on my lower back. I just shouted but got back on the job; I could not even hold my back which was aching like hell. I just had to ignore it and keep going or else I risked another slap, but was looking forward to a rest and a wash. Someone in the toilets said my back was in a mess with black and blue marks right across it.

In the third week I was emptying carts again. Now, however, I had a good idea of how to do this; once you broke into the cart you had to make a decent hole and the beet just rolled towards you. I would have preferred to be on this job all the time as nobody bothered you unless you stopped for a good while. This was warm work and shortly we would be getting bad weather and that was why they were hurrying to get as much done as possible. You did not have time to relax or have a chat with your mates; the only time was your half hour break. The days were getting shorter and there were lights all over the place and we hoped we did not have an air raid as with Krupps just down the road we would all be blown to kingdom come.

Someone said that a Polish driver had told him that the Russians had the Germans on the run which was good news and gave our morale a lift.

I got few blisters on my hands and what I did was to pee on them until they stung and then gave them a good wash then burst them with a needle later. This was meant to stop them scarring and there must have been something in it.

That day I did all of seven carts and had just started on the eighth which would give my relief a good start; then it was not long before we had our meal. One of the lads detailed to this duty was Harry who asked how I was. I told him I really wanted some salt for my hands and he said, 'You are dead right, I always believe in salt as it soothes sores very much.'

In the fifth week it was back to cutting leaves off turnips at the grid and I was on the right side which was better than before because I could use either hand. On the Sunday afternoon I was on till 6 o'clock the next morning and then back for 6 p.m. on Monday night. It was all work and sleep. It was bitterly cold with weather coming straight from the Russian steppes according to the driver who had just pulled away. I had my dinner and whilst the lad who relieved me was away I just thought if I got back inside the first cart I would get warm again. When he came back he said this was the first time in his life he had had to use any kind of fork or shovel. I said I had been doing it since I was 12½ years old, moving 15 cwts of coal for people and only asking sixpence so that I could go to the cinema. At Shiremoor if you did not work you got nowhere at all and many times I used to put my mother's coal into the coalhouse.

Here we were into December 1943 and Christmas just round the corner. I was in the factory again with the horse-faced guard. The pace was not too bad as I was getting used to it. The lads who were tying the bags were also doing well and then the bags had to be wheeled away to the end of the building where we were waiting for a wagon. I stacked them as well as I could but the machine started over-spilling onto the floor and the guard hit me again, just above where he had hit me last time. I managed to get up and start again but the machine kept on over-spilling and I tried my best to clear it with the terrible pain. The lads said they would try to clear things up a bit. They said, 'Go on, have your break, we will have ours later.' They had taken a lad away.

I had just one scoop of cold soup; some people always took a bit more so that when the last people came there was none left. It is a shame when someone takes a ration from someone else. At the end of the day

I got a lovely wash down in cold water which did take the sting out of it. I got three hours sleep before being woken for dinner time.

For the second week in December I was back on unloading carts. This might be our last eighteen-hour shift as they must have all the sugar beet harvested as the ground had a very heavy frosts. I had the lads with me that I had had before. There seemed to be only four carts to be emptied so maybe we could have a break. The three of us together was just great, to have someone to talk to for a change. They said if only you keep a steady pace we can cope. This driver was one who could speak a bit of English and I asked him how the war was getting on. He said that a lot of German soldiers had been caught by the Russians though he did not know where; that was good news; and Italy was still fighting. The next truck was a difficult one with a bad bottom, a bar of wood across every foot so I took my time digging in and as soon as I got a couple of feet in the beet started to roll towards me. The next one had side boards which were a bit of a problem and I had to do it by hand for a good while until I was deep enough to work with the fork. Just as I was halfway through I saw another two carts approaching. They would be for the night shift, however, and to my relief I saw the two lads approaching.

As December continued the loads became smaller as the frost was hindering them. If the sun came out it helped the people in the fields but if it snowed there would not be any beet coming out of the ground at all. We had very little food and one shift there was no soup left for me which was a long time to wait for something to eat especially on the grid again. We had three potatoes each; they were cold so it did not matter when we had them. But this bloke came on the scene and started to tell one lad to hurry his dinner as he had another job for him in the factory. We ate all the potatoes, black bits and all. We took turns emptying the carts as it gave my back a bit of a rest and then the other lad said he would do the emptying and I could stay at the grid.

He was halfway through the cart when our relief came. I was standing outside when three lads started talking to me. One said, 'Come and have a fight with me, I am a boxer.'

'I am not,' I said.

The other two lads kept saying, 'Come on, have a go,' and I said, 'No, can you take a telling?'

He hit me again so I just lifted my left hand and grabbed him by the throat and he dropped to the ground. The other two fled as their mate was out on the deck; they must have thought I was a pushover. I never saw them again. I think they got the message that I was not a fighter but a lad who had been trained in combat tactics.

It was nearly Christmas and we still had not had any letter forms to send home so our families would be wondering where we were after the mail we sent from Stalag 8C at Sagan. If only I could send a Christmas card to Edie as I had not done this since 1940.

Eventually the chap who was always spying on us and who spoke English came onto the scene and said, 'I am quite pleased with your work. You are finished now. You can have Christmas Day and Boxing day off and the next few days as well as at the moment no sugar beet will be processed until next year as we have nearly all the crop in. You can stay in the billets but you will be going to another factory soon. '

So we could relax a bit for the next few days. The lads asked how my back was and I showed them and they said it was still black and blue; it was a wonder I had not broken a bone. They said that guard seemed to have it in for me.

The chap who had been spying on us came and said, 'Could you come with me.' He took me right through the factory; it was a beautiful and clean place. We spent a good while then he asked me where I was from and I said 'Northumberland.' When we got to the top end he said, 'It is a lovely factory,' and I agreed.

Then we had a good rest for a few days before being taken off in three trucks to the next one on 4 January 1944. Again there were thirty men.

These new billets had three-tier bunks and a fire at the back of the room, with coal and wood outside in the corner and a small pail to carry it in. It was very dirty indeed; the people who had been here before must have lived like pigs. There was barbed wire all the way round and the gate was very high. On the post was a hose so if you had a shower you had many onlookers: German men, women and children but there was nothing you could do about it.

The sergeant in charge told us his name and said he wanted no one escaping as if we did we might get shot. He said he had been on the phone about rations for us and they were on their way. I had a middle bunk which was not too bad but in the corner were four buckets and when we asked what they were for he said that the door was locked every night so we had to use the buckets. He spoke canny English.

Eventually a van came with our potatoes and black bread; the sergeant cut up the loaves and the lads dished out the pigswill potatoes. They were terrible but being hungry we just ate them. Again we had no water to drink but at least something in our stomachs.

The sergeant said that we would be woken at quarter to five and outside by five o'clock and at the factory by six. Everyone had to be in bed by 9.30 and lights would be put out then. I went to bed straight away.

Using the pails was terrible and I told the rest about the situation at Bari when there was a complaint and something was done but we agreed to let a few days go by first and then talk to this German sergeant.

We left the camp at 5.15 and marched in columns of three down the road, past a lovely field then a good few houses. There were a few shops too. Then we arrived at the factory and were taken to the canteen which was run by the Germans. There were two sections: the German guards were one side and us on the other. A German girl served us with tea or coffee; the coffee was lovely and hot but with an awful taste so I left it.

We were taken to different parts of the factory. I was by myself in a small place with a round concrete roller and a strong steel round ring. He started it up and showed me how to put newspapers and cardboard boxes and rubbish into it to be chewed up. This was a tedious job, just by myself, and German workers came in with wicker baskets with paper and cardboard boxes. They just dropped them, gave me a stare, and went. Eventually a guard came to tell me to go to the canteen and I asked him the time. He showed me his watch and it said 11.55. We were allowed half an hour and got three potatoes and a thin slice of black bread; and we were all to go there again at 5.30. We went to the toilets which were in a filthy state so one lad saw this civilian guard and told him about it. He said we had better see the sergeant; and also discuss the one at the camp.

When I got back to my workplace there were loads of papers and I just took my time with them as I was not going anywhere. Then another five people came in with more baskets full and they all gave me a good stare; they must not have seen an Englishman before. I had a stupid beard as I had not had a razor or soap for a shave. I found some stones in a corner and put them in as well and they made a lovely crunching sound. I just heard the last sound when the guard came in; I was really lucky. He took me back to the canteen for the same sort of food as at dinner and then went back to the billet.

Work continued in this sort of routine all week. On the Sunday there were wagons of stones, some small and some large. We had to take them along a wooden plank quite a long way. No one had any ideas as to what they could be for. It was very hard work and sweat was rolling from us though it was very cold. As I was on the plank some stupid person threw a large stone on it and I toppled, carrying a stone in my hands. It would have been serious if I had broken an arm or leg but no one owned up. Some were so big we had to roll them. The next truck had smaller ones, say 56 lbs. After dinner we started on another truck but were taken away from it by the factory boss to a secure truck. In it were bags of sugar. Someone stayed in it to lift the bags onto our backs. All this was in snow and we were soaked through.

Next day it was still snowing and it was like a skating rink as we were taken to the factory and particularly difficult going down a small incline. It was about three and a half miles and we were frozen to the bone. We got the acorn coffee when we arrived and at least it warmed us up. We were still wet through from the day before. We continued to unload stones but it was very dangerous carrying them. The guard was frozen too and kept moving around. Eventually the boss said to just leave it. There were going to be twenty wagons coming in to this area and paper to unload. We had to carry the paper a long way; one man had to carry bundles about 80–100 lbs in weight tied up with string which gave a good grip. We must have had to walk four or five hundred yards with them in the snow. We had done four wagons and this chap came up and asked if we could do two more. Some were really heavy (110–120lbs) and took two men to carry them; sometimes they fell off our backs but this was on purpose, just to waste time. We managed to finish one more wagon which was full to the roof, which left five more for the next day.

At least the billet was snug and warm. Everyone had a detailed job in the billet: getting coal, paper from the toilet, pieces of wood from the factory. People in the paper warehouse brought paper. We all had to help each other.

The next day was the same; the civilian guard kept warm in the warehouse while we unloaded the wagons. He told us where to put the bales and it was nice to be inside while we unloaded. The heavier bales took two of us and we left those till last and we took our time going up the hill of paper. The guard sliced open the bale and we sometimes had a rummage to see if we could find anything of value but no such luck. When he came out to open another wagon the ones inside had a look too. If they found anything they had to cause a distraction perhaps by a fight and the guard would try to calm things down while the person hid what they had found. We would have to make sure it was really safe in case we were searched. We had completed the seventh wagon by the time to go to the canteen at 5.30 p.m. As we got to the door of the billet the sergeant came with bundles of letters and cards to send home. Harry asked if we could have some disinfectant for the toilet as it was in a terrible state and he said he would try to get some. The sergeant said we were to put the Malsch-on-Oder address on the mail as our post would all go through there to Sagan. He also said we might get Red Cross parcels soon.

One lad brought a piece of paper from under his bunk and it was a map, not good but a start. Harry asked who could sew well and one lad said he could and I said I could a bit. The lad said, 'See what you can do,' and we left it like that. The map was of large towns which seemed to be important but Harry said to be careful as we would all be involved if we were caught.

The next day someone signalled to cause a diversion and this chap landed me one on the nose. The guard came up and said, 'What did you do that for?'

The lad said, 'He put all the weight on my side and so I just landed him one.'

There was another signal so the lad must have got away safely, but

I could not stop my nose from bleeding so the guard just said to sit down for a while. He kept talking to me and said he had been a prisoner in the First World War, somewhere around the Wash; he worked on a farm and they were good to him and his three mates. That was why he spoke English. He said we were getting treated so badly as there was very little food and that everything was stuck in the fields with this bad weather.

My nose kept bleeding all over my jacket and I hoped it was not broken. The lad that did it apologised when I went outside and I said it was in a good cause.

Harry had cut the map into four pieces and we discussed what could be done. I tried some sewing and got a bit of paper and tried to keep a straight line, just as if I was doing a seam; and he showed me different stitches. He said we would have to work out ways to sew it into material, as we could not leave this valuable map lying around so Harry hid it. The next day I suggested trouser seams and the top band of trousers and he agreed; he also suggested lapels. Someone had an old razor so we could open the seams. During that evening Harry managed to get it all hidden in this way in the billet.

The next few days passed in much the same way as before: more wagons to unload. The snow kept off but the sky was still black. One lad, Colin, was feeling ill; if he kept on he would have to see the doctor but at least there was a doctor to see. The guard made him lie down among the papers and when he was not better, called the guard. The guard said he had to ask the sergeant; and the sergeant had to consult the officer before he could be taken to the doctor, but he was taken to the warm canteen meanwhile. He eventually went to the doctor and was back in his bunk at the billet. He was to go the next day to Sagan hospital as he had pneumonia; and was asked if he would take a bit of map with him as it might help someone to escape. Everyone shook his hand and thanked him. Just then the sergeant came in to say the parcels and cigarettes had still not arrived so it was just as well we had not started sewing. We got it done eventually that night. The lad was really ill and had a high temperature; we thought he should really have gone to hospital straight away.

That day we found a wagon full of loose paper which had to be loaded into wicker baskets so that weighed quite a bit. But we had a chance to look through the paper for anything interesting, though we decided that bales were a lot easier. We were told that parcels and post would come very soon; and one of the lads said he was going to use a card to send to the Red Cross in Switzerland to ask for some music or games: records perhaps and a gramophone, pencils and pens and ink. We also thought of jigsaw puzzles as they would pass the time in the evenings.

But three days later there was still no sign of parcels or cigarettes and the next day would be February. I was told to go back on the machine again, however, and it was nice and dry in there with no heavy lifting. I had just made a hole on one side when three Polish people came in and tipped their hats, as if to say Good Morning so I did the same to them, like a small salute. I could not find any stones to put through this time and although it was warm it was terrible with no one to talk to. Getting back to the billet was difficult with the wind blowing very hard indeed and snow coming right across the Oder from Poland; it took all your time to walk, never mind march.

But then the German sergeant came in with mail from home and twenty cigarettes each, and told us we would get Red Cross parcels the next day. That was a real morale booster, three things on one night. I had a letter from my mother who was frantic about missing me again but at least told me that the building beside the Ritz had been sold – why couldn't she have told me earlier? My last cigarette had been in October and the first one now would probably make me dizzy.

The next day the place was full of paper and cardboard; they must have been saving them up all night. I had a look at it while I was putting it into the machine in case there was anything useful. I had just made a hole in the heaps when two people came in with wicker baskets full and put them there so I could not get the fork in. I kept on rummaging in between. At least my clothes were not wet like the other lads as it was impossible to get things dry; the fire in the billet was just small, perhaps big enough to boil a can or two.

The march home was very dark with just one or two cars passing with small lights front and back. We went through Malsh on Oder and up a long rise to get back. Our parcels were there so we could have a nice cup of tea if we could find a tin big enough to boil water in, so we started with a cold tin of soup just to get the container. We had to wait our turn and we would have to make a larger tin by joining a few together which would take time. Harry seemed to know what he was doing. We could not make tea before our march to work as it took time to get the fire going.

The next day I was back to unloading trucks and was carrying bales with the lad who had punched me on the nose. He was still saying he was sorry so I told him to forget it and he shook my hand on it. He came from the Transvaal in South Africa and looked very young, and said that he was 19. He had told his sergeant that he was 18 when he had joined up but in fact was only 16. He had been captured in Tobruk in 1942. I told him I had been captured at El Duda and had fought in the Tobruk Corridor and he said he was in Cairo at that time. The two lads with him were caught with him. We kept on carrying the bales and had a rummage while the guards were elsewhere and just then he said, 'I have found another map.' He put it in his breast pocket and if he had a chance he would put it in his boot later. He just kept on chatting about South Africa; it was a lovely place where he lived with his mother and father.

We had some wicker baskets to carry which were very unwieldy but at least it was not snowing and our clothes were nice and dry for a change. We were glad to get inside the billet to a nice cup of tea at the end of the day; the South African brought out his map from his boot. It was cut it into four sections and hidden in the billet by Harry. After that whenever anyone went sick to Sagan Hospital they put them into parts of their clothes and then stamped on them till they went flat.

Quite a few days passed and then one night at 11.15 we were told to get out of our beds as someone had escaped and we were counted; it was no one from our place. It was very cold indeed; I had a blanket round me but some had rushed out with very little on. We were kept out five hours, just in time to go to the factory so they must not have caught whoever it was. Eventually they told us to get us ready for work and then we could hardly get our marching feet right. Someone told the civilian guard at the wagons that we had been up all night and warned him that we were tired out and would just take things steady. We kept trying to find some up to date news from a newspaper as the three lads from South Africa could read and speak German, but had to be careful. We were going to have a meeting about this the next day at lunch time – we took up three or four tables and the three South Africans were at the end of ours.

I had had a practice with my sewing as someone had found a piece of cloth and was shown blanket stitch; it was very interesting; the lad said he would show me how to darn socks as well. If socks were too bad he pulled them apart to get wool to darn others; nothing was ever wasted.

We were really jiggered that day and most of us falling asleep so it was early to bed that night.

The sergeant came to the billet one morning and said during the next week we might go down to the cinema at Malsh; and also that Red Cross parcels, cigarettes and mail would be with us soon so we were very happy. That day we had our meeting about the South African lads and told them that if they were caught talking in German they would be dealt with; they would have their names taken to England. Meanwhile we would keep an eye on them in their various groups. In the evening we got to the canteen at 5.45 and as we had to wait to be served, we were holding our food in our hands to eat when the guard said 'Outside.' As usual I kept my piece of bread for the next morning.

The next days were much the same; sometimes it snowed and sometimes it did not; the wagons had bales of paper weighing anything between 80 and 120 lbs. Once there was a civilian guard on and I asked him if there was any chance of some food; but he said he dared not as if he was caught he would lose his job. My back was a bit better with very little pain but I was frightened it might flare up again, and indeed it did with a very heavy bale. What could you do with no medical help or tablets to relieve the pain? When we had to fill wicker baskets we tried filling them only three quarters full as they were very heavy and explained to the civilian guard; he said we would see how it went. That night we had post and cigarettes and a parcel between two men; my card said very little except that everyone was well but that John was to go into hospital again.

At the beginning of March was our trip to the cinema. We formed columns of three to march and were told by the sergeant that we had to march properly and not talk. As we came into the town there was a group of Hitler Youth standing on either side of the road; they started spitting at us and then throwing stones and calling us names in German. We were glad when we had passed them, and then we came to the cinema. It was a matinee performance and we were the only people there. First they showed us the Russian Front and what they had achieved there; and then the desert and what had happened there, about Tobruk in 1942; it was about the places they had taken like Mersa Matruh and Bardia. They showed us tanks, armoured cars, troops and lorries in one plane; they must have thought they were wonderful but it was the same plane each time. We were in this place an hour and a half but it was better than going to work. The sergeant said he was going to bring us again in six weeks time. We got out of our seats, formed into columns and marched back. When we arrived everyone had a good laugh about the flea pit type of cinema with a very old screen.

The sergeant came and said he was going to take us down to the canteen for our dinner and we would bring back our tea with us and it was worth the trip down and back to get fed. We passed the place where the Hitler Youth had been standing and wondered if it was a put-up job. As usual we were given potatoes and were so hungry we just ate them as they were; and I had coffee as it was warm and had sugar in. Harry had a word with the sergeant about the toilet but he said it was nothing to do with him as it belonged to the factory but he would talk to them about it. So once more we lined up, this time holding our teatime meal wrapped in newspaper.

During the second week of March, the work and conditions were much the same but I felt I had a cold coming on. While on my way to the warehouse with one bale, I just stopped and sat on top of it. The guard came up and asked me how I felt. I said I felt terrible and just kept on sneezing with my head ringing with pain; it felt as if the sweat was pouring out of me. He told me to just lie there for a while; I was quite dizzy. He said he would talk to the sergeant about me and thought I had flu; maybe a day in the billet would help. I was shivering and just could not keep warm though I was inside. Two lads came and put bales close to me to keep out the draught from the door. They were very good to me, being a loner; I did not think they would care but they did and I appreciated it very much.

The sergeant said that if I felt no better I could stay in the billet the next day and either he would leave a guard with me so that I could go out to the toilet, or he would lock me in. I marched at the back of the file going back in case I had to drop out, but I made it although it was hard keeping up and I was never so glad as seeing that gate. I must have fallen asleep straight away as it was dark when I woke up to go to the toilet.

I did go to work the next day as I felt a bit better; the sleep and a good sweat may have helped. We saw an engine on the other line taking a large wagon down to the warehouse area. They started loading it from the warehouse side. Much later the guard and driver came to couple up the engine. The door would not open as it was frozen so someone got a piece of iron and started hacking at it. But the guard forgot to move his left hand and the door jammed on his fingers and he lost four parts of them. There was blood everywhere and he was shouting. The civilian guard came out and one of the lads told him to get some string to use as a tourniquet, to stop the bleeding. He just lay against the wagon till it was tied then was taken to the hospital in Malsh. We continued but the driver could not move the engine as he had no guard.

When we got back there were parcels, one between two, mail and ten cigarettes each. Everyone was really pleased. I had a nice English meal and a cup of tea with milk and sugar, and read my post from my mother and a card from Eva and Mary.

On the last day of March when we were having our cup of coffee Harry was chatting to some of the lads in the canteen and saying that anyone who could not read, write or do sums should get in touch with him at dinner time. I said I would not mind and he said the more the merrier.

Next morning I asked to go to the toilet and I just could not believe it. The place had been cleaned and disinfected. The other amazing thing was that I saw Colin, the lad who had gone sick a while before, sitting at the next table which would take our total up again and help a bit. He told us that it had been pneumonia and that he had stayed in the camp hospital till he recovered and was then sent to a billet for a few weeks. Very early that morning he had been put on a train with a guard, handcuffed, until he arrived back at 11.45 as this was a long jouorney.

I had a word with Harry about his class and told him I would not mind joining them as I felt a bit backward and explained the reason. He said there would be six of us and it would be for three nights a week. Someone found a large piece of cardboard to use in the lessons and he asked the civilian guard if it would be all right to take it.

Now we were into April 1944. Four Polish lads and a German had made some schnapps and in the morning were dead, according to the sergeant. Spring was starting and there were lumps of ice floating in the Oder and at least we could march without slipping all over the place.

I was taken to the place where you put in logs that were bark free; there was a good heap of them in the alleyway. He said, '*Langsam*' and '*Schnell*' (slow and fast) but I decided to reverse the commands. After two hours he came back raging with temper because I had gone slow when he said fast and vice versa. He said 'Do you speak German?' and I said, 'No,' He took me back to the wagons. I never told anyone about this as sometimes Germans speaking English could get into camps and you could be taken away and thrashed.

Harry took one subject at a time and made it interesting and simple. He had patience with everyone and never rushed anybody. We asked the civilian guard if we could take pieces of blank paper to use for writing and he said we had to show him before we left the building. Only one person could carry it and he would tell the sergeant. It was another way of rummaging without being caught, looking for a map or newspaper headlines.

A few days later coming out of the canteen Patrick collapsed. One of the guards came and asked him what was wrong but there was no response. When he came to he said that he had a pain in his stomach so they put him inside the canteen where it was warm. He was taken back to the billet. We started unloading and someone signalled he had found something, so someone found a piece of blank paper and asked him if he could put it beside the door and managed to get the secret piece into his pocket. That evening we concentrated on a hiding place in the billet, and Patrick did take two pieces with him to Sagan.

The next day the sun was shining and lo and behold the first long boat appeared pulling another, with logs and other materials. This might release traffic on the busy roads. I went with another lad to the toilets, unescorted as they were short of guards, and he found an elderberry bush and took most of the leaves off. As we came round the corner we saw one of the girls from the canteen and a soldier who was disabled as he must have been shot. They went into different toilets. The lad found a small hole in the walls and managed to tickle their buttocks with his stick. They rushed out but we were back in other toilets and came out adjusting our trousers as if we had just come out. We later had a good laugh as she was trying to keep her skirt up and he had his trousers round his ankles.

On Saturday was our next trip to the cinema. Again the Hitler Youth were waiting for us to spit and throw stones; we just put up our hands to shield our faces and were pleased when we had passed them, just stupid hooligans. The films showed Rumania, Bulgaria and what they had achieved, right to the outskirts of Moscow, then switched to the desert They showed pictures of lots of troops grouped together to make more men, all propaganda. We were bored stiff as they showed the films for an hour and a half and we had seen parts before. The rest of the day we spent looking through the barbed wire at a German girl sunbathing on her verandah in just a bra and pants. Someone heard she was a German actress. Then the sergeant came and made us strip naked to have a shower with the hosepipe in the compound; it was very embarrassing as girls, kids and women passed so usually we had showers in the evening after work.

We six asked Harry if he would give us a lesson, to put the night in, and he put on the white board places each of us had been in. We needed to rummage for a dictionary to help us. I was learning a lot and it opened my eyes as to what education was all about.

We had worked out a new method for emptying trucks and it paid dividends: one man was on the truck filling baskets and two were taking them away; and we each took a turn. When they were all emptied we just sat on the wagons until it was time to go to the canteen. Although it was starting to get hot we did not get any water; just the coffee morning and evening. That was the day we got our parcels though so that evening we had a good English cup of tea with sugar and milk and some English food as well. We stayed out for a good while in the pleasant evening and when it got dark we went in and I did a sock for one of the others.

But that night we again got called out at 12.30 and had to stand out on the parade ground for three hours. I managed to get my clothes on and it was not a bad night; some of the others had only a blanket. We got a little sleep but were all very bleary. Later I asked the German civilian guard if there was any chance of getting extra food, some potatoes or an egg, and he said, 'I do not think so. Food is very tight. You English soldiers should be all right as you get Red Cross parcels.'

'I said, 'But they are between two soldiers.'

'But you still get better food than us.'

I said to myself that this country was in a very bad way.

That evening a lad pulled a chicken out from his coat. He had chased it, he said, and it had gone behind a wood pile so he waited till it came out and caught it and wrung its neck. He plucked it and put the feathers into the fire to get rid of the evidence, but they did smell. He boiled it in a tin but there was very little meat on it, just enough for himself. I had a very good spelling lesson but it was quite hard to grasp as many a words sound the same.

The next day was 11 May 1944 and Edie's twentieth birthday. I wished I could have sent her a card to say that again I had missed her birthday; the first was in Egypt, the next when I sent her the letter breaking things off; then I was in various camps. But I would still go on loving her.

Towards the end of the month, late May 1944, we we were told that Red Cross parcels would be sent up from Sagan that day. I talked to the civilian guard about perhaps getting some extra potatoes and he said he would try but I would not have to say anything about it. He said that the man who had escaped last month had been caught with a girlfriend whom he had met but that now he was in prison camp. I said to myself that he was a courageous chap to try when he knew he could be beaten or even shot; and would tell the others about this but they would have to keep quiet, not to get the guard into trouble.

That evening we got twenty cigarettes, the Red Cross parcel between two and some mail from England. Nothing much happened after that for a few days except that the South African lads had gone away and we were short-handed. One lad found an English dictionary. It was in very bad condition but it was put away until we could hide it. We had to show all the blank paper we found, too. It was Colin who was detailed to do it as he had a good trouser pocket and a long Italian coat. It was my turn to go in the truck and bring out the bales and someone suggested it might be easier if two people did this until there was a way in. It was a great help to me as my back still gave me lots of pain. I asked the guard again about potatoes but he said he was frightened of getting caught; so I said I would not bother him again. That day we found a map too, and managed to get it back to the billet. It was a good one; and the English/German dictionary would help us to look up words in the headlines.

One day at the beginning of June the guard called me over and we were talking when he said, 'Just put your hand behind your back.' And there was a hardboiled egg. I just could not believe it and asked if I could go to the toilet; he knew that I would eat it there and get rid of the shell. It was unbelievable and I enjoyed it very much as it was the first since I left Egypt in 1941, the night we left to go to Mustafa barracks when I had been bitten by bugs. That evening we had parcels and we had a cup of tea and something to eat; Harry had made a rota which changed daily and we were nearly last at this point. The sergeant had given us each twenty cigarettes earlier and some mail. My mother told me John was home from hospital. Our supper was a can of vegetable soup between us which was lovely.

Owen, the lad I shared parcels with, was from Stoke and he had a safety razor which had been sent from home and he lent it to me which was good of him. Colin was back, of course, which we were pleased about, and he had had a word with a corporal who was at the camp hospital, a medical orderly. He asked if he could get in touch with an officer as they were in a separate compound. He said he had two pieces of a map that he wanted to hand over. The orderly was amazed when he saw them and said he would contact the officer straight away as they were so important. The officer apparently said that he would try to tell someone in England of the good work we were doing at the factory.

One day in June when we arrived back the sergeant gave us a parcel addressed to our billet. It was from the Red Cross in Switzerland and inside was a gramophone and some records. We were a little disappointed as we expected to hear English songs and it was a foreign band playing, but it was a lot better than nothing.

We were told that at the weekend a doctor would come to see us all in the evening after work. That day we found a front page of a newspaper with the word '*Engländer*' on and the lad put it in his pocket until we could get back and read it. He would not talk about it till we got back to the billet where there was a committee including Harry and six other persons who got the news first and then came round and talked to us in groups. After the sergeant had brought us some mail and gone out and locked the door we could try to read this front page. A committee member told us that British, American and Canadian troops had landed in France, some by parachute, and this could be the second front we had been waiting for.

Anyone lying on his bed when the guard came in the morning got quite a good thump on the body and this seemed to have started since the British invasion of France. Everyone was getting up a lot earlier now.

The doctor came that Sunday and it was a woman. She was wearing jodhpurs and a riding coat and carried a whip. With her were two big minders with swastikas on their armbands. She made everyone strip off all their clothes and then went down each line lifting everyone's private parts and giving everyone a whack on the buttocks. Those hefty men just laughed their heads off at our downfall and then made us all go to the gate where we had a hosepipe shower, one at a time, with women and children and old men passing. We put our hands over ourselves but she made us take them away. We were all very pleased this was over.

One day a lad caught a rabbit and hid it in the woodpile. I suggested he took some blank paper to stop the bleeding when he had it in his pocket, and if anyone asked him what he was doing with it to make writing gestures. He managed to retrieve the rabbit and all went to plan; it was lucky his trousers were quite large. A week later as we arrived at the billet the doctor was there again; everyone was made to take their clothes off and she did the inspection again; and then told the guards to hold each person's shoulders while she put a slender needle into their nipples. Again we had to have the shower and just ran to the billet where the first person had put the fire on. The rabbit was put under the fire, which was on bricks, but it was more bone than flesh so he had it himself.

The doctor was there again the next Sunday with the same inspection but this time some people had no needles and some had two. It was not a very nice experience. The same thing happened the next Sunday too and some had the needle once, every third or fourth person, and a whack across the backside. It was very painful. She must have got some sort of a kick out of this and you could see the sergeant was not too pleased.

We found another newspaper headline which said something about the English being held around Caen but we would be able to read it properly later in the billet. Later that week Colin said he had been told by the corporal that we must not try to escape. He was told to keep up the good work with the maps. We were doing well that day with lighter bales of paper and time to have a good rummage but you had to be careful in case there were bits of glass or nails sticking up.

That evening we were waiting for our Red Cross parcels when there was a commotion and the next thing I saw was this lad, Robert Burns, from West Allotment. I nearly had a fit. He came over and said, 'I cannot believe it, Tommy! I knew you were a prisoner but never expected to find you here!' He just gave me a hug and shook my hand.

'How long have you been a prisoner?' he asked.

'Since 1941.'

'It was a million to one chance seeing you here.'

He was there with another three lads. We just sat talking about different people who lived at West Allotment where we lived before the war until we moved to Forest Hall. He told me about my brother Stephen and said he had been killed in 1942. I told him I had been receiving letters and then they stopped, but my mother never mentioned him. He said he was caught at Anzio in Italy and I told him about my time in Italy and that I would see him in the morning.

The next morning he was beside me on the march and although we were not allowed to speak I kept smiling at him and he was doing the same. At the canteen I asked someone to change tables so that Robert could be beside me and I could hear a lot of information about things that had happened in the world. We went separate ways after that and I went back to the warehouse but we had an extra man so were up to full strength. The new man in our team was told about looking for newspaper headlines and blank paper. The guard spoke to me and said that I was going to be moved from the warehouse on Monday and I wondered if it had something to do with my back which had been giving me a lot of pain and maybe he had noticed it.

Robert joined me in the canteen and told me about his brother Lionel who was in the Army and I told him about John being in the hospital. When we got our potatoes, Robert said, 'I am not eating them!' but I said he had to as he could not work on an empty stomach and there were no Red Cross parcels yet.

That evening we got our parcels and it was a parcel between two with a half left over. Harry gave the last person half a parcel plus an extra tin, and the rest would be divided amongst the other lads; but he would make a rota so that a different person would be in this position next time.

Robert Burns told me a great deal about the war in Libya; about the battle of El Alamein in 1942 and landings in Morocco.

On Monday I was taken to the logging area and a Welsh lad, Taffy, showed me how to operate a knife with two handles and a trestle fixed on two pairs of legs with a steel spike to put the log on. I had to put a log on this and take the bark off. I had a quota of so many feet long and so many feet high. I tried small logs till I got the hang of it. I took my time and made a few blunders, digging too deep. I did not seem to get the rhythm of it but I just had to practise.

Chapter 20

This was the last week in July and it was another lovely day. I was getting the hang of the knife and log situation and realised that it had to take time. Last evening I got a letter from England saying that they had sent a parcel to me but I had not yet received it. I had no idea what it was but anything would be most acceptable. When each log was done it was laid in an area 20 feet long by 4 feet high which was a lot of space to fill each day. I had to leave the bigger logs until I could get some help to lift them and just carried on with the smaller ones. Robert was not feeling too well so I told him to go to speak to the guard. Taffy came and I asked him to help, explaining about my back and the beatings by the guard at the last factory. He said just to give him a shout if I needed him. I did nearly half during the day but my hands ended up with a few blisters. The guard came to lock away the knives at teatime and then away we went.

The next day Robert Burns was quite ill with a very high temperature and the doctor had told him to stay in the billet. It was a problem when someone was ill and left on their own because how could they get in touch with anybody if necessary? I arrived at the wood area and looked for nice slim logs and when I met the large ones I would give a shout for help. Someone had found a hedgehog amongst his logs but just let it lie there and went to the other side, not to frighten it away. I told him to ask Taffy for advice how to deal with it. Apparently you need clay, so we were to look for some. Later the lad gave a shout: he had found some clay under his wood pile and using a stick he dug it up till he had a good round ball. Taffy had worked on a farm many years ago and had had many a cooked hedgehog when he was with his sheep and his dog on the hills. He said to put plenty of clay round the animal so he could pick it up and if anybody asked him, to say he was trying to make a cup. Amazingly nobody stopped him at all, all the way back to the billet and we cooked it later; there was enough for four of us: him, me, Taffy and the singer, Denny from Wales.

When we got there the sergeant told us we could be playing football in the evenings, maybe half an hour a day, at first just five a side and ten men watching. Everybody gave him a good cheer, and we thought he was astounded; mind, he had been very fair with us and with us not trying to escape had pleased him.

Robert looked a little better; the rest had done him good. His mate George was from West Hartlepool. Just across in the next bunk was a lad, Sidney, who had played the guitar with Hughie Green's band before the war but he was sacked as they knew he would be called up. He started playing and Denny was singing with him as he used to sing in a group in the Rhonnda. So there was a small concert before lights out.

Robert Burns was in his bunk for four days but felt like a limp rag. George had been very good in looking after him; they shared a parcel and it was good that they had some things left from it. I went over every night for a while for some tales about when we were young; he would say this person was in the Army, this one still working at the pits. I told him how I had met Johnny Leighton from Turner Street on the *Louis Pasteur* in 1941 which was now a good long time ago.

We had news that Caen had fallen to the British troops and that Paris was an open city; our troops were pushing on towards Belgium.

The sergeant asked us who would like to play football. Ten of us stepped forward, and another ten to go as spectators. We went to the lefthand side of the field and picked sides. I was a sort of back-cum-goalkeeper and could not handle the ball in a certain area or it would be a foul. I did not exert myself too much as it was a long time since I had handled a ball and we were all stiff for a while and would probably suffer later. We were one-nil down at half-time when we changed ends, but towards the end of the game one of our lads scored: one all. Not a bad game and quite friendly.

I had a surprise that evening, a parcel from my parents with two vests and two pairs of long-johns which would keep me warm this winter if we were still here. It was most welcome. Two days afterwards we got more Red Cross parcels and had another game of football which we lost two-nil but it was a nice friendly game. My back had flared up again however and I told Taffy I would not be playing again as I was frightened I would hurt it more.

The sergeant brought some books in English and gave everyone one without saying anything. I read through it but could not understand it at all. Later the six of us went to the lad Harry from Norfolk and asked; and he explained bit by bit what it was all about: we had to put our names on to join the German Army and fight the Russians, but would be given a month's holiday at the German stadium where the 1936 Olympic games were held, where we would have women, plenty of good food, a new uniform and whatever we needed. My book went straight into the bucket and later into the fire and so did most people's though some kept theirs for a read. Nobody signed it in our room, though we heard of some who did. Then Sidney with the guitar played and we all sang or whistled.

One day was very windy and I called Taffy over to give me a hand to lift this heavy log. As he walked away the strong wind blew the log off the trestle and onto my right leg. As I went to pick the knife up. It came crashing down onto my leg and I was trapped by the weight of the trestle; also the steel spike was embedded in my leg. I shouted for people to come and help me. Four of them came and Taffy held my head till they had taken away the trestle and removed the spike. There was blood everywhere.

Four lads took me on their clasped hands to an ambulance first aid area. There was only crepe paper there for dressings so one lad took a piece of his shirt and wrapped it round my leg as a tourniquet. They carried me to an old wheelchair and two of them with a guard pushed me all the way to Malsh where there was a doctor. He put two butterfly clips on my leg and then they took me back to the billet and carried me to my bunk. They put a bucket beside me as I could not get to the toilet without someone to lean on. I was in a great deal of pain and did not get much sleep that night.

Four days passed and I was told that I had to go to the factory again: three and a half miles hopping along with two men and a guard. It took a long while and I was really pounding with pain. Eventually we arrived and I collapsed. The civilian German guard came in and could not believe it when he saw me there; he went straight over and talked to the sergeant and made him get a guard and two of our men to take me back. I was really tired out with all that hopping there but at least could rest on my bunk. The lad who pushed me must have really been sick at having to do the journey again and by the time he got there there it would only be an hour or so before he had to come back again. This all happened twice within four days.

I was brought food each day by the guard as he opened the door, and one of the lads brought me my dinner. It was very boring. Sometimes I hopped over and put on the gramophone and listened to all the records over and over again. It did cut the loneliness but I had time to go over all my time with Edie. Some people were saying that the war could be home by Christmas and it would be worth all the money in the world to see that Mona Lisa smile. A lad brought in another headline which told that some high-up people had been killed and wounded; another map was found, the best yet with small villages on. Harry disposed of it in a safe place. I would have to ask to see the doctor again as I was in a lot of pain. If it had been in the front of my leg I could have seen to it myself but it was behind my knee in an awkward place. I could not put the fire on as our supply of coal and wood was limited.

I could hear the sergeant dismissing the others so asked about the doctor and he said he would try. He said we might get a supply of Red Cross parcels soon which would be just as well as it was three weeks since the last was finished. They did in fact arrive after a couple of days together with twenty cigarettes each. The first one always made you feel faint so I just took a few draws and had the rest later; I did not share with anyone as that made you get through them faster. I spent some time darning as one of the lads had a pair with no foot in at all so I could use the wool; and it kept me busy and helped me ignore the pain in my leg.

Two days after that the sergeant said I was to go to the doctor the next day; two lads would take me there and they would go to work later. There was also mail from England – I had a card and later a letter.

It took us quite a while to get to the doctor and with every hop it was painful. I thought there must be poison all around the area and tears were streaming down my face and it seemed an eternity getting there. He made me lie down on his couch and looked at it then he had a few words with the guard. We went away with the guard who was told to see the sergeant. I was told that I would be going in a few days to a camp hospital at Sagan, by truck and then by train. I would have a guard to escort me and this all had to be arranged. When we got back to the billet the two lads who had helped me had to go back to the factory.

When the rest came back I told my news to Robert Burns and he said he would miss me when I had gone to Sagan. I asked the lad I share parcels with if I could take a tin of something with me when I went, just to have something when I arrived and he said that would be all right but there would be very little left by then. Harry came over and asked if I would take a couple of pieces of map with me and I said I could take one in my trouser bottom and one in my waistband. My sewing was improving and they said it was all right but not to keep looking at the places or I might give the game away, just to try to doze off as trains do make you sleepy.

I was glad when the sergeant came and said I was going that morning. This was in October 1944. I had a good wash and then I heard a truck pull up outside. I got hold of the bunks to try to get me to the door but the guard came over and gave me his shoulder and then a hand up into the truck; it was really decent of him to help me. The time was 8.30. As I was going to arrive about teatime it looked as if I was going to have nothing for my dinner; and all our tins had run out so I could not anyway take anything with me. Quite soon we stopped and I heard the tailboard drop; we were at the station and it must have been Malsh on Oder. He must have driven a long way round.

The train came within twenty minutes and the guard helped me on but before that he put handcuffs on me and I put my jacket over to hide them. I wanted to go to the toilet but he did not take the handcuffs off for this. The train went on and stopped and started and I felt we were going to be late getting to Sagan. We were due to get there between six and seven at night; that was if we did not have any more stops. I was really hungry. We eventually arrived about seven and I hopped the two hundred yards to the camp with the help of the guard. He took off the handcuffs as soon as we were off the train.

After the gates I hopped along to the hospital and I was really glad when we got there. The orderly said, 'Where have you been? We expected you a lot sooner,' so I told him we had problems on the line. He said the doctor would see me soon and asked if I had had anything to eat. I said I had had nothing since this time yesterday so he said he would try to get something for me, just some soup and black bread and a cup of English coffee.

After a short time a doctor came with interpreter, a corporal with two stripes, who spoke French, and a nurse. I pulled up my trouser leg for him to have a look. The doctor asked what had happened: had I been shot? The orderly interpreted as I told him about the trestle with the spike. They both said it was a nasty wound; the doctor gave me an injection of penicillin and bandaged it and gave me some tablets which they said would make me sleep as it looked as if I could do with some.

Just as I was getting seen to, the corporal said to me, 'Do you mind if I take your bed as a young lad has come in badly injured.' I said yes then he told me that I would get a bed later. The lad had come from a Polish mine and died three days later.

The other orderly brought me some food and took me to a bed in a ward. It was lovely and clean. They said lights out would be at nine o'clock.

I had the best sleep for ages. The ward had about twenty people in. In the morning I had my first breakfast for a long time; it was porridge with sugar and milk, really lovely. The orderly told me my clothes were in a cupboard. I asked him if he remembered the other lad from our camp who had been there before and who gave him something to take to an officer and eventually he remembered. I told him that the other two parts of the map were in my trousers and if he gave me something sharp I could take them out and he could give them to the officer.

He said, 'Do you mind if I have a look now?'

'Not at this moment in case someone comes in and sees them, as you never know who is looking around. These lads' lives might be at stake.'

'You are dead right. Maybe later, in a safe place. Oh, I nearly forgot. You have to see the doctor shortly.'

I said, 'Thanks very much.'

'How did you sleep?'

'Wonderful, the best for a long time.'

It was not long before the orderlies helped me along to see the doctor. He said that he would take a bit away each day until it was time for me to go into a billet. I lay on my stomach on a bed while he saw to my leg, putting a needle in. While the doctor was away the corporal said it was all right to give him the maps and he would try to get over to the officers' compound. Then the doctor came back and started to take pieces of stuff from my leg and put them on a piece of paper. I could hear him talking in French to the corporal and then he gave me a tap on the back to get up. The corporal helped me to my bed with my leg heavily bandaged. I was still in a bit of pain and it was going to take a while to get the poison out but I was in the best place and in good hands.

The corporal said I should see the doctor again in a couple of days to get out more poison. He said the doctor still thought I had been shot and said he thought I was very lucky to get there when I did. I was given two more tablets in case the pain got worse.

In a while orderlies came with dinner; it was a slice of ham, two potatoes, peas, gravy and a slice of bread. After that I lay down and I was out like a light in that really comfortable bed with its white sheets and straw mattress. After a good while in dreamland an orderly woke me with a nice cup of tea and a biscuit. I thought I would just like to stay there till the war ended. Later I asked for some water to take my tablets and then just slept again. I was in great hands now and sleep was what I needed to recover. Later the orderlies brought a big bowl of soup which smelt lovely, not like what I had had recently, and we had another thin slice of black bread.

In the morning an orderly came with warm water and a towel – this was small but a lot better than drying yourself on your jacket. He asked if I wanted a shave and I said I would not mind so away he went and brought me a razor, shaving soap and three spare blades. I was quite amazed getting this sort of treatment and it simply boosted your morale. I felt like a new man, after weeks not shaving. Warm water was another good thing. We had tea and porridge and I waited to see the doctor.

There were many worse off than me who had to be seen first. Some were from Polish mines and some from factories like me. The doctor took off the bandages and put in some more needles; he told me I would stay in hospital another couple of days but would then have to come back every other day for dressings. I was given tablets and a bandage and when I got back to the ward they were just putting the dinners out; this time it was corned beef, mashed potatoes and gravy with bread and coffee.

The next day was much the same, but after I had seen the doctor he sent me away with the orderly as the corporal wanted to speak to me, At first I thought it was about my leg but he wanted to talk about the maps. He said he had given it to the officers and they were pleased as now they had a full map. They thought it was brilliant and that we were very courageous people. I was to thank everyone in the camp. He shook hands with me and said to take care when I got back. I might be in a billet by the end of the week.

Apparently I should have been brought in a lot sooner and the butterfly clips should have been off as the wound was very badly infected. They should have come off in eight to ten days and that was a fortnight. The corporal said that I was on the mend as long as I did not hit it as there was only a thin layer of skin.

I had missed dinner so the orderly went to the cook and brought me back sandwiches. I took a tablet with my tea and lay down to sleep; when I woke up I could not believe it as it was teatime and once more hot soup.

Two days later I was waiting to see the doctor. It took a good while as there were another two people admitted. The orderly said that never a day went by without receiving people who were injured or sick from different camps. I limped along to the washroom for a wash and shave and was told that in the billet I would be able to get some washing done as there was a good washroom there where I could hang out my clothes, but to keep an eye on them as they might take a walk. I could limp now rather than hop and it was good to go to the toilet and washroom by myself.

Lunch that day was bacon and chips, not a lot but I really enjoyed them. I would miss this wonderful treatment. I didn't see the doctor till the afternoon, when he said I would go to the billet the next day. They would get back to him to say if there was a bunk for me which had to be a bottom one as I was not to climb at all. I went to the washroom and had a good wash down as this might be my last in warm water.

As the corporal was passing I said. 'Thank you both for all your help,' and he said he would tell the doctor what I said.

The next day, waiting to go to the billet, I had another wash and enjoyed my breakfast and a lovely lie on my bed. The doctor examined me again in the afternoon and said that I would go to the billet later with an orderly and a guard. The corporal said again that I must not climb at all and just walk a little way; it would be a while before I could go round the compound. It should be done in stages, say about a hundred yards for a few days and then increase it. I was to come back in three days to see the doctor. After tea they came for me and I shook hands with the corporal and the French doctor and thanked them for the help they had given me.

The billet was a very different kettle of fish. There was a long table and two benches to sit on and very dull lighting; everywhere you looked clothes hung around. The lad next to me, Tim, said that he would be sharing the Red cross parcel with me when it came but they had none at the moment and the German rations were not very good. He must have thought I was a newcomer so I told him I had been a prisoner for nearly three years and he just could not believe it. I told him of all my travels since my capture.

During the next couple of days I had a small walk; I was going to try a hundred yards but to no avail as my leg started to pain, so I just turned and went back, not to overdo it. I would try again later. The food here was not good: no breakfast and just two potatoes at dinnertime and at tea two potatoes and a thin slice of bread. There was a small loaf between eight people. You always had another person to cut it as it saved a lot of trouble; there were some people who would cause trouble over crumbs. I asked why there were so many clothes hanging and Tim said that there was a wireless somewhere though no one knew where. Maybe later we would get some news from the BBC overseas broadcasts.

When we were served with food two lads from each billet were on a rota for a whole week's work if they were well enough but I would be exempt with my leg problem.

After dinner on the third day a guard came for me to take me to the doctor. He started to go quickly so I said 'Go slowly' in German and he did just that. I had to stop three times as it was a good way. Eventually we arrived there and I asked for a seat as my leg was paining like mad. I went in to see the doctor and lay on my stomach while he examined the leg. He said it was bleeding and what had I been doing? I said I just came from the billet.

'Did the guard hurry you?'

'No, we stopped three times.'

He said to do no more walking practice and to come to the hospital every day as he was not pleased with it and that I had to try to get help to come. He bandaged me up and said he would send an orderly over for me until I was better.

Back at the billet Tim said another lad had been round with some news about a hold-up near the Rhine and also in Belgium, but that Russia were improving their advance on all fronts. We only got news once a day at different times as they were afraid they would be caught. It was better than getting newspapers that were weeks late.

Some people were playing cards and Monopoly and I spoke to Tim who helped me go to the toilet area but I did not want to get involved with anyone after leaving my friend in Italy.

After a week I had very little pain but the doctor said I still had to take it easy. I would be very pleased when I could get right round the compound and I would know I was getting better. I was certainly getting good treatment and I was glad I was there. I told Tim all my story and how I had hurt my leg. He asked what it was like in the factory.

'Blooming hard work, eleven and a half hours a day,' I replied.

'I hope they do not send me to any work place,' he said.

I said, 'According to the news we might be home in New Year 1944.'

I had to see the doctor and by the time I got it was getting on to our teatime meal and Tim said that the Red Cross parcels had arrived and perhaps mail from England. He said he had not received any yet. I told him that it did take time; when a letter left Germany it could take six to eight weeks and you might get one back in four or five. I told him about my brother Stephen being killed in the Navy sometime in 1942 and how it had been my friend who lived near me who told me.

The parcels were going to be Canadian ones and there were also twenty cigarettes each. I got a card and the other lad got one too and then my name was called again and there was a small package from my parents. When I opened it I found it was a book which did seem funny as I had been wishing all day that I had something to read to pass the time.

It was good to have a cup of coffee and a biscuit after all that time. Tim said we could save our potatoes for breakfast and have a tin of meat or soup for our dinner. The Klim milk was always very good, lovely and creamy, and we could have coffee with a half spoonful of sugar. Meanwhile I went off to the doctor again. He said that I could do some walking by myself, maybe as far as the toilet and back, but that I was coming along well with the cream and the needles. I asked what was in the injections and the corporal said it was penicillin, a new drug. I had very little pain now. When I got back to the billet I saw Tim coming with coffee and a bowl of soup. It smelt really lovely and the black bread just finished it off.

The lad who ran the billet came over to me and asked if I would like a new pair of boots; I said it all depended on the size and that I took size 10. 'No problem,' he said and in ten minutes was back with a pair and they were a perfect fit. I thanked him very much indeed as the ones I had then would not last much longer; I had got them in Moosburg to replace my clogs.

Morning roll call was just outside the hut and very quick, not like Italy, and in wet and windy weather it was a lot easier; just a corporal or a sergeant came and counted you, so simple in every way. Tim, the lad I shared with, was very kind; he went off to get our potatoes even though I said I would, but he said it was something to do as it got very boring just walking round the compound. I told him what it had been like being counted in Bari and that he was very lucky, that it was like paradise here.

The doctor that day was pleased with me and said I could start to walk a little more, say fifty yards, but to take someone with me as a precaution. While I was out the next day in the compound someone came over and told us that the Russians were advancing on all fronts but the British and Americans were at a standstill around the Rhine and in Belgium. They might be just consolidating and this seemed good news all round. I would be able to tell the people in Malsh on Oder if I got back there. After my fifty yards I thought perhaps I could do more later, and I enjoyed talking to Tim while we walked, telling him about my work in the mines in the north-east. I told the doctor about this next time I went: that I had done fifty yards twice and then a hundred yards; he was pleased and said that I need not come back for four days. Before that time I managed to go round three quarters of the compound with only one stop on the way and two on the way back.

We were waiting for another issue of parcels and we knew there were still some in the storehouse but as this was a large camp we did not know if there were sufficient in there. After roll call we had a friendly game of cards with seven cards but I cannot remember its name; it whiled away the time. Our dinner potatoes were really black and must have been caught by the frost, really terrible but we had to eat them or starve. That was the day to see the doctor who was still pleased with me and I told him about my walking round the compound. He said to keep going but to take great care and to do everything a bit at a time. If anything happened I was to tell the man in charge of the billet who would be able to contact him.

We spent the rest of November getting me round the compound and managed it with no break at all with no pain. Going to the toilet was now no bother at all. The doctor was very pleased with my progress and told me to get in touch when I could go round twice. I kept practising until I could do this and then asked the lad in charge to arrange for me to see him again. When I got there however there was blood on the bandages and he told me I had overdone it and was not at all pleased with me after all their good work and I got a good telling-off from the corporal. I had to keep off my leg now as much as possible and get someone to go with me again.

When I got back to the billet I went straight to my bunk and Tim asked me what was wrong, so I told him my problem and that I had to have someone with me again to go even to the toilet. He was very willing to help me though and while I was there I decided to have a good wash-down, and by, was the water cold. I just dried myself on my jacket and we took our time back to the billet.

We heard then that the Russians were giving the Germans a good thrashing, that the English and American forces were still standing on the Rhine and Belgium but that in Italy things were moving and villages and towns had fallen.

I spent the next few days in the billet and I hoped that the tear in my leg had mended. Tim went with me all the time to the toilet and back and he has been really good to me in many ways; going for our parcel, getting cups of coffee. The weather had been awful with wind, rain and sometimes squalls of snow, so it was just as well we had not been going round the compound, but it had been very wearying just sitting round the billet. The doctor said it was starting to knit again but that I had to be very careful still.

Post came and I was unlucky but Tim received a card and a letter. He was very pleased with himself, but you just had to get on with life. especially inside a prisoner of war camp. You just had to take each day as it came along, no good wishing this or that as it never happened at all. I didn't tell people what we had done at the paper factory except the routine business as they might have reported us and made other people suffer. A close mouth was my best policy.

The weather was really awful, with very heavy rain, so they counted us inside the billet and it did not take long. We only just made it back from the toilets in time; if you were not there they classified you as missing and would be in trouble not only with the German corporal but also with the lad in charge of the billet.

At my next check the doctor said the wound was healing properly again and that I could do fifty yards twice a day and gradually increase it. I did this; and at the next check-up I was up to 250 yards each way. We had another Red Cross parcel at this time and it was a godsend to have some good food, starting with a couple of biscuits with butter and jam and a lovely cup of coffee. I had no pain at all in my leg.

This time the exercise did not hurt my leg and the doctor said I could go up to one circuit and then a hundred yards and gradually increase until I got to two circuits.

We were talking about the officers who had escaped from this camp earlier in that year, but we did not know the result of the escape. There were a lot of trees on the left hand side in the distance which would have given them cover if they had reached them. It was starting to snow quite heavily and at the billet my jacket came off straight away to get dry before my visit to the doctor.

That day in December they were very pleased with my progress as I told them about my walking; they were both smiling when they saw the wound; and the corporal said that I might be going back to Malsh in a few days time, though it took time to arrange things: someone to take me there and transport. The lad in charge would notify me of the day and it might be early in the morning; it would depend on the trains.

The news that day was that the Germans were on the run from many places in Russia and there was bitter fighting in Belgium. This was 12 December 1944

I said goodbye to the lads in the billet and thanked again Tim who had been going round the compound with me for all his help and support. He came and said, 'Give me your hand, and do take care of yourself.' He shook my hand and away I went with the guard.

We went to the main gate and then to the station. Just before the train arrived he just put his hands out and I knew he meant to handcuff me; he made me take off my jacket to hide the cuffs. Once again we were in the conductor's place. The people stared at me as if they had never seen an English person before. When I went to the toilet I had real problems with my buttons and the handcuffs. The day wore on and I was very thirsty and it seemed a long time since I had had anything to drink. The conductor was talking to the guard and they were laughing at me. But then, much later, the train was stopping; the guard gave me a sign to get up and we alighted on the small station platform. There was a truck waiting to take us to the billet.

Chapter 21

Robbie Burns was there to greet me and I asked if they had anything to eat. He said they were sorry but they were still waiting for Red Cross parcels so it looked as if I would have to wait till the next day.

I was glad to lie down on my bunk; it was a top one again so they must have switched round while I was away. Robbie said that he had had a letter from his parents saying his brother had been wounded in the face and he seemed very upset about it. It was nice to be among friends again, especially Robbie.

It was a struggle for me to get up the next morning after my journey especially as I was really hungry and a cup of coffee at the factory would not help me much. I went to have a wash and then hoped I would manage the three and a half mile march. The sky was very black. I felt a bit of pain in my leg but managed it, and after a cup of coffee went back to my old job at the wood section. I took the small round logs first and if I found any larger ones I just had to shout for Taffy and he would give me a hand. I took my time as I was going to just take things easy for a bit and was careful with the spike. Dinner was the usual black potatoes, not nearly as good as the ones at Sagan and it seemed odd that they were different unless they came from a different part of the country. I was so hungry I just ate the lot.

On the way back the wind was blowing very hard and we had a few showers which turned to snow. We were hindered by the wind blowing in our faces and it felt like one step forward and two back. When the billet was in sight that put a spring in our step to try and get there a bit quicker. The sergeant had the gate open ready for us and we were glad to get inside and take our clothes off.

The sergeant came in and said that the next day we would have Red Cross parcels and some extra coming as well in case the weather got bad; and that he would shortly be leaving and a corporal would take his place. We were cock-a-hoop at the news, especially about the parcels and there could be mail to send to England as well, and cigarettes. We settled down and Sidney, the lad with the guitar, started playing war songs and some by Vera Lynn so it turned out a good evening. He said he was going to make a stage and put on a story about prisoners with a lot of new songs he had written and that we should tell him what we thought of them. The Welsh lad Denny might help as he was a good singer. Over the next few days they discussed the new songs and sang them and decided which were good.

It was really difficult marching through the snow, with the roads very treacherous. We were so late we did not get any coffee at all, just straight to our jobs. We had to put up the trestles first and then try to put on a log; it was a bit gusty and I had to use my leg to keep the log on. It started to snow again, coming right from Russia and Poland and it was hard to work in these conditions. The wind went right through you as our clothes were not suitable for this sort of weather. We were pleased when the guard came to put the knives in the steel box and to take us to dinner. Back at work the snow was really getting deep and the trestles had blown down in the wind; we had to dig the logs out with our hands and by the time we had managed that our hands were frozen. Now and again we had to put them inside our coats or give them a good thump against our chests. At least the work kept us a bit warm; the guards were just walking around and wishing they were inside too. In fact they stopped work a bit early.

The new corporal was waiting in the canteen. He was very old, say in his late thirties, and must have been wounded as he was wearing the same stripe as his sergeant. It was lovely and warm in there but we knew we would soon have to go out in the weather again. Our clothes were soaking and everyone was unhappy; there was not a word spoken as we marched home. The wind made tears run down our faces and I was numb all over. Going up the incline was treacherous as our feet slid all over the place. I had my hands up my sleeves to try to get warm. Even the German guards looked like snowmen.

The next week would take us into Christmas Day and we were not going home as we had hoped. I needed urgently to go to the toilet one morning and asked a lad in front of me if I could have his turn in return for darning his socks. When I thanked him he said he had two pairs for me to darn as when I was away nobody had taken over this task. Our clothes had never really got dry as the snow had been going on and off and this day was a another soaking. Again there was no coffee on arrival and snow and wind in the log yard. My morale was as low as it could be. The guard came for us and we all started to complain but all he did was to shrug his shoulders as much as to say that he had to battle with these conditions as well as us. The canteen was wonderful and warm but we had to go out again afterwards and just try to do what we could.

On the way home someone spotted a Christmas tree in a window with lights on. It made your mind go back to earlier ones at home, some not very good as my father had been out of work since the 1926 strike. Then he got a job at the Rising Sun pit near Wallsend which made Christmases a lot better. I wondered how the family at home were going to cope with Christmas this year. It would have been a lovely Christmas if we had all got home safe and well, but this would now be my fourth one away.

On Christmas Eve it was so bad underfoot that we decided to go in single file to see if it was any better but we still had snow blowing in our faces all the way. I had had a letter from my parents wishing me a nice Christmas and a happy New Year in 1945; at least everyone was all right. I wondered how Edie was in this holiday period and I could not wait to get home and hold her in my arms and tell her how much I loved her. I knew that the mistakes I made should never have happened and only wished I could go back and start afresh. The war must surely finish one day but it felt very bleak at this time of year. We stopped that day at 4.00, early because of the holiday period, ate our meal and went back again in single file. We were to have two days off and it would be lovely not to have to get up at 4.30 and go out in the wind and snow.

That evening a key turned in the door of the billet and two guards came in with a box and a rifle. They seemed drunk. They picked ten men, including me, and lined us up. Then they opened the box and inside were rotten cheeses. Starting at the beginning of the line, they told the man to open his mouth; he refused, so the guard put the rifle to the side of his head and told him to eat it or get shot. So he put the cheese in his mouth, but the other one did fire the gun though it did not go off. It was like Russian roulette. They went to the next and did the same to him and eventually went down the whole line, each one eating the cheese and still firing at each person. When they had finished with us they started laughing till they got to the door which they locked behind them. The next thing we heard was a rifle shot, so we did not know if there had actually been a bullet in it. It was a rather scary incident. We did not report it to anyone as to them it was only a prank, though very unpleasant for us. We shook for a long time after this ordeal.

The New Year was still very snowy and there were drifts three feet high along the hedges. We were all wondering what sort of a New Year it would be. It was still the same job in the snow and wind and we got a real soaking. One day in the session after dinner the guard came early to collect the knives and then made us go towards the billet. It was 8 January 1945. We did not know what was going on. They tried to make us go faster and when we got there we were told to collect our personal belongings and put Red Cross parcels on a large sledge that was beside the gate.

Eventually there were 125 parcels on the sledge and the guard opened the gate and we were on the road again. By this time there was very little daylight left. We all had to take turns pulling the sledge. Going down the incline we had to reverse it. We did not know what was happening till the corporal said that just across the River Oder the Russians were consolidating just three miles from us. We all started talking, wondering what they were doing, moving us into a danger zone.

Later we had a ten minute break while another six people took over pulling and pushing the sledge. We were glad we had some food with us; and the guard gave us twenty cigarettes each but told us not to smoke them on the march as the lighted matches would give away our position. We kept changing the teams pulling; Harry thought we would be fresher if we did short turns rather than long hauls. Eventually we arrived at a farm and were very pleased to get a bit of shelter. We stayed there a couple of hours and the next thing was he said, 'Everyone out of here.'

We asked how far we had gone and he said it was about twenty miles. There was still no let-up with the weather but at least we were warm walking with one hand in our trousers pocket. After forty miles we arrived at another farm and he said we could stay there till the morning. It was about 1.30 a.m. We were upstairs in a loft but some of the lads stayed downstairs in empty byres watching the parcels. We got a few hours rest and then they got us up at six o'clock to do another march. This was the early morning of 9 January 1945.

We went across the fields, again taking turns with the sledge. It was very cold and rather dark and we walked in single file; The wind was blowing at 50 or 60 miles an hour and the snow had drifted to each side. We hoped for better luck at the next farm as we needed something hot to eat; we had only had cold food from the parcels and nothing to drink at all. In front of us were a lot of people and when we caught them up we recognised the girl who worked in the canteen and the disabled corporal she was going around with. They had a small hand cart with their belongings on and her family were helping her to pull it. They too were trying to escape from the Russians.

I was dying for the toilet so I asked one of the guards, the oldest one; he said all right but only two or three minutes. I was a bit longer and he was going to use the bayonet to hurry me, so just jumped up, pulled up my trousers and kept on walking and did it in my trousers, which was better than getting a stab in the bottom. People were passing but I just did not care.

The guards took us across a field, just fifty-six of us with some still pulling the sledge and we could see the bobbins on the top of the telegraph poles above the deep snow. Some parcels fell off the sledge and we stopped but we carried on afterwards. I was worried about my leg as this was the furthest I had walked since Sagan. We saw a farm in the distance but it still seemed miles away to us and we still kept going till we reached it.

We took the parcels up the ladder in the barn with a chain of us passing them up. I went out to see if there might be anything to eat but everything was covered in snow. We asked the guard for his knife so we could open our parcels; everyone had his own with his name on it. Later we went to a lean-to for a smoke and had to make sure all cigarette ends were out.

In the morning we were woken at 5.30 and tried to get a wash but the only water was in a trough and looked rather dirty; we decided to keep the dirt on our faces instead. We were going along fine just like the day before when Geordie came and said that Robbie Burns was not at all well. I told him to keep an eye on him and I would take his place on the sledge. I was carrying a pair of boots round my neck, with two pairs of long-johns and two vests wrapped in a parcel and I might be able to barter them later with one of the guards. We just kept on going without a break with the wind blowing from the north-east while we seemed to be travelling south-west.

Eventually we had a break and I had a word with the lads about me taking Robbie's turn on the sledge so they said they would put me on the front turn and then midway through so I would have a rest between. Then Geordie said he would try to do a turn so. I went to see about Robbie and he said he had dysentery with terrible pains in his stomach. I told him to keep away from any water as it could be contaminated, even while washing it could run into your mouth. I said he should just eat to keep up his strength. He said he just wanted to go to hospital, but I said that the SS soldiers would just shoot him. I went over to one of the guards with my long-johns and vests and asked in sign language if he would barter them for some bread. I got Harry to barter as he spoke a good bit of German. Harry told me he would not budge and I knew he had the upper hand. So Harry took a pair of long-johns and gave me a loaf and with some butter and jam this might help my friend. We stopped the sledge for a bit to give him some straight away and Geordie was looking after him.

We just kept going and I was getting very tired as I had done two stints pulling the sledge. It was getting a bit dark when all of a sudden we stopped and made our way towards a farm just a few yards away. Again all hands got the parcels up to the loft and that done, we had a look around the farm, but no luck. We found a small shed and had a smoke then decided to go up for something to eat. We borrowed the knife from the guards, who stayed downstairs. I cut some bread for Geordie and Robbie and me and we all sat together. I had a tin of cold soup with my bread; it was better than nothing and everyone was very pleased to get a a good break till the morning. We heard one of the guards say something like 'Lubin' and that was a name I had heard when I was travelling to Sagan.

Robbie was not well at all and I did not want him to go to a German hospital; what would his folks think of me if I let him go there and get shot? I was depending on God to help me with this problem. I had had a similar illness twice before and nearly lost my life because of it. You just have to keep food down if you can. The bread might give him a bit of strength but all this marching was not helping him and he might get behind sometimes. It would be good if he could keep his temperature down.

I hoped we would be lucky in finding something hot and we had in fact to keep looking for anything at all as the parcels would not last forever; sometimes you could see places in the field where the wind had blown the snow away. but every step we took was one towards our troops. A map would have been really useful at this time but we were in such a rush to get our personal things when we left. I still had Edie's photo though.

At least it was not snowing but the wind was enough to cut you in two. I was on the sledge again, this time for Robbie, but everyone had been very good helping each other; this was what Army camaraderie was about. At the second break Geordie came and asked for some bread for Robbie and took some butter and jam out of Robbie's parcel. He seemed to be holding a bit better that day and I told Geordie to come for some more later if he wanted it.

The wind was behind us now which was better than facing it. As it got dark, we were walking up an incline and in the distance was a shape which we could only hope was a farmhouse. We had been very lucky finding these places and we just put an extra spirit into our walking. I had a scout around but could not find anything; then we went indoors, had something to eat and then fell asleep as we were all shattered.

Now it was 14 January 1945. The weather had been awful and everything was terrible and Robbie was still not well. Once more we were up at 5.30 but our parcels were nearly all gone, just bits and prices like sugar and tea left, so we would be starting on our second issue that night and could add the odd bits to them. We would have our names on them again. The last few days we had been doing twenty, fifteen and twenty miles, but the sledge was getting lighter as the food went: a godsend in a way because it took only four men to pull it now, but where was the next food to come from? Once again we were travelling in single file and we had not seen a soul. We just wished they would tell us where we were going; there would be no good trying to escape anyway as we would not last long.

We had passed Lubin on the 11th and saw a tank and on board was the sergeant who had been at Malsh on Oder. He looked at us and was amazed so he just put his hand to his brow and saluted us as we passed. We all shouted, 'Good luck, Sarge!' and he and the tank went on their way to the Front, to face the Russians.

We were travelling south with the wind from the north-east. We seemed to be sleeping a bit better which was good as we needed all our strength to keep going each day. It was not snowing but the wind went right through you as our clothes were so thin. At least walking kept you warm except your head and hands. We crossed fields and were away from roads and signposts. The sledge was very heavy. That night we were relieved to get to a farm and the first thing was to find a toilet, which we did and it was quite clean which was unusual; and then I went to see Robbie who was not too good. Again he asked if he could go to a hospital but I said no, as the SS would just shoot him. It would be safer with us and he would be OK with Geordie to look after him. Once again Harry bartered with the guard for my vests; he said just one loaf. He told him my friend was sick and he still said just one so I had to take it. Harry said that the guard offered three loaves for my spare boots but I said no as my left sole was breaking away from the upper and it would get worse. I found a sack lying around; and then when I went up the ladder I heard the lads talking about Hitler and how he had been involved in a bomb explosion, a while ago while I was in Sagan, and that he had been injured.

It was a bit flatter for a while which was a blessing as going uphill made the sledge very heavy. Robbie was a bit better, not relieving himself so often. I gave him two slices of bread with butter and meat out of his parcel and at least it stayed down which was a good sign. I had to discard my boot and sat on the sledge to put some of the sack round my foot and ankle. I would have to save my other boots as you never knew when you would need them. We passed a small hamlet on the way to another farm. It looked quite nice so we thought our luck might be in. We looked around to see if there was anything we could eat here, even pig swill would have been warm and I did not think this would hurt us. But there was nothing so once again we had just cold food. I was wondering about our families at home who might be getting our last letters from Malsh and who would be worrying about us as we were about them.

We were pulling the sledge now with a one parcel each plus thirteen after that. When I came off the sledge I found that my back was starting to play up so I asked Geordie if he would take over from me as I had jarred my back as, the sledge being lighter now, it kept on sticking in the snow. and I would look after Robbie. He said, 'No problem at all; it will give you a break.' I told Robbie to tell me if there was blood in his stool. If we had been allowed a fire I might have helped as my mother used to mix ash into a paste when she was a bit loose.

Eventually we came across a railway line which seemed familiar and then arrived at Sagan camp; it had across the gate Sagan VIIIC; just to think that I was here in December and had had to walk all the way back. All the perimeter fences were down so I could cross to where the Russians, the Dutch and the officers had been. It was where the great escape had taken place.

The cookhouse area was full of stuff: beans and peas mixed for broth and sugar all in bags. I found a piece of glass and started cutting off the corners to put a bit of each in and when I thought I had enough I carried them back to the camp. As I approached, a German corporal said to put them all on the ground. We could not believe it. He said, 'No fires are allowed,' and the next thing we knew he said, 'Everyone out.' We must only have been there a couple of hours.

The next morning was the middle of January and the guards started to get us up. Sidney, the lad with the guitar, said quietly that he wanted to stay and get taken by the Russians and a few people started to hide him under straw. We went down with our parcels and started putting them on the sledge. The guard counted us with one missing and we said there was no one upstairs; he must have gone in the night. At least he had a parcel with a few days' food.

We continued south-east then south and found a farm for the night. In the morning the oldest guard was looking very bad and looking all in but none of the others came to see if he was all right. The sack on my foot started coming off so I stopped and threw it away and put my other boots on. I found that the left foot had frostbite in my three smallest toes; and one toe on the right foot was starting to go too. The old guard stood next to me while I did this and we just took our time to catch up. The poor old soul was just about all in. When we reached them the guards gathered round him and we also went over to have a look; He just sat there and the next minute he just rolled over and he was dead.

They asked if they could put him on the sledge; we all nodded, they put him on and away we went. This was going to be a shock for his family but we thought at least they would be able to get him buried. If he had been in the front line he would just have been thrown into a hole and have no grave at all, like so many others. But we stopped at a hamlet and laid the dead man on the ground; they went to the door of a house and an old chap came out. They must have explained what to do, then they came back to us and once again we were on our way.

Harry said that while there was some light we should open up the last thirteen parcels and see how many pieces were in each and see how far they would go. He counted six with sixteen articles, five with fourteen and two with thirteen. Everyone could have something of the smaller articles, and of the larger ones there was enough for one each except for one person; he said that would be him. We all said we would try and give him something from ours. We still had to pull the sledge for a bit as the parcels were heavy but would dispose of it soon and all of us would carry a bit of extra weight ourselves. Robbie was a lot better and still managing to keep walking which was the main thing. It was not snowing but must have been during the night as you could see new snow white against the old. At a village we saw some young ones on a small sledge, so someone said, 'Why not do a swap?' Everyone agreed so one of the lads took it and we reloaded that one instead of the other. Away we went a bit happier as only two lads pulled it. The guards just laughed at what we had done.

That night we stopped at a large farm and Harry said we should keep our ears to the ground and try to get some information about a large village nearby. A few of us took a look round the farmyard and found two big sacks of corn. Straight away we started filling our pockets; then one told his mate and everyone came down but Robbie. Geordie said, go upstairs and fill Robbie's pockets, then come again and fill yours, so everyone of us could have food along the way the next day. It was maize and we would have to be careful with it and have a chew or suck to make it soft before swallowing and not to have too much. As we were starting off we saw another group of guys forming up too and we followed along behind. We went along nicely with only two men pulling as there was very little left of the parcels. We would shortly be able to abandon the sledge as what we had left could go in our pockets; we could ration out the sugar and perhaps barter the tea as there was a packet between two men. We could perhaps leave it to Harry as he seemed to be able to talk to Germans of late – having that dictionary helped a great deal.

The group in front stopped and so did we for a break. Some of them were Australians. They were eating the maize just like us and one man was eating it almost continuously until his mate told him it would expand in his stomach and make him ill. One told me that the last village we had passed was called Zary; their guards told them the place names. They continued up front and started singing 'Waltzing Matilda' and we joined in; this put a spring into our step. The Aussie I was talking to said they had come from Breslau and that at least they were making their way to Blighty, that was what kept them going. He said he had not seen his family since 1940 as he was in the desert around Bug Bug and through to Benghazi with Wavell's command. With the singing and some whistling we seemed to eat the miles up.

That evening we just had small articles left like condensed milk and small tins enough for one person so we had what we could. Harry was arguing with the guard and just walked away but the guard called him back and said that the best we could have was two packets of tea for a loaf. We told him to take it; we had about a hundred and twenty packets of about half a pound each and it would be better than carrying them around. We thought we should give them just a few packets a day. So at least we had something to eat for the time being. If necessary we would have to take the sledge for one or two more days to carry the tea.

The next day was 21 January 1945. Harry had got twenty loaves of bread; he cut them with the guard's knife and gave everyone a slice saying that was all. I still had my tin of Nestlé's milk for a rainy day. The snow was easing and the wind had changed to northerly so it was on our backs. After a break as we came back to the group the Aussie who had been eating the corn turned round and his stomach exploded and he died within seconds. His mates gathered round him but there was nothing they could do. They asked if they could put him on our sledge, and they pulled him all the way till they found a village with someone to look after him.

Robbie was looking a lot better and only relieving himself say three times a day, though he was still a bit white. The bread would do him good and it was a pity we could not have a fire as burnt toast would help a great deal. We hoped we would make a settlement soon also so these lads could hand over their mate and say a farewell to him. It was not long afterwards that we found a farm so we went up the ladders to find the loft full of straw. I had a good look round, but no luck. The other group was next door to us so they could perhaps find out where their friend was buried.

The next morning we shouted us up at 5.30 and I went to the toilet and tried to clean myself as best I could with the straw which was not very nice as it was very rough, though better than nothing. When I got down they were ready to go and I was glad as I did not want to be left behind as I would not know which way to go as it was so dark out there. We went in single file and were averaging 15 to 20 miles a day. We wanted to keep up with the other group in front of us and they were being told the names of the places they were going to; if their group could know why not ours? I asked the Aussie I had been talking to and he said we were at somewhere called Tuphee. We had ditched the sledge at the farm as we were really carrying very little. We were really desperate for food and hoped we would get some soon.

As I walked I remembered the first time I saw Edie. It was in summer 1938. I was on afternoon shift at the Algernon Pit near New York and West Allotment and I went to call on my mate Sam Appleby who lived in Nicholson Terrace, Forest Hall. We set off on our bikes and I said, 'What do you call that girl who just passed?'

He said, 'Edith Robinson,' and I just left it at that. I saw her a few times during the summer holidays.

At that point we stopped for a break. That night I would try to find a stone to open my milk or maybe ask the guard for his knife, though I did not know what to say to him even in sign language. If I could make a small hole then there would be something to drink on the way along. The guys in front started singing and whistling so we all did too and it put a spring in our step.

The next farm had nothing to eat and the day after that was 23 January. There was deep snow and it was bitterly cold and we could not see any stars for direction. We were going along quite nicely when the snow hit us, not just snow but hailstones which gave you a nasty hit on the face and head. This slowed us up a bit and it was still very dark and we did not know where we were going. We seemed to be going on with no break and the corporal didn't seem to like us stopping; you would have thought that the Russians were just behind us. At least we could get a drink from the snow and hail. I spoke to the Aussies who said we were at a place called Forst; and this was where they were going to leave us as the next day they would be going a separate way. We both wished each other good luck.

I thought again about Edie. That day was my birthday, 5 July 1940, around about dinner time. I had just been talking to my brother Steve who was sixteen; he was learning to lay kerbstones and flagstones. As I went down towards my home she came across to me and said, 'Could you get that bird out from my mother's house?'

'Of course I will,' I said so I just went upstairs and closed the room door so it would not fly downstairs. I was quite a while but at last I caught it and took it across to my mother's and put it in the cage where my mother had a budgie. They started a racket but soon settled down. Later I saw her at the gate and asked her if she would like to go for a walk.

We went walking for quite a while. She said, 'Yes,' then came with me. She stopped and said, 'Wait a moment, I have to see someone,' and when she returned she told me that Richard Campbell was going to take her to a show in Newcastle. He had two tickets but she told him to take her sister instead to see Joe Loss and his band.

Eventually we made our way home and asked if I could see her late after tea. She said she did not know so I said that I would walk past her gate and if she was free she could come out with me. So that evening I went past slowly and the next thing I knew she was coming to meet me and I asked her to go to the movies with me. She said yes, and I was ever so pleased. I had told her my name and she said, 'Tommy, will you wait?' I stopped till she caught me up and I could not believe that she had come into my life; this was the best birthday present ever. She met me again the next day.

All of a sudden the group in front stopped, ten minutes only but better than nothing as I needed a toilet break; I only just made it. That night at a farm the Australians went to the left and we went to the right; straight away I went to have a look round and I found a cauldron half full of pig swill. It was not very warm. I gave Geordie a shout and he came down the ladder with several other people including Robbie. It was full of carrots and potatoes and other vegetables. We had no containers so we just ate it in our hands as quickly as we could. We managed three cupped handfuls each and at least we would have something in our stomachs.

The next morning we formed into threes and went away into the dark; after a while the Aussies turned off south-south-east while we continued south. I decided to ask Harry if he would ask the guards if we could have the names of places as there were still no signposts. At least with the guards we got shelter every night and if we were on our own we might get handed in to the Gestapo to be shot: not after what I had been through.

I was telling you about how Edie met me and we went for a walk, quite happy in each other's company. I told her I was going to see someone the next day about work. I went to two collieries but was refused because they knew I was going to be called up soon. I came round from Backworth to Shiremoor crossroads then onto Holystone, Palmersville as I was going to go home; then up to Killingworth and through the fields to Burradon, on to Gramlington, down Hartley Bank, up to Guide Post then onto the Hirst near Ashington on to Pont Street to my Auntie Martha's: John and Doris's mother. I asked if I could stay and she said, 'Of course; you can stay all week if you want.' I told her I came to try and get down one or two pits if they would have me.

On the Wednesday morning we saw twenty-five German planes going over my aunt's house. I tried two pits and thought if I was rejected I might as well go home, but my aunt said, 'No, stay till Saturday as John is going to your Mam's and you can share the bike.'

The days continued like all the rest while I thought about the past. One night we were attacked by rats. By now we had nothing to eat at all. Every step though took us nearer to home.

I carried on with my reminiscences. John and I set off, first just walking towards the Hirst, then we did a cycle turn: first he cycled and I walked; then he would leave the bike and I would ride it and pass him, then I would leave it for him. We did this all the way to Forest Hall where I had a meal and was really looking forward to meeting Edie, though she would not be pleased at me being away and not writing to her but I was afraid to ask my Aunt for a stamp, which was 1½d., second class. I went to Edie's house and her sister came to the door and shouted, 'Tommy's here!'

I waited a while and nearly walked away but she came to the door and said, 'I will see you later.'

I said, 'All right, but first I want to tell you I am sorry – I have been over to my Aunt Martha in Ashington.'

She said, 'Just tell me later,' so I went away home.

Later when I met her outside her gate she said, 'Tommy, I thought you did not want me.'

'You are wrong, I went to try the pits there, but no luck and I don't want to go into the Forces.'

She just put her hand in mine and we went on walking and talking. To me she was my Mona Lisa as she had that little smile and I could not believe my luck. I said to myself I was going to spend as much time as possible with her because you did not know what was around the corner. I think it was love the first time I saw her; I thought I was too old for her but age does not matter when you love someone.

There seemed no let-up with the blizzard and it seemed to come from all directions; we were getting a real soaking. My trousers were very wet and my legs were freezing. It was hard not knowing our destination and we were weary and hungry. The sky was full of black clouds. Robbie was still not well but was trying to battle along. He said he was really hungry and I said, 'Just think of the lovely dinners you have had in the past – soup, home-made bread, this is what I do all the time, but it does not fill your stomach.' He started to smile.

Harry had asked the guard if we could know the names of places and he said we would be at a place called Cottbus, and that was all. That day we started singing old first world war songs and this put a new spring in our step. The day after that was Spremberg, but the days were much the same. Now it was 1 February. One evening Geordie found a bag with carrots in it – not a lot but enough to share around. It was under a lot of paper bags; you had to go through everything. It was snowing again and I kept having handfuls of it to drink which was lovely and fresh. It was like manna from heaven.

Harry was getting on well with the guard he had bartered with and he said that the next place was Hoyerswerda and that we were making our way towards Dresden. We kept saying to Robbie, 'Just a few more miles,' and he would give us a little smile which pleased us. There were only fifty-five of us and we were like a family, sharing all the time. It would be lovely to have a bath and a shave; it seemed weeks since I had shaved, even a cold one would do.

Time went on. They say an army marches on its stomach but we were marching on empty ones. On 3 Februry one of the guards fell down and we halted and milled around, trying to keep the cold out as much as possible; when we started again the guard was limping so that was going to hold us up, unless we could find another farm nearer. At this rate we were going to have more casualties. Suddenly the guard called a halt and we could not believe it: we were just outside a farm and we had not seen it through the snow. We were at a place called Bernsdorf. When we started we had five guards and a corporal; now we we down to three and a corporal; we could be left on our own sometime.

This was 5 February 1945. We were on our way again. Robbie was still suffering, but at least not passing any blood which was good as that saps your strength. If only we could have had a nice sunny day it would have made all the difference, but we were struggling over miles upon miles of fields and they seemed to never end. Harry was going to have a word with the corporal to see if we could be told the name of each village, large or small, and also the larger towns and cities. We were soaking wet and very hungry and so relieved to arrive at a farm. While searching around we found a small lean-to and inside was a boiler with hot pig swill. Geordie told the lads upstairs and I told the ones down there; but it was so hot we could not put our hands in and everyone looked around for a can or a scoop; surely the farmer must have had something like this. Eventually we found something but time was against us as the corporal was telling us to go to the loft. In the morning the pig swill was cold but much better than nothing at all; when you are really hungry you will eat anything within reason. The corporal had told Harry the name of the village and it was Kametz; the next place we passed was Radeberg.

On the 7th we seemed to change from south-south-east to south, quite suddenly and we also seemed to get attached to another group of lads in front of us. The next thing was that we came close to Dresden as we could just see buildings sometimes through the blown snow. There was a bridge and a lot of people waiting to cross it and we just followed behind the group in front. Suddenly however someone shouted, 'Back, they are going to drop the bridge into the river, it is mined!' so there was a rush to try and get off. We must have been nearly a quarter way over when this happened. We ran as fast as our legs would carry us but there was a lot of pushing and shoving. We were all over the place so we just kept shouting the names of people we knew; Robbie and Geordie were not there though they had been just behind me. Then I spotted them not far from me and they came over. This place was Radebeul, according to the corporal.

We walked down to the next bridge. It was lovely walking on a road. When we reached it it was packed with people but we just kept going for a while then someone shouted, 'Back, they are going to blow this one as well!' We did an about turn and tried to get off but it seemed impossible as while we were trying to get off others were trying to cross and some people did not understand the language. Then someone said Boom and clapped his hands and they seemed to understand this and turned round. This place was called Coswig. When we had all found each other we went on to the next bridge. Still there were a lot of people, it seemed never-ending. This time we managed to keep together and got eventually to the other side. This bridge was Meissen and the second bridge had just been blown.

We were on the outskirts of Dresden and the corporal went into the city. We came across an old building to spend the night in and I do not think many people slept at all as it was a concrete floor; but one consolation was that we were out of the cold wind and snow. We could not even build a fire, why we did not know.

We were glad when it was time to go. At first we were sheltered by the buildings and we were marching in threes on a proper road with a fair amount of traffic. We stayed near the kerb as we did not want to be knocked down. We seemed to circle Dresden and then went off into the fields. We came across our farm quite suddenly and there was just a small ladder to the loft which was just as well as I do not think we would have had the energy to go up a long one. At least there was plenty of straw. Everyone was feeling the effect of the night at Coswig.

We were still doing 15 or 20 miles a day. The next night we found more pig swill, warm this time, and we all had handfuls until it was empty. We passed Freiberg and it was 11 February, just travelling in single file thinking of lovely dinners of the past, which only made our hunger worse; but also thinking that every step took us closer to the American or British troops. We had soaking wet clothes and I do not know why no one had fallen ill with pneumonia. On 13 February we stayed at a large farm on the outskirts of Chemnitz. Sleep was the most wonderful thing; when you were asleep you had no worries till you got up and saw what kind of day lay ahead. This was a place called Fiona.

On St Valentine's Day I thought I should make up a poem for the day with great thoughts of the days we were courting. This morning of the 14th, St Valentines Day, one of the lads said 'Sky is very red' and this guard said, 'It must be a house on fire.' All of a sudden a storm broke, with snow and wild wind in all directions; we just carried on as best we could, sometimes blown off our feet and hardly seeing anything in front of us. It slowed our pace; we were just like snails crawling along. All we could hope for was to get under cover but when we were called to a halt, we were milling around and still the corporal had not said go. It looked as if we had missed our destination. Even the corporal and the guards were clapping their arms across their chests and stamping their feet and they too would have to do without anything to eat for a change.

Robbie and Geordie and I wondered how our families were doing as they must be worried sick about us and I said this was my Five Times Missing; the others could not believe this so I started to tell them the whole story. At least this took up a part of this long long night. When I had finished I thought up my poem:

> I will always love you till I die
> As you will always be mine
> As I have a tear in my eye
> And you will always be my Valentine.
> It was short but sweet.

We spent the night milling around, just going in circles; as we moved inside others were coming out, just to try to keep warm. It did not let up all night and we would all be glad when the corporal said 'March', in German of course. The guards had black capes to keep off the snow.

It was better when we started, still in biting wind and flurries of snow, but a lot warmer when moving, The left sides of our faces were cold but when I had the chance I put my left hand over my face and ear as they were really frozen. The sky was very black. We had had nothing in our stomachs and were really feeling the strain; our poor legs were really aching. I was glad that my leg had not opened up again as I had thought I was going to have a problem with it but the doctor had done a really good job on it, together with the English corporal and my friend in the camp at Sagan. Eventually we found a farm and just to lie down was wonderful. There was a large loft with plenty of straw but although we scouted around for a good while there was no food, so that was another night without eating, even after our great ordeal of the night before. This was outside a large village called Glauchau and apparently we had done twenty-eight miles over the last two days.

There was no food that night, nor the next, and the only thing we could do was to keep whistling and singing to show the Germans they were not getting us down. The pace was going along fine as we knew we could see the light at the end of the tunnel and we must at all cost keep going. We had not been fed for while and we hoped that at the next farm there would be something for us. It was not long before there was a halt and a mad rush to get to the snowdrifts to relieve ourselves. Robbie had been a lot better. We continued until it was nearly dark, with a town visible four or five miles away, and there was a farm.

Geordie found a small bag of potatoes and we ate them raw, better than nothing but we would have to take it easy to give our stomachs a chance to digest them. There were just enough for two each. It seemed to take away the hunger pangs for the time being.

The next day the wind was still blowing hard, from all directions, but there was no snow which was marvellous for a change. We kept on singing and whistling and got into our stride; we seemed happier than before, just like a small family. It was unbelievable what we had been through together. The sun came out and it was really lovely. I asked the corporal at a halt the name of the last place and he said it was Gera. We were generally moving south-east and south, then later south-west. We got to a farm near Kraftdorf but there was no luck at all as to food. The following day was much the same, still with some sun. I thought that I had nearly done a full circle, from Gourock in 1941, and here I was marching my way home. The evenings were getting a bit brighter so it gave us more time to look for things. Today was 19 February. The farm that night seemed really poor and again we found nothing. With marching all those miles every day, it was really nice just to get down and rest your weary bones.

Some time on the 21st we passed Burgel and were very pleased to walk for a while on a road which had been cleared. There was a lot of water and puddles at the farm gate with lots of mud but this didn't matter as we could clean it off our boots with straw in the loft. There was no food and we were very hungry indeed. Robbie was again not feeling too good and kept talking about going to a hospital, so Geordie said, 'Do you want to die with us or go to a German hospital and get shot and left in a gutter? At least you are getting looked after by me and Tommy.' Just then he fell down, so we helped him, held onto his arms and told him to try to carry on as best he could. We were really dragging him along as he had no stamina left. We were not going to desert him now but it was a pity we did not have that sledge as it would have made it a lot easier. The corporal sent a guard back to us as we were lagging behind. Robbie asked why we were not stopping for halts and Geordie explained that we had to keep in touch with the others as we did not want to stay outside that night. Robbie was complaining all the time but we told him this was the only way we could do it. If only we could find some good food. The Germans had not put themselves out to help us in any way, but perhaps they had very little themselves.

We could not see the lads in front any more but the guards said, 'Look over there,' and there was the farm. We struggled there as best we could and through a quagmire at the farm gate. Several of the lads came to help us get Robbie up the ladder. One of them said he had a temperature so they covered him with straw to keep him warm. They said, 'You have done enough for today so we will look after him; you go downstairs and see if you can find anything to eat, even if it is only for Robbie.' But there was nothing.

In the morning Robbie was still not well, even after his long sleep. He went to the corner and it was my turn to look after him; Geordie and I took alternate hours as it did give us a bit of a break. He could hardly clean himself so I got some straw to try to help; he had dysentery again but not too bad and at least no blood. He pulled up his trousers with my help and we went down the ladder, Geordie in front and me behind. We walked beside him to steady him and he seemed a lot better walking at first but there was a long way to go. He stopped needing to go to the toilet so we pulled his trousers down while he just sat there and he was in a mess and had lost a little blood. We did not know what to do, but then dug with our hands for some clean snow and used it to clean him. Once more the guard had been sent back to look after us as we were still a long way behind. We could see the lads ahead having a break so we just pushed forward. We told Robbie he was doing wonderfully since he had been taken ill as we had done a lot of miles and he was still here with us. At least it was not snowing and we would have dry clothing that night to lie down in. That night we just made the farm before the light went and the other lads took over; Robbie was asleep straight away.

In the morning early we were called by the corporal and told to get down as soon as possible, which was unusual. Geordie and I got up and shouted at Robbie who just opened his eyes. He just opened his eyes and we could see his pale white face. We told him he had to get up or they would come up and shoot him; this was just to get him to move. I took him to the corner and he still had dysentery but I could not see if there was any blood as it was very dark; I managed to crumple some straw to make it soft and cleaned him up as well as I could. With the help of the lads we got him down the ladder and onto the road which was tarmac but not for long as we hit the snow covered field and drifts.

Again we helped Robbie along and we were not lagging behind as much as other days so we kept our fingers crossed he would be able to go on like this. We supported him with one hand on his shoulder but if we felt tired one held him while we changed places. Your arm certainly got tired. It was a lovely morning for a change with a bit of sunshine. The corporal had said we were to go fast, why we did not know, so Geordie told Robbie he must not fall behind like on other days. We kept telling him he was doing a good job and we were proud of him. There was a group ahead of us and as they were heading west and we were travelling south-south-east we were getting ahead of them. Much later we saw another group coming from the east, and one from the west, and we were in the middle, so this German corporal said '*Schnell*' (quick) and we did and we reached the tarmac first. Then the one from the east came behind us, and the ones from the west came behind them.

We were going along lovely when out of the blue two white aeroplanes started machine gunning us. We jumped in the ditch which was full of water. When we got out we saw people lying about dead or wounded. One chap said, 'I am soaking wet,' and another beside him said, 'We are all wet but we can get dried; those lying over there cannot.' If the corporal had not kept us moving it could have been us lying there. Robbie messed his pants with the fright, poor soul, but there was nothing we could do for him then, as we had to keep going in case the planes came back. One of the lads said he had seen them before, and they were Russian Migs. As they were white it was difficult to spot them.

In the distance we could see a large town, Weimar, and we were on the outskirts; within a short while we were on snowfields again. One lad shouted that there were pigs in a field and so we hoped we were lucky this time with food. The road around the farm gate was in a state with puddles and mud everywhere, but we managed to get to the loft. The lads said they would take Robbie up while we looked around. Within ten minutes we found a half full container of pig swill; it was barely warm but better than nothing. The lad Harry from Norfolk said that everyone should have two handfuls, and then a smaller handful each if there was any left. We had to confess that we had already had three handfuls but he said at least we were honest about it, and everyone should be thankful that we had found it. We only hoped that the food would do Robbie some good.

We tried to clean up Robbie's trousers, and it was easier with them being wet; it took quite a while softening the straw for it. All Robbie wanted to do was sleep. The next day he was walking better than before but still slowly as we gave him encouragement all the time; we said each mile got us nearer to England, and he would give us a smile of appreciation. We were trying to catch up with the others when Robbie said suddenly, 'I have to go,' and we tried to find a place in the snowdrifts in case anyone passed by. The lads in front had not moved on from their break until we nearly caught up. We went through a small village where people were perhaps going to work, or out for a walk. That night we stayed at Apolda and it was 25 February 1945.

The next day Robbie was really walking quite well and we were keeping up with the others, walking on the tarmac which was so much easier. Suddenly someone started whistling and this made it even better; everyone got in step and started marching. Of course we got left behind then because the pace was too fast for Robbie, but at least he was on his feet. Now and again we saw the odd motor or truck but we had to beware. We were still talking about what happened the other day and Robbie said, 'I am lucky to be alive!' All of a sudden Robbie got a new lease of life; we did not know how but he seemed to walk a lot better than he had done for a long time. We were really pleased for him and he just said, 'Life is worth living.' That night we stayed at Bad Sulza, but there was no food to be found.

In the morning Robbie got himself up straight away and we were amazed; we only hoped this was a good sign. We would still keep an eye on him on the Death March as we called it after the events of the other day. We swung along with whistling and singing and we passed people going to work and motors and trucks going in different directions; we picked up our pace as we went along to show these people that we were not downhearted. All of a sudden the corporal called a halt and it was great to have a break. We asked Robbie about the toilet and he said no. We told him we were very pleased with that morning's effort.

At the farm that night someone found a barrel of water with thick ice on top. Someone broke the ice with a large stone and threw it away. One of the lads went into the very cold water, but before long there was a queue as lads wanted to have a bath, the first for a long time. I told one of the lads to go and get Robbie as it would really do him good and perhaps warmed a little by the lads who had been in earlier. Then it was my turn and it was really great; I just dried myself with my jacket. The sign said that this place was Naumberg.

Robbie continued to do well over the next few days. We were on the outskirts of Leipzig at the beginning of March and thought we must have gone well over a hundred miles. Then came Weissenfels on 2 March and now there were many more hamlets and villages lying back in the distance as we went along. The road seemed to twist and turn and we saw quite a few vehicles. The approach to the farm that night was another quagmire and the loft quite small. Geordie and I had a scout round; we turned the place upside down and were just going to give up when we spotted this bag. We thought it was rubbish, but not so; it was half full of carrots and between us we carried it quickly up the ladder, in case any Germans saw us. As we got to the top, Robbie came over to give us a hand and we asked Harry to dish them out as up to then he had been very fair regarding food. He said that others had been out looking and had not spotted the bag. There was enough for one and a half each, to have then or keep for tomorrow. This place was called Lutzen.

On 4 March we were walking south-east on a cloudy day but with no snow or rain, and were on a proper tarmac road. A few people passed us on cycles or just walking and it was lovely, with the sun just trying to break through. One of the lads started singing 'Tipperary' and we all joined in; we went on to other first world war songs and then Vera Lynn, Judy Garland's 'Over the Rainbow' and many others. Robbie was coping fine at the moment but you could never take chances. That night we were at Merseburg. Robbie said something about Rommel and I asked him what he was talking about.

He said, 'Rommel is dead.'

'How do you know?'

'Ask Harry, he read it in one of the papers from the paper factory.'

I asked him if he had been killed in action.

'No,' said Harry, 'He was made to take something, as far as we know. It was just before Christmas.'

I could not believe that he had gone. He was well liked in the desert and very good with his men: a good field officer.

On the 6 March, we had a resting place with plenty of straw which made a difference as you could get deep inside it to keep warm. We all slept well, but in the morning I did not feel well as I wanted to be sick. Maybe it was the carrot I had the other day, but none of the others was complaining. I went to one of the corners and was violently sick. Robbie and Geordie came over to see me and asked what was the matter, and said I was white as a sheet. Then I had to rush to the corner with dysentery and it came away like water but at least no blood. The others were good and tried to make handfuls of straw soft for me to try and clean myself.

We travelled along on snow-covered fields again but I had to stop – I just ran to the snowdrift and only just made it. I could not clean myself much but tried with handfuls of snow. The lads in front got quite a way ahead. We just hoped that the guard with us knew where he was going. We were on a proper road and then Robbie said he could see the others in the distance and they were having a break, but before we caught them up they were on their way again. Once more I had to find a hedge, as we were on the main road and children or their parents might have passed. The other lads must have known something was up so they just took their time to give us a chance to catch up and when we saw them just in front this put a stride into our step and when we reached them they all gave us a cheer as if to say, Nice to see you.

That evening as we were going up the ladder to the loft I put a hand on my neck and found a louse which must have come from the last farm. Harry told the corporal about it, but what could he do? We were at Hollenben, on the outskirts of Halle. I went to the corner and was still very loose. I was up a couple of times during the night too but would just have to put up with it.

We were just going along nicely the next day, and the others were keeping with me in case I felt dizzy, when the heavens opened and within ten minutes we were soaked to the skin. It was pretty windy as well making the rain swirl against our bodies. It made walking very difficult as rain on snow made the place like a skating rink. Later we came to a road and formed threes; this was a lot better: firm ground, you cannot beat it. We sang our way along and caught up the time we had lost. That night of course we stayed at a farm and were on our way to another. I tried my best to keep up although I had to stop occasionally when I could not hold it in any longer. I got Geordie to watch that the guard did not leave us as I did not want to be left on my own, and tried to clean myself with handfuls of snow; and then I dug deep to wash my hands in it. The lads in front were on a break, so we managed to catch up. That night was 7 March and we were in Bennstedt. We slept naked and just burrowed into the straw to try to get the wet out of our clothes.

I was feeling so ill but had to put a brave face on it, mostly for Robbie – when he had been ill he had wanted to go to hospital and Geordie and I persuaded him not to go and now here was I in the same predicament. I just did my hardest to keep up; we started off along snowfields but not for long and when we reached the tarmac we were surprised and all started singing. People were passing and kept looking at us, as much as to say, 'So this is what an English soldier looks like.' We enjoyed those moments and it gave us pride in ourselves, also knowing we were getting nearer to England. We were going easterly at that time, and the day was brighter than it had been for a while, with moderate wind. Someone started singing 'Blaydon Races' which made our day because it took us straight back to home and a lot of memories. That night I had not been too bad. We were at Lutherstadt and it was two months to the day since we had left Malsh on Oder.

I felt a lot better the next day and had not had to get up in the night. Walking was difficult as the snow was melting underfoot but people seemed to be in a happy mood and as it got light it was good to see houses beside the road. I saw Harry talking to the corporal and just before we moved away from a break he told us that we would be coming to a place later in the afternoon where there would be a shower and our clothes could get cleaned. Everyone gave a hip hip hooray at the thought that at last we were getting something done. We kept up a good pace as there was something to make for.

When we arrived everything was set up and curtained off so no one could see us. At each end we had a man watching that nothing happened to us, as it had to the Jews. We were taken to a machine that cleaned the clothes in a slow process but just as it got to my turn the air raid sirens went off and we had to make our way to a shelter. We had to put our hands to hide our dignity as there were people of all ages going in: young children, lads and lasses. It was freezing and no clothes made it worse. After an hour the all-clear went and we ran across the road towards the showers. People were staring at us and laughing their heads off at our downfall. We went through to try to get warm as we were freezing and at the end got our clothes back. It was a good job it was a bit lighter in the evening as we only just made our farm for the night.

The weather was better next day and we were going along a good straight road singing 'Pack up your troubles' and other songs from the first war; and songs from our own time from Crosby and Robeson. After the break we continued on the straight road – it was like a roller coaster and you could see lovely scenery; a lot of hamlets and scattered farms and a good few villages. In the afternoon by a small town there was an avenue of trees and the leaves were just coming out; to us this was really beautiful after the rotten snow dykes all the way. It was a pleasure marching along on a lovely day like this though at the end of it there was still no food. I was feeling much better however. This village was Aschersleben.

Leaving the farm our feet and trouser bottoms got soaking through the wet fields but eventually we arrived at the road. It really seemed like the start of spring as the hedges were starting to bud. I thought of Edie as I walked along; it was such a shame that two people in love got broken apart by someone else. I hoped to meet her again soon as I loved her with all my heart, body and soul. The last letter I received from her was with her photo in 1941. At a break Harry came over and asked how I was, and I thanked him and told him I was a lot better. He said that that evening we would be coming up to Egeln and that was 13 March. We sang past the fields and villages; we could see green grass now and very little snow. We came to an airfield and as we got nearer saw it was one hell of a mess – our planes must have done a great job as there were aircraft all smashed by our bombing, just heaps of rubble. We sang and whistled 'Colonel Bogey' as we passed and the guards just gave us a look.

The next day went the same, on the way past Magdeburg and staying at Wanzleben. We past a factory that must have been bombed by our forces; it was all flattened except the chimney. Daffodils were starting to come out. Harry was really concerned that we needed to find some food soon as he thought we were at the end of our tether.

The next day however, we saw a building, a brick factory, and when we got to it we saw quite a large group of prisoners also lying around. We sat down in small groups and I was with Robbie and Geordie. Shortly Harry came up and said, 'I want a man to go with me and four other lads to the village as they have food for us.'

We just could not believe it and straight away I said 'Yes,' and Robbie and Geordie said they would try to build a place to try and keep the cold out. I went to meet the other lads who had a small wagon with medium shafts that we could pull. There was a lid on top of it – it was barrel shaped – and the lad lifted the lid to see if it was clean inside. It looked all right, so away we went with a guard, quite a distance downhill. When we got there there were three German women who filled the wagon with soup and when they had finished one of them gave me a white pail full of soup too, and a scoop. Then we moved away, with two of us in the front, on the shafts, and two of us at the back. I asked this other lad to carry my pail in return for a couple of scoops; the woman had given us a small ladle.

We took turns on the way up the hill and Harry organised everyone into a queue. Everyone had a scoop each and then went back to the queue again so they could have another; but I had my two scoops first for bringing the wagon up.

Robbie and Geordie were in this brick lean-to and I was just putting my foot over to join them when this tall French soldier tried to take my pail of soup off me. I just took a brick and put it straight into his face. I must have broken his nose as there was blood all over the place. He never came back. Nobody was going to take food off me after I had brought it all back.

Harry came over and thanked me for going and I offered him a ladleful of soup out of my pail; he said later, if that was all right. He said this place was Duderstadt and that we would be staying there that day and the next and them moving the next day. It would be lovely to have a break though a pity we could not put a roof on our brick walls; but it was lovely to have food for today and maybe tomorrow. It was lovely thick soup with plenty of vegetables in it. This was the first time we had been fed by the Germans.

We moved on on 17 March. Some of the other parties had left already and we were not up very early. Harry asked me about my trouble with the Frenchman and he said, 'Well, you were defending your property and it serves him right for interfering with an Englishman.'

There was a great difference in our step now after the food and the rest. We went along lovely country roads; sometimes we saw livestock. The air was nice and warm with a gentle breeze. we were on our way to Wefensleben. At one point we passed a lot of German people including children, maybe coming out of school and then as we turned the corner there were a large gate and people there dressed in black and white stripes with a star on their chests. They were putting their hands to their mouths, asking us for food, but we could only shrug our shoulders.

The next day was much the same, and we stayed at Helmstedt, near Brauscheig. We had to cross an autobahn at one point which was difficult as it was pretty busy and we had to cross a few at a time. Then there was a winding road to our next farm and the next day carried on in the same way, when we ended up at Königslutter, with another group of prisoners just across from us. Here we had a day off, so a long lie in. This was a great big place, just like an aeroplane hangar. Some of the other lads came out and we had an exchange of places we had been. They too had been prisoners in Italy and said that I must have been a prisoner a long time: it was nearly three and a half years now. One said there were potatoes in the field over there and that he was going to try to get some.

Geordie said, 'Lad, you will be a fool if you do: you see just inside that door there's a German guard and he must be planted there just in case someone makes a move on those heaps.' There were four long heaps altogether.

We were not allowed fires and we all understood why as the other day we saw the trail of white smoke in the sky and one lad said, 'Those are Flying Fortresses.'

'What are they?' we asked

'They are large American planes.'

Someone asked the corporal if we were to get any food and he said no. But there was food just lying in heaps and they were not going to give us any. One lad said that when it got a bit darker he was going to try but we said it was not worth it to get shot.

He said, 'If you're hungry you will do anything.'

In the afternoon we again saw the trails of white smoke, quite high. Someone said they must be bombing somewhere. We had another long sleep which would do us a power of good and went to the toilets which were pitiful, who knew when they were last cleaned and the smell knocked you over. We strolled around and at one point a guard told us to go back; there was a guard each side of this place so we just turned back. We sent inside and the next we heard was a rifle shot. It was at the lad who had said he was going to the potato clamps and luckily they had fired over his head, but had then given him a crack across the face. He could have been killed, just because he felt hungry. He had thought no one was looking. When the shot came he had run back as fast as his legs would carry him.

After our rest day we kept marching as usual, past the outskirts of Brauscheig, where we sang and whistled or hummed, with everyone trying to keep in step; the German people were looking on thinking we must be mad to do that at this time of the morning. We stayed that night at Lehre, just a few miles out of the town, and the other group were still with us.

Daffodils were coming out, and some primroses, and it was nice just to see flowers again after such a long time. Everyone was wondering how far were our troops as most of us thought that they would have met us by now. The next night was at Peine and after that Harry said he had found out that we were to go to Hannover where there was a camp.

We were up later than usual at Peine and as we reached the road we saw the other group coming across the fields to meet us so we waited till they caught up and they followed on behind. We were the only ones on the road, not even one vehicle at the moment. We were travelling north-west and thought that tomorrow at least we might get some food as we could be in a large town. Denny started singing something his mother used to sing to him and it was such a lovely song and with such beautiful words that we all applauded him at the end. I asked Harry where we were going and he said it would be Hamelerwald and that the other lads would go to another farm that night and we would meet up again in the morning to go to Hannover. That was 24 March.

We were on the outskirts of Hannover and could see people waiting for their transport into the town. We could see aeroplane trails in the sky but they seemed to be by-passing us which we were pleased about as we didn't want anything to happen to us after all the trouble to get here. Sometimes we could see fighters streak across the sky protecting them. Hannover seemed four or five miles away and we sang 'The White Cliffs of Dover' and many more songs. As we approached the city we could see that it had had a real bombing as we could see the beds in bedrooms of bombed houses with the rest of the house lying in a heap of rubble. There were a lot of gaps in the rows of houses and tramlines broken with the burnt-out trams. We ended up in a camp in the middle of the city; we arrived at an iron gate and through it was a mess as if it too had been bombed recently. There was no water or electricity and no food either. This was about six o'clock in the evening and as some of the huts were damaged we just had to make ourselves as comfortable as possible.

Chapter 22

Last night trucks came and brought us some palliasses so we could sleep on bunks instead of the floor as we had imagined. In the morning we were called out of our beds by the new guards who formed us in threes to march to a place of work. We went through the gate onto a tarmac road and on either side pretty well every building had been damaged. The railway station and the tram depot were both badly hit. When we stopped an officer counted out fifty of us including me; Geordie and Robbie were in the second group.

We were made to go up an embankment onto the railway tracks. Some were buckled and and there were lots of holes. They made us stand so many paces apart along the track then gave us shovels: no handles, just a long shaft with a shovel at the end. We had to fill in the holes with ballast that was lying on the side of the track. The shovels were difficult to handle and one lad from Yorkshire was just resting on the end when the officer just knocked it out from under him and he nearly fell. He picked up the shovel and was just going to hit the officer but the guard nearby lifted his rifle. Ten of us were on this work and the lads next to us were doing the same. In the distance we could see a train stopped but we did not know if it had been bombed or hit by fragments or if it had been blown off the line. Then the officer made forty of us lift the twisted railway line; it took all our strength as we had had nothing to eat for so long. It was not right, making us do this. The officer was a real Nazi, with rimless glasses – a real pain in the backside. We carried on in this way through dinner time, with nothing to eat, until it was time to go back to our camp. That evening a truck came with potatoes – three each, not fit for pig swill.

We sat by our bunks for a while and later tried to clean the place up. We found a cupboard with a brush and shovel and everyone did a little bit and we would try to do a little bit each day to get the place ship-shape.

Two days later we had still not had anything to eat though doing the same work. We were further away now, nearer the engine. The officer was a very nasty person; he liked giving orders and hitting people in different ways; he liked drawing his revolver and threatening people with it. He was a young Nazi lout. We were still filling in holes and lifting the twisted lines and then the new ones as well as the German railway men had to come after us and lay these. In the afternoon was an air raid; the sirens went and we all ran to the fields nearby: plus the officer and the guards. The sky was full of planes. Just to our left a Flying Fortress was hit and the men were jumping out as it was on fire. It went down with the pilot still on board and there was a big bang as it exploded a few miles from us.

That evening a truck arrived with three potatoes each – that was better than nothing – and later some German cigarettes. Some lads went to the guard and found out he was Polish; someone gave him a cigarette and he told them to go down the chute which was where the carrots and potatoes were kept. The lad and his mate managed to get some and the three of us decided to try and get some the next day. It was a risk but where food was concerned it was worth it. This was 28 March 1945.

The next day we were again called for work but four lads were taken back to the hut: what for we did not know. We had to fill in the holes with rubble from the side, and someone said the best way to do it would be for two men to throw shovelfuls upwards, because if we all kept going up and down our legs would be exhausted by the end of the day. We were all like skeletons and doing those lines was not doing my back any good but what could you do with a stupid Nazi officer? We were getting very weak so the whisper went along the row of men – One Two Three – and we dropped a rail and stood a while for a breather. Just then the sirens started and we all fled to the field; we could see the sky filled with planes and someone said that a thousand bombers did daylight bombing. All of a sudden we looked up and saw a large object in the sky with a parachute attached. It descended slowly and nobody knew what it was. Then this long thing eventually opened and a load of pieces of paper started floating down over our heads. Then they started dropping bombs in the distance but not far away. When the all-clear went we could see the planes going back to England and how we wished we could go too.

When we got back to the camp we found that Robbie and the other lads had been in the canteen kitchen cutting up carrots and potatoes for the officer and guards. Some people had to carry them there in buckets and others kept peeling them; Robbie had put carrot tops and potato peel in his pockets. Everyone was hoping we would get some food but the officer said there would be none because of the American bombing. The water had been put on however and we could light a fire as it was still early and cook our peelings.

A tall Coldstream Guard came over and asked if we could spare a little food. We had a little left over that we were going to save for the next day but said, 'Why not give it to him?' It was nearly ready when he just keeled over and died on the spot. This was after coming all those miles and nearly being at the end of the war. Someone told the German officer who ordered the guards to go for a stretcher and take him away.

The next day I was taken with three others out of the ranks and went back to the hut to wait for orders. I was thinking of Edie and wondering if we would make it, considering that guardsman dying like that. I was pleased to be off the railway work that day. When I saw Edie again she would be a mature woman but to me she would always be my Mona Lisa. The guard took us to the kitchen to do some potato peeling and some carrots. I was picked to get the potatoes down some steps. It did not take long and when we had finished we had to give the lads a hand to prepare them. I had an Army hat which had borrowed to put the peelings in but the guard caught me putting some in my pocket and made me and the others empty our pockets so it looked like nothing tonight unless I got down the chute. The Polish guard was on and I still had two cigarettes left. I now knew the way in which was even better than going down the chute. I gave the guard the cigarettes and got four potatoes and three carrots – better than nothing even if we had to eat them raw.

After a while there was a commotion. It was the Yorkshire lad and the guard that caught him handed him over to the officer who was beating him with a piece of rubber tubing. He was lashing into the lad; he hit every part of his body and face before he let him go. His mates went to console him; he must have been in agony. Later I dished out the potatoes and carrots and we ate them raw, skins and all, as we did not want to leave any trace.

It was in this camp that I met a lad in the washroom and we started talking. I told him about when and where I was taken and he said he was taken in Italy in late 1943; he was one of the hundred or so that came to this camp. He said that he was Jewish but with an English name and his parents had come to England just after the first world war. He said, 'I do hope I get back to England,' and I said I hoped so too and would not say anything about him. We just shook hands and I wished him all the best.

Next morning we were called by the guards again and we went to our rotten job on the railway. We went to near where the derailed engine had been but it was gone now. We had once more to move mangled railway tracks, which was a struggle, and then we had the long shovels to fill the deep holes. Three or four lads moved the rubble to us by relay. The officer kept patrolling the area, watching that everyone was working; you would think he had X-ray eyes as he kept turning round hoping to catch someone leaning on his shovel. If he saw someone he came running back and gave him a clout on the ear, and then walked back, grinning like a Cheshire cat. On the way back the heavens opened and by the time we arrived at the camp we were soaked through.

At least we had a fire like a round stove and some of the lads laid their things on the floor to get them dry; it was done by rota with movement every half hour. Nothing got really dry but at least some of the wet went. Robbie had found bits of cloth and suggested we made a sergeant major, two sergeants and corporal stripes, as NCOs did not have to work.

The Yorkshire lad and his mates said they were definitely going to get the officer by hook or by crook, when our forces arrived at the camp.

Work next day was as usual, but it was very warm and some people took off their jackets. They looked like skeletons with all their ribs sticking out. I did not take my jacket off when I saw them, so sweat was just pouring out of my body. We had no water which made me feel quite ill but you had to keep on or risk a thrashing.

Robbie had found some cloth which might do for stripes under some rubble. When we got to the hut Geordie said he had some pieces of carrot and potato peelings and said if there were any fires outside we could ask if we could take over when they were finished. Just then a lad from America came over and said,

'Could you give me something to eat, if I'm not too cheeky.'

We said, 'Of course not, we will just try to stretch it between the four of us.'

He said, 'I have had very little to eat since I came out of a German hospital. My wrists and leg and ankle were all broken; I was a glider pilot.'

Geordie said, 'You must have been an officer or an NCO.'

He said, 'Staff sergeant.'

'Well, you must get out of here because NCOs do not work.'

Robbie asked if I could do the sewiing and I said no.

As we were cooking we asked the American if he had any sharp items to cut the cloth. As we were showing him, another lad came across and said,

'I heard you say all that – I have a small knife and will do the cutting if you will give me some. I also have a needle and thread.'

We could not believe this. He said that in Civvy Street he had worked in the 50 Shilling Tailors and had done a lot of repairs. He got the knife and started cutting the cloth gently into strips. He said he would cut two for me, three for Geordie as he was a lance jack, so that is why he made Robbie sergeant major; and the lad said, 'If you don't mind I shall make myself a sergeant. Then I can cut out a circle for your crown and try to make some sort of laurel.'

He added, 'There is very little left but you never know, we may trick these Germans.'

The American said, 'My things are in my jacket, Could you be so kind as to sew them on for me?' and the lad sewing said that was no problem.

We decided that the best thing to do in the morning was to go on parade and stand at the front so the officer and guards could see our stripes and see what they would do. We did just this and when they came to us they told us all to go back to the huts. The American was over the moon at what we had achieved. We were all lined up with twenty-six others and marched off with a corporal in charge, through the city. It was in a terrible state; there was hardly a street or a place that had not been hit by a bomb or an incendiary. Shops were damaged and there was scarcely a person in the streets. Before long we came to the end of the city on a nice straight road; one of the lads started singing and we all joined in whistling, we were so pleased to get out of that hell-hole. We did a good few miles onto a country road, just twisting and turning, through lovely countryside with lots of flowers. All of a sudden the corporal called a halt and we all ran to the hedges but at least there were no houses to see us. I got a chance to thank the lad who had helped last night but he said it should be him thanking me and my mates for getting him out of there.

We were all enjoying ourselves instead of working our butts off, walking freely along this lovely country road. Geordie said, 'Every step we take is one nearer to our troops.'

We turned off to a farm which was the first one we had seen which was dry with no mud, though a few ruts in different places. We could find no food at all so just climbed the ladder and found a spot where we could all lie together. The other lad came over and thanked us again. I said, 'I do wish I could find out what this place is called,' so he said he would go and find out. The corporal spoke a lot of English and told us we were at Elzec and on our way to Fallingbostel Camp.

The next day was nice and bright and we thought it might be our last day before we got to the new camp. It was so peaceful you would not know there was a war on. The fields were full of wild flowers and the trees with different shades of green. But while we went to the hedge in a break we heard that a group who left a few days before us to go to Fallingsbostel were machine-gunned by American planes; some were killed and some injured and the rest were sent back to Hannover.

Trees on either side of the road gave us some welcome shade as we marched and sang; eventually we reached a small farm and went up the ladder to the loft. We could find no food and did not want to risk drinking any water on this last lap. The place was Hottenhagen and that was 3 April.

The next day as we were walking along I thought, If I do get back to England, I would like to get off the train and walk all the way from the Central Station to the Haymarket Bus Station even if I was carrying all my Army gear; and it would be nice if Edie was there to meet me. It would be grand if we could come across our forces on the way to the camp; but eventually we arrived there. There was a funny smell as we approached, which grew stronger: a putrid smell that we could not put our finger on. We did hope that we would get something to eat when we got there and even the smell would not put us off.

Chapter 23

A staff sergeant said that we would have a hot meal later. 'Later?' we said, 'We have had nothing for days.'

'Nothing to do with me; it is up to the German guards and cooks, but you will get a parcel each tomorrow.'

We thought that all our birthdays had come at once. We got detailed to go to different old wooden buildings, but Robbie said, 'If it is possible, could we three stick together and also the American. We have been looking after him.'

'All right, there are six spaces in this one,' so Robbie said we would take four of them. It would be lovely to have a bunk with a good padded mattress and some blankets, we hoped. While we were getting ourselves sorted, they shouted the meal was up and the staff sergeant gave us mess tins, not big but at least we could get some food. They dished us out a slice of black bread and some soup with a few vegetables and a lot of potatoes. It was most welcome and took the hunger pangs away.

I had the best sleep for ages with no disruptions, no getting up early; even after going to the toilet, which was not far away, being able to crawl back to bed. There was not even a parade to get counted. Later we thirty were taken to the warehouse with the parcels and were given one each; we decided to share them between two as this was the best way not to waste food. I did not think our stomachs could take a lot. I told the American I would do the cooking for us two as he could not manage with his injuries, but he was trying hard to massage his hands. Robbie and Geordie had soup and we had two sardines each in olive oil; he drank the oil off one side and I off the other as it would be a shame to waste it.

We heard the rumble of gunfire in the distance and went out to look but could see nothing. At dinner time we had two potatoes and a slice of black bread; the potatoes were lovely and clean and you could eat the skin. Some of the lads had fires going and they made a lovely smell, not like the one yesterday, but the wind was now coming from the east. We heard the gunfire again, this time from the south-west so our lads did not seem so far away. We had a lie down before our evening meal which we really needed.

The days passed in the same way though we were coming to the end of our parcel. Just as I was cooking one day I saw a lad coming towards me.

'Hallo, Tommy,' he said.

'Hallo again, when did you arrive?'

'We came late last night. We left Hannover three days ago, just ten of us.'

Then he told me this story. He, together with the lad who had been whipped by the officer and four others, attacked the officer along the road, just before they came to the station. One of them was carrying a nice thin rope round his waist. They put the rope round his neck and hung it round a lamp post; they all pulled the rope tight and stayed till he died so he would not hurt anyone any more. The guards did not interfere. He had been a vicious man, perhaps taught to be so by a Nazi organisation or the Hitler Youth.

'You did a great job,' I said. 'Stay and have a cup of tea with us.'

In the meantime Robbie and Geordie came out and he told the story again.

The American and I were just eating a tin of beans when there came one almighty bang and the building started to shake. After a while we heard the shells landing and then it happened again. Just then the staff sergeant came along bringing us each twenty cigarettes. He told us that the guns were manned by 16- and 17-year olds and that they were guarding the River Weser.

He said, 'Our troops are only a few days away so we may get some heavy shelling. They know about us here as the last group before you ran away and hid until some were taken by our lads.'

The guard had given him all this information; perhaps he was looking after his own skin or perhaps he hated Hitler as did a lot of guards who dared not show it, like that civilian guard at Malsh on Oder.

On 15 April we got another parcel. I had taken some bits of wood out of my bunk to start a fire; and the other day Robbie had asked a guard for matches for his cigarette and was given the whole box, which was kind of him. I found some paper and got the fire going and suddenly there was a mighty bang and again we heard the shell explode in the distance. Then there was another so it looked as if something was happening around there. We could smell that putrid smell which really put you off your breakfast. I managed to get the water boiling for a cup of tea; then Robbie said he would take over the fire while the American and I had our sardines on biscuits. This time they were in tomato sauce.

I was telling them about this funny thing yesterday morning: as I woke up I could see an outline of sailors' uniform with no faces or legs; and a voice said, 'Everything will be all right, Tommy.' It sounded like my brother Steve. I had never seen him in his uniform and Robbie had told me he had been killed in 1942.

At dinner we had three potatoes each plus a slice of bread – we were amazed; everything in a few days after having had nothing for weeks. Just then the sky was black with planes going overhead; we just hoped they would not bomb us. They seemed to go on and on. The banging came from both sides plus the guns from the River Weser. The ones from the west seemed to be getting nearer. We had a very scary night with the guns and the shaking building. At times we thought the roof would fall in. I decided to go out to make some breakfast and had a tin of bacon in my hand, but I heard this noise and next thing I knew, there was a lad on an armoured car throwing loaves of white bread to the ground and lads were standing there trying to catch them, but some didn't have the strength and they fell to the ground.

I went over and said, 'It has taken you a long time to catch up with me as you were meant to meet me at El Duda.'

It was the 7th Armoured Division. Tears were running down my face with being released after all this time. I shouted to the others to come out and they were so happy and we all shook hands with each other. So the ordeal was over and we would be going back soon to England.

After dinner I went towards the main gate and straight in front of me was the large barracks for the Germans Army. In front were great big batches of rifles, with only two guards looking after them. I walked through the gate and made my way down the road and on my right was a field with two pigs belly up and a cow, all with bullets in their carcasses. The smell was terrible, just as it had been for days.

I passed some of the lads from the camp smashing shops up but carried on a little bit and met a man from the invasion force. We had a long talk about different things. He said when they left here they were going to Berlin if the war lasted that long; I told him about my three and a half years and he was amazed. He had heard me shout about them taking a long time to catch up with me and we just started laughing. It was a long time since I had done that. He brought me out a plate of chicken, peas, potatoes, carrots and gravy and I ate as much as I could; he said 'Come on, eat up!' and I said I could not as my stomach had shrunk so much. I only wished I could have eaten more. I said I should get back, but he asked me to stay the night with them.

There was a corporal who was the major's driver, and the major had been shot by a sniper. So they went out for a while with guns and when they came back said they had shot out every window in the street, but two lads were watching in case the sniper tried to get away. They told me the major had been a good officer for the men.

This Geordie lad said, 'Your bed is inside this truck.' I looked inside and there were plenty of blankets to keep me warm, I had not seen so many since I left England in 1941. I lay down and had a lovely sleep and the cook called me with a lovely cup of tea in the morning and asked if I wanted any breakfast. I said a bacon sandwich would go down well with my tea and he said he would not be long bringing it over. When the lad came and asked if I had slept all right, he pulled the bedding off and said, 'Look, you have slept all night on a truck of ammunition.'

On the way back I saw a warehouse on fire. I went inside and found cigarette papers and a roller to make them, and also took half a dozen lighters and bottles of perfume; but further in I saw this beautiful sable fur coat. It was so lovely. I just took it and ran out thinking this would be a wonderful present to take to Edie; if it did not fit I could sell it and buy her another.

I walked back to the block and they said, 'Where have you been? They have been twice for you to go to Minden aerodrome; you could have been in England by now.'

I said, 'Why worry, one day is not going to hurt me; not with what I have on my arm. It will be really worth it when I see Edie's face.' They got a cup of tea and I said, 'If I do go today, you can have my parcel.' They had a few sandwiches of spreading cheese, and I told them where I had been and about the bed in the truck. They just killed themselves laughing. I said, 'It is no laughing matter; I could have been blown to kingdom come,' but then I too saw the funny side.

In a while a sergeant came and said, 'Is Thomas Sample here?'

I said, 'I'm here.'

'Get yourself ready and collect what personal things you have. A truck will take you to Minden Aerodrome and you will stay there till you get a flight back to England today or sometime tomorrow.'

I said farewell to everybody and shook hands with them all; the American gave me his home address. Geordie and Robbie both said thanks. Robbie said, 'When I see you again I am buying the drinks, as you saved my life, and thanks a million.'

In the truck I waved until I could not see them. We were passing places we had marched through along the way but by truck it was much quicker. We went westwards to the bridge over the Weser, then went onto an autobahn and just kept going to the aerodrome where we were handed over to some RAF personnel. We were issued with razor blades and other toiletries and forty cigarettes. The we were taken to the mess to get something to eat. We told them that we could only manage small portions, so we had half a sausage, a bit of mash and a few beans, with a cup of tea. We were told that the NAAFI would be coming around at different times that afternoon and evening if we wanted anything else.

I went to the gate and told the guard I was going out for a while to this German house. He said, 'All right, but don't go far in case you are called for a flight home.' I told him my name and he wrote it down. I went just outside the perimeter fence and up to a house; I knocked on the door. I asked in a bit of German, and demonstrated with gestures, if I could have a shave; of course I took out my shaving brush and soap and cloth. A young girl came down the stairs and her mother ran up to her and told her to go back to her bedroom; she must have thought I was going to rape her, looking as I did like a ragamuffin. I had a lovely wash and shave and thanked her in German.

Back at the hangar I saw the NAAFI van and asked for a cup of tea; she gave me a chocolate biscuit as well plus twenty cigarettes. We had been issued with a small haversack to keep our personal things in. Later I went back and had some coffee and another biscuit and more cigarettes. As I turned round there was another NAAFI van with a queue, so I made my way towards it and got another cup of coffee and cigarettes. I kept on in this way till me pockets were full and had to put some round my waist to hide them from view.

Back at the hangar I gave a lad who had been looking after my things some cigarettes. I put all the other cigarettes into the haversack and used it as a pillow.

In the morning, 18 April, we were told to go down to the mess whenever we felt like it so long as it was before 9 o'clock, when it closed. We were told to stay in the aerodrome area as if we wandered away we might lose our flight to England. I took my belongings down to the mess with me as I had around two hundred cigarettes and the coat and if I got a chance I would get more. We were asked what we wanted to eat, and I asked for a bacon and egg sandwich and a cup of coffee with plenty of milk and one spoonful of sugar, and he wrote it all down. I asked if I could possibly also have a tin of corned beef and a white loaf; he said I could have anything I wanted. I asked the lad if he would guard my things again while I went a message; I wanted to take the things to the German people who had let me have a shave the day before.

The girl came to the door and ran in to tell her mother. I gave her the food and she said thank you; but went to the mantelpiece and took down a cuckoo clock and tried to give it to me, but I refused.

Back at the hangar I said I was going to get more cigarettes from the NAAFI van and that as there were four of them I could get coffee and cigarettes from each. I suggested he did the same but he said he did not smoke. I said, 'Hold this packet in your hand and they will know what brand to give you,' and away he went to do the four of them. I said that they might be short at home when we got back so I was taking a lot home with me. I went round again and had over three hundred which should keep me going for a time.

Our dinner was soup, pork, a spoonful of potato and some peas, then some ice cream. We still could not eat large portions. We were looked after as if we were royalty. I went back to the hangar and the next thing was a lad saying, 'Wake up, you are on stand-by to go back to England. So I got all my things together and said goodbye to the lad and shook hands and thanked him for looking after my things. He had only been a few months a prisoner, having been taken in France in 1944.

We were taken to a room near the runway. The sky was full of Dakotas and now and then one landed. Eventually our names were called. I walked over the tarmac and one of the officers shouted at me. He said, 'I am afraid you cannot take that coat on board as you are going to have extra weight on this plane. You will have to drop it on the tarmac.'

I did so and was really angry, having got it all this way, so my lovely surprise was lost.

We got on the plane as the sun was going down in the west. I asked the pilot where our parachutes were and he said there were none but that he had none either. Before long we were in the air and I felt funny; somehow a bit dizzy. When we levelled off I felt better though and much later someone said they could see the white cliffs of Dover through the pilot's window. He told us to keep sitting down as it would be a lot safer. Next thing, we were going down again and I got the funny feeling again. I put it down to the lack of food over the last years.

Then the plane stopped and put ladders up so we could get off. We were guided through the hallway where they called out our names. In the hallway was a girl in uniform and I said to her, 'You are the first English girl I have seen since 1941,' so she gave me a kiss and I gave her a bottle of 4711 perfume; she was really pleased. Each person that was called went to the left as we were going to hospital and we waited to get into an ambulance.

We landed in England on 19 April 1941 at 1.35 a.m. at Wing Oxford. I was not interrogated and got my liberation papers.

Chapter 24

I was sitting in the front of the ambulance by the driver when I heard a voice I recognised. I just could not believe it. It was the sergeant major I saw at Derna in 1941, with the lads he had been captured with; and there he was on the same ambulance as me.

The hospital was a Canadian one and we were taken to a ward with six empty beds. I had some Horlicks and a few biscuits and went to bed, hoping they would soon get in touch with our families. In the morning a Canadian nurse took my temperature and some blood for tests, after giving me the bacon sandwich and cup of tea I had ordered the night before. I thanked her again and again and she said she was here to look after me and that she had to take my height and weight and take me to see a doctor later. After breakfast, which I really enjoyed, I took off my pyjamas, got into my trousers and shirt, and just sat in the armchair listening to the radio; it seemed a lifetime since I heard one and it was as if I was in Wonderland.

My height was 5 ft 10½ inches and I weighed just over 6½ stone. I just could not believe it; in Poland I had weighed well under 10 stone. I asked the doctor if I could tell my story but he said he had only half an hour to examine me. The nurse took me back to the ward and said that dinner would be baked fish with mashed potato and peas; I said, 'That sounds nice but I hope it is a small portion.'

'It does not matter how much you eat, but try your best as we are trying to build you up; you have had very few vitamins the last few months.'

I then had a lie down and a nurse took some blood and my blood pressure and then I fell asleep till teatime which was soup and apple pudding.

The nurse came over. 'You are going to another hospital, and I have sent a telegram to your parents. You have no sweetheart, have you?'

'I had a fiancée once but some meddling people broke us up just two days before I was captured.'

I decided to write to Edie before I went to bed and the nurse said she would bring writing paper and a stamp, all free. I had a few tries at writing but just could not find the right words; so decided just to send a letter asking what she was doing. I did say how much I missed her and how much I loved her, and would leave the rest till I saw her.

The hospital was in Oxford. On the fifth day, after my cereal, boiled egg and toast, I was told that I would be going off to another one, a British one. I followed the nurse to the kitchen for a drink of milk and she told me I had to get ready with my uniform on instead of just my trousers and a shirt. I went to the washroom in the ward to have another wash; I had had a shave and shower in the morning as it was lovely going into a proper toiler and washroom with everything spick and span. You could just turn on a tap and get hot or cold water.

I just sat in the chair and waited till they came for me, listening to the radio; the next thing I saw was the nurse with my dinner: chicken, peas, mashed potatoes, carrots, turnip and Yorkshire pudding and gravy; this was the meal I dreamt of on the death march. Just a week or so ago we were very hungry and now I was getting a lovely meal, just like manna from Heaven. I tried very hard to eat it all but only managed to get halfway through.

After a good while she came back and collected me; we went through a few doors to the entrance and there were other lads too waiting to get into the ambulance. There was not much conversation so I just wondered when I would get a letter from Edie, she was so much on my mind now. I had left her a teenager and now she would be a grown woman. It was over four years since I had seen her; it would be wonderful if she could come down and see me and I would be the proudest man in the hospital. Anything she said would do for me so long as we could be together and make me a very happy man. Her birthday was not far off and she would be 21. As I am writing this the tears are starting to flow from my eyes and I just keep putting my hand up to stop them trickling down my face.

I needed the toilet and so did a couple of the other lads so we gave the driver a knock on the partition and he stopped and came round. He said we were stopping soon at this place where we could all go and have a bite to eat as we still had a long way to go. He asked if we could hang on for fifteen minutes but we said he was going to have a lot of water in his ambulance if he did not stop then. He kept his word and pulled in to a place with lorries. We asked him not to be so long next time. We had a bite to eat and some tea and he said that we were going to Hemel Hempstead near Luton; but we were none the wiser. We dozed to the rocking of the vehicle and talked to pass the time; we did not talk of our war experiences but about our families and how they would react when they saw us. We had another break at a transport café; we were ready for the toilets and we had a bacon and egg sandwich and a pot of tea. We asked the driver how much longer we had and the time: it was 9.30 p.m. He said he was going to have a snooze for at least half an hour so we said he should have an hour as we did not want any accidents and that we would wake him when we thought he had had a good rest. We just went on talking about all sorts of things except war: football, cricket and where we used to work. After an hour we went on and I fell asleep and the next thing I knew we had arrived. It was one o'clock in the morning.

We were allocated to wards, chose our breakfasts and fell asleep. Next day I went out into the grounds but was told not to go outside them. It was a lovely place with plenty of places to walk around, flowers and trees. After a while I went into the kitchen and asked if I could have some milk to drink and the nurse said I could just help myself from the fridge whenever I liked. Just as I was going to my bed area she came up and said my parents were on their way to see me and it could be some time that afternoon. She asked when I had last seen them.

'The 23 April 1941,' I said.

'All that time? Well, you will be pleased to see them.'

I asked if there was any mail but she said no; I explained that it might be from my ex-fiancée and she said if it came she would bring it straight away. After dinner I sat outside for a while and then said to myself, That must be my parents looking for me, so I went towards them.

I said, 'It is lovely to see you both again.'

They said, 'You do look well.'

I said to myself, If you had seen me last week you would have thought differently. I gave my mother a hug and a kiss and shook my Dad's hand, then he gave me a cuddle and there was a tear in their eyes. We went along the path and talked about things at home, especially about my brothers, but they never mentioned my brother who was killed, just said he could be in a foreign country. I just fell in with what they said but my mother was in black. My father had to get time off to come down to see me and must have travelled all night. I told him that I had some cigarettes and he said he had not had any for a few days as they were rather scarce.

I mentioned Edie's name and my mother just went berserk. 'She went out with a married man while you were away!' I said nothing; I did not even tell her about the letter I wrote because that was none of her business; I was nearly twenty-five years old and I had a mind of my own.

We went back to the Matron's office and she said everything was arranged for my parents to stay till the next day. They went to the canteen to have a lovely three-course meal and I went to my haversack and got two packets of cigarettes for my father and said that I had some 4711 for my mother. She asked how I got it: 'Ways and means,' I said.

As I gave my father the cigarettes, I asked him how Edie was. He said she was fine and that he saw her sometimes without my mother knowing. 'I go to the top of the street as if I was going to your Aunt Sadie's house and stay about twenty minutes or so; I always give her the news when you write.'

My mother got off the bench and said, 'What are you two talking about?'

'I was just telling him I was in the Middle East.'

'Oh I see, he can tell me about it later then.'

My mother was deaf in one ear so I went on talking a bit about the Middle East so he could tell her and I did not mention anything about writing to Edie as I did not want anyone to know.

My meal arrived, with corned beef and salad and my mother said, 'Why are you not eating your food?'

I said that at the moment I did not fancy much, which was all I could say as I did not want to tell her what weight I was when I got to England.

Next day I warned the nurse not to give me any letters while my parents were there and she said she would be careful. She said that a taxi would come shortly to take them to the station and I would be told so I could say goodbye. After breakfast they said the taxi would be there in half an hour so I went to talk to my parents and tell them that I would be home the next week but that the hospital would send a telegram and let them know when.

After they went I took a stroll around the grounds for a while just wondering what had been going on: my father goes over to Edie but my mother seems to hate her for some reason. I thought of the last few weeks of what I had been through and how I was now living like a lord. Now and again I could not help looking round to see if anybody was following me as I expected the Nazi guards. It was going to take a while before I knew I was free.

I was still not eating much food and in fact slept right through dinner time so I missed it. When I woke I did not feel very well so the nurse said she would get a doctor to have a look at me. She asked if I wanted any tea and I said I did not know so she brought me some soup. I tried my hardest to keep it down but I as violently sick and it was all over the bed and floor so I just sat on the chair.

The doctor came and took my temperature and asked how I felt. I said, 'Not too good,' so they took me to a side ward and did a lot of examinations and again I was sick. He thought I had a virus and said they would keep me there so the nurse could keep an eye on me. He said, 'You have not put on much weight since you came here; they say you are not eating all your food.'

'Doctor,' I said, 'I am always hungry when I get my meals but after a bit I just cannot take any more.'

He said, 'We will not give you any more to eat today, but have whatever you want to drink,' so I asked for a glass of milk. He said it should always be warm, not cold.

'How long were you a prisoner of war?' he asked.

'Three and a half years; and I have just done a thousand miles from Poland to Fallingsbostel in West Germany.'

'That is a long way; did you get much to eat?'

'Sir, we just had to live on what was available.'

'You have really been through the mill.'

'Yes sir, but there could be people worse than me,' and away they went.

During the night they woke me as I was sweating and shaking and the doctor put me on antibiotic tablets to try to help, every four hours. The nurse brought me warm milk and sat with me for a while, asking different questions, but I just could not be bothered as I just wanted to go to sleep. They woke me later for my tablets and I felt like I had been pulled through a hedge; I asked for a lovely cup of tea as I was very thirsty.

I must have fallen asleep again and when I woke it was daylight. The nurse came in with a letter in her hand. I couldn't believe it: it was from Edie. I opened it straight away.

She said: 'I am organising at this moment and really busy so I shall see you when you come home. I send all my love and I miss you very much. I am really glad you are back in England. The four people who sent the Dear John letter were your brother Steve, nephew John, and cousins Greta and Olive. Steve was killed; John was in a pit accident and died in hospital; Greta is in Birmingham and Olive lives in Forest Hall with her mother.'

So they were the culprits; they should be ashamed of what they had done with people's lives. We had done them no harm.

Edie went on: 'I just wish you were home so I could see you again, it has been such a long time. I love you with all my heart. Kisses and love.' It was so long since I had heard from her. I had a tear in my eye now I knew she loved me; this was the best tonic anyone could have and would give me the strength to get better for her sake.

On 5 May I was told I would be leaving today. We would be taken by truck to the station and it would carry all our personal things like kitbags, our uniforms, our rifles with rounds of ammunition. We would be given our pay books and tickets. We would not be discharged till we got to the nearest barracks, mine being at Fenham Barracks, Newcastle, Everyone was on edge while we waited for the doctor to discharge us. He came eventually and saw us one at a time: he examined me then handed me my discharge papers, shook hands with me and said, 'Take care.' There were four of us leaving. We got dressed again in lovely clean clothes and it did feel funny. What lay ahead was going to be tough, getting to know people again after all we had been through. I was still having problems eating.

The driver gave us our tickets. We all had to go to Euston then I had to go to King's Cross. The train was really full so we sat on our kitbags in the guard's van and this train stopped all the way to London. King's Cross was very near and I got into the guard's van again on the train north. I talked to the guard and told him where I was going and what I had been doing but that I now had six weeks leave; he said that the train was very full as with the end of the war near there were a lot of soldiers on leave. He also said that it would be five o'clock when we got to Newcastle as it was a stopping train. I asked him to give me a nudge if I dozed off but he said he was getting off at York to go back to London. I told him about what had happened to me during the last three and a half years. He got off at York with a lot of parcels, a dog and a cat. He said that I had only Darlington and Durham to go before Newcastle and that we were ahead of time. I said to myself, I am going to do that walk to the Haymarket and then get a bus to the Ritz, Forest Hall, as I saw this getting built in 1938.

At Newcastle I got off the train and walked over the bridge. I passed a taxi rank and the driver said, 'Are you a prisoner of war; if so I will take you home for nothing to say thank you for what you have done.'

I said, 'No, not me,' and away I went towards the Haymarket. On the bus a girl said, 'You are Tommy Sample, welcome home. Everybody is talking about you.' When we got off she asked if she could carry my kit bag or my rifle, but I said No, but she could carry my haversack if she liked. As we approached the top of the street I could see bunting, flags and 'Welcome Home Tommy' and I saw my Aunt Jennie standing at the front door of our house. She said, 'They are all gone to the Central Station for you to come off the train and you were supposed to get a taxi home.'

'Well, I'm here now,' I said, and dropped my kitbag beside the front door.

My aunt gave me a kiss and a hug and said, 'Our Mary and me put these up as your mother did not want them; she said only one of her sons had come home, not Stephen. She thinks he might be in another country and have lost his memory.'

I was desperately waiting to see Edie and was telling my aunt all that had happened, with the Dear John letter and all; and just then my father and mother, with John, Robert and Fred, were all coming down the street; also Ned Blake, the one who had refused to give my address to Edie.

I said later, 'I am going over to see Edie to see what has been going on.'

My mother said, 'You cannot just now, maybe later.'

Why was she saying this? I was entitled to see her as she was going to be my wife. I said, 'All right,' just to keep the peace, 'But I do want to see her, and soon; she will think I do not want her, and I do.' I told my mother that if I had been in Scotland longer we would have been married. No one could stop us now as we would be of age.

And eventually we did get married.

Two people involved in the letter died horrible deaths – interfering in other people's lives always get paid back sometime. It was going to take me some time to get used to Army life, not to mention civilian life, and my health was not good. All I wanted was a good life with the one I loved.

A few days later Edie and I went down to Whitley Bay by bus. We walked down to the Promenade, as we had done regularly in 1940. We went towards St Mary's lighthouse on a really lovely day, just kissing and cuddling each other after being away so long. It brought back many happy memories. People were looking at us but we had not a care in the world. Nothing mattered but being together. We walked so far along it was well past dinner time so went back towards the Spanish City and found an Italian restaurant with reasonable prices. We had soup, ham salad and ice cream and peaches. When we finished Edie went to the door and held it open, but I said to the proprietor, 'I am not paying for these meals.'

'Why not?'

'Your people the Italians starved me nearly to death when I was in Greece and Italy.' I explained all I had been through there.

'But I was born in England.'

'You are still Italian to me and they gave me a rough time.'

He came round the counter, shook hands and said, 'The meals are on the house.'

A while later, as we were going towards Cullercoats Bay, Edie played war with me about it, and it just sank in and we both had a good laugh about it. Later we found a small café and had some tea and a sandwich then went to this small picture house on the front. I bought her some chocolate as I had some sweet coupons; then as we went into the passage she gave me a lovely kiss and a hug and I did the same back.

She said, 'It is lovely, just to have you for life.'

I said, 'As long as I live there will be no one else but you.'

We watched the show cuddling in the back row and then went to the bus station to go home.

Edie kept pestering me to go to the Council to see about getting a place for us. I said I would try to find something for us before I went back to the Army as I had six weeks leave. Next morning I went to the Council office at Forest Hall and this young chap said he could find me a place temporarily and I could have a look round to see what I thought. He took me to Tinkers Turn, where the AckAck guns had been during the war, and showed me a place full of old railway sleepers and a ground sheet and told me where the toilets and the cooking place were.

I said, 'You must be joking, I have been halfway round Europe, sleeping in worse places than this and you expect me to live here? You can forget it.'

He said, 'If you don't you won't get housed.'

I was really gutted and just walked away. After all I had been through, to come home to live in a pigsty.

Every step I take
Every mile I make is to hold you in my arms
As you are so beautiful in charms
Your love will live in my heart
As it did from the very start.